T0135784

Bibliografische Information der Deutschen Nationalbibliothek

Die Deutsche Nationalbibliothek verzeichnet diese Publikation in der
Deutschen Nationalbibliografie; detaillierte bibliografische Daten sind
im Internet über http://dnb.d-nb.de abrufbar.

zugleich: Dissertation der Fakultät für Informatik und Elektrotechnik
der Universität Rostock, 2011

ISBN 978-3-8325-2948-2

Logos Verlag Berlin GmbH
Comeniushof, Gubener Str. 47,
10243 Berlin
Tel.: +49 (0)30 42 85 10 90
Fax: +49 (0)30 42 85 10 92
INTERNET: http://www.logos-verlag.de

Maik Wurdel

An Integrated Formal Task Specification
Method for Smart Environments

Die vorliegende Arbeit wurde von der Fakultät für Informatik und Elektrotechnik der Universität Rostock als Dissertation zur Erlangung des akademischen Grades Doktor-Ingenieur (Dr.-Ing.) angenommen. Die Verteidigung der Dissertation fand am 29.06.2011 statt.

Gutachter:

Prof.-Dr.-Ing. habil. Peter Forbrig

Universität Rostock, Lehrstuhl für Softwaretechnik

Prof. Dr.-Ing. Thomas Kirste

Universität Rostock, Lehrstuhl für Mobile Multimediale Informationssysteme

Prof. Jean Vanderdonckt

Université catholique de Louvain, Louvain School of Management

ABSTRACT

This thesis is concerned with the development of interactive systems for smart environments. One of the characteristic of smart environments is the need to support different interaction paradigms at runtime. On the one hand interaction is performed explicitly: the user performs an action in order to interact with the system (e.g., pressing a button to adjust the light). On the other hand actions of the user are interpreted by the smart environment, even though they have not been performed primarily to interact with the system: implicit interactions (e.g., walking to the speaker's desk to give a talk). A smart environment tries to infer those interactions to assist the user in her work (e.g., display slides at the projection canvas). Both interaction paradigms originate from different research fields and are currently treated independently although implicit and explicit interaction mutually influence each other and occur interleaved.

To address this shortcoming, in this thesis a holistic approach to interaction development integrating both interaction paradigms is proposed. For this purpose task models are utilized which have been proven successful in Human-Computer Interaction for user interface design (a special branch of explicit interaction). User tasks are specified and transformed in diverse model-based development steps in order to semi-automatically generate the user interface. An analogous approach based on task models for implicit interaction is proposed in this thesis. To base the development of implicit and explicit interaction on task models leads to better integration of both interaction paradigms and supports the alternation and transition from one paradigm to the other at runtime.

Through the new field of application for task models, namely smart environments, additional requirements for task modeling languages have been revealed as tasks are tightly coupled to the technologies present in the smart environment and the contextual dependencies of tasks are of high relevance for implicit interaction (e.g., where is a certain task executable in the smart environment?). Thus, a part of this thesis is the newly designed task modeling language, CTML, which support typical features of task modeling, such as hierarchical decomposition and temporal operators, but also comprises new concepts like preconditions and effects based on location, device and domain knowledge. In smart environments cooperative aspects of task performance are of particular importance because tasks are usually performed by multiple users. Therefore concepts for synchronization of tasks of different users and teams are integrated in the language.

Another research objectives tackled in this thesis was the development of an integrated development approach based on task models for interaction development in smart environments. An iterative, incremental model has been selected since it supports user feedback and experience better than classical software engineering methods. In such an approach, models are not created in one sweep but iteratively being evaluated and perfected with each iteration. Model adaptation is therefore a common issue and needs to be supported. Different refinement relations for CTML models are part of the development methodology which determine whether a certain adaptation is valid with respect to the base model. The relations are categorized into structural and behavioral refinement. In case of the latter one can further distinguish between fully-automated refinement checks and interactive priorization of tasks by so called meta operators. In particular, behavioral refinement is a helpful device to verify adaptations with respect to their base model. Different refinement relations are employed depending on the current phase of development: While models in early phases are compared with less stringent relations, during specification and design rather strict relations are advocated. The integration of these refinement relations into the development approach is another contribution towards the methodic development of smart environments.

With this thesis a practical as well as methodical contribution to the research field of smart environments is accomplished. The developed concepts are utilized through tool support.

Keywords: Task Modeling, Smart Environment, implicit and explicit Interaction, Refinement

Computing-Reviews-Classification: D.2.1 Requirements/Specification, H.1 Models and Principles, H.5.2 User Interfaces

ZUSAMMENFASSUNG

Die vorliegende Arbeit behandelt die Entwicklung von interaktiven Systemen in intelligenten Umgebungen. Als Besonderheit dieser Umgebungen ist zu beachten, dass verschiedene Interaktionsparadigmen während der Benutzung zu unterstützen sind. Auf der einen Seite erfolgt die Interaktion explizit: der Nutzer führt Aktionen aus, um zu interagieren (z.b. Drücken eines Knopfes um die Helligkeit anzupassen). Auf der anderen Seite werden auch Aktionen des Nutzers durch die intelligente Umgebung interpretiert, die jedoch nicht primär zur Interaktion ausgeführt wurden, sogenannte implizite Interaktionen (z.b. Vortreten zum Rednerpult, um einen Vortrag zu halten). Eine intelligente Umgebung versucht diese implizite Interaktion zu erkennen, um dem Nutzer zu assistieren (z.b. Projektion der Vortragsfolien). Diese beiden Paradigmen der Interaktion stammen aus verschiedenen Forschungsbereichen und wurden bisher weitestgehend isoliert betrachtet, obwohl sie sich wechselseitig beeinflussen und gleichzeitig auftreten.

Daher wird in dieser Arbeit ein ganzheitlicher Lösungsansatz bezüglich beider Interaktionsformen vorgeschlagen. Dazu wird auf Aufgabenmodelle zurückgegriffen, die sich im Forschungsbereich der Mensch-Maschine Interaktion für die Oberflächenentwicklung (ein spezieller Zweig der expliziten Interaktion) bewährt haben. Mittels solcher Modelle werden die Aufgaben des Nutzers spezifiziert, um daraus durch verschiedene modellbasierte Entwicklungsverfahren eine Oberfläche zu erzeugen. Eine analoge Verfahrensweise basierend auf Aufgabenmodellen für die Entwicklung der impliziten Interaktion wird in dieser Arbeit vorgeschlagen. Implizite und explizite Interaktion auf Aufgabenmodellen beruhen zu lassen, resultiert in einer besseren Integration beider Paradigmen und der Unterstützung von Wechseln der Interaktionsform während des Betriebs der intelligenten Umgebung.

Durch die Verwendung von Aufgabenmodellen für die implizite und explizite Interaktion in intelligenten Umgebungen ergeben sich neue Anforderungen an eine Aufgabenmodellierungssprache, da die Aufgaben und deren Ausführbarkeit in einer intelligenten Umgebung stark an die Technologien innerhalb der Umgebung gebunden sind und die kontextabhängige Ausführbarkeit der Aufgaben für die implizite Interaktion von großer Bedeutung ist (z.b.: An welchem Ort innerhalb einer intelligenten Umgebung ist eine Aufgabe ausführbar?). Daher wurde im Rahmen dieser Arbeit eine neue Aufgabenmodellierungssprache, CTML, entwickelt, die sowohl klassische Konzepte der Aufgabenmodellierung, wie z.b. hierarchische Dekomposition und temporale Operatoren unterstützt, aber auch neue Konzepte wie Vorbedingungen und Effekte basierend auf Orts-, Geräte- und Domänenwissen unterstützt. Eine besondere Bedeutung im Umfeld der intelligenten Umgebungen fällt dem kooperativen Aspekt der Aufgabenausführung zu, da im Allgemeinen mehrere Nutzer gemeinsam an Aktivitäten beteiligt sind. Daher sind Konzepte zur Synchronisation von Aufgaben verschiedener Nutzer und von Teams in der Sprache integriert.

Ein weiteres Ziel der Arbeit bestand in der Herausarbeitung eines integrierten Entwicklungsansatzes basierend auf Aufgabenmodellen für die Interaktion in intelligenten Umgebungen. Ein iteratives, inkrementelles Modell wird vorgeschlagen, da es unter anderem Nutzerfeedback besser als klassische Softwareentwicklungsmethoden unterstützt. Dabei werden Modelle „Schritt für Schritt" entwickelt und gegenüber dem Nutzer evaluiert und gegebenenfalls adaptiert. Eine Herausforderung bei dieser Art von Vorgehen ist die Konsistenz des weiterentwickelten Modells bezüglich des Ausgangsmodells. Daher wurden in dieser Arbeit sogenannte Verfeinerungsrelationen für CTML Modelle entwickelt, die auf der formalen Syntax und Semantik von CTML basieren. Grundsätzlich wird zwischen struktureller Verfeinerung und Verhaltensverfeinerung unterschieden. Bei der Verhaltensverfeinerung ist zwischen vollautomatisierten Verfahren und interaktiver Priorisierung von Aufgaben mittels Meta-Operatoren zu unterscheiden. Insbesondere die Verhaltensverfeinerung ist ein sehr hilfreiches Werkzeug, um Adaptionen auf ihre Korrektheit bezüglich des Ausgangsmodells zu überprüfen. Die entwickelten Relationen zur Beschränkung der Änderbarkeit von Modellen kommen jeweils in unterschiedlichen Entwicklungsphasen zum Einsatz: Während weniger stringente Relationen zumeist in der Analyse verwendet werden, sind die Relationen während der Spezifikation und des Designs wesentlich strenger. Die Einbettung der Relationen in den modellbasierten Entwicklungsansatz stellt einen weiteren Beitrag dieser Arbeit zur methodischen Entwicklung intelligenter Umgebungen dar.

Mit der Arbeit wird sowohl ein methodischer als praktischer Beitrag im Forschungsfeld der intelligenten Umgebungen geleistet. Für die entwickelten Konzepte wurde eine Werkzeugunterstützung bereitgestellt.

Schlüsselwörter: Aufgabenmodellierung, intelligente Umgebung, implizite und explizite Interaktion, Verfeinerung

Computing-Reviews-Klassifizierung: D.2.1 Requirements/Specification, H.1 Models and Principles, H.5.2 User Interfaces

ACKNOWLEDGEMENTS

Research is never done alone. Numerous people have been involved while writing this thesis. I am grateful to a number of individuals and organizations:

First and foremost I thank my supervisor Prof. Forbrig who gave me the chance of doing the PhD in his group. His critical thinking and way of listening made this thesis what it is.

My co-supervisors, Prof. Kirste and Prof. Vanderdonckt, for their feedback and ideas especially in the last year. I am thankful for the cooperation with Prof. Kirste in the last four years and in particular in the last year in MuSAMA. I deeply appreciate the numerous discussions at conferences with Prof. Vanderdonckt and his way of connecting people.

The German Research Foundation for the financial support over a protracted period of time.

My colleagues from my research group Softwaretechnik, especially Gregor and Jens, who have been striving with the same issues. Gregor for the unreasonable amount of proofreading.

The Graduate School MuSAMA for the opportunity to work in an interesting field of diverse research areas. The former and current scholars of MuSAMA for invaluable discussions and moral backup over the last four years. Special thanks to Florian, Christoph, Christian, Henry, Christiane, and Michael.

I thank the following colleagues and friends: Dr. Daniel Sinnig for the endless paper writing sessions, Dr. Krishnan for his support during my diploma thesis who motivated me doing the PhD. Frank and Andre for the coffee breaks. My friends who helped me relaxing from problems during research.

My family, my sister Caroline, my mother and father, and my grandparents for the backup and support over the years as student. Without you there wouldn't be a thesis today.

Above all, I am grateful for my own little family. My love, Jana, and the sunshine in our life, Lion.

TABLE OF CONTENTS

LIST OF FIGURES

LIST OF TABLES

LIST OF ABBREVIATIONS

ACP	Algebra of Communicating Processes
AI	Artificial Intelligence
AmI	Ambient Intelligence
AUI	Abstract User Interface
BPEL	Business Process Execution Language
BPMN	Business Process Modeling Notation
CSCW	Computer Supported Cooperative Work
CSP	Communicating Sequential Processes
CCS	Calculus of Communicating Systems
CCTT	Cooperative Concur Task Trees
CTT	Concur Task Trees
CUI	Concrete User Interface
FDR	Failures Divergence Refinement
GOMS	Goals Operators Methods Selection Rules
GTA	Groupware Task Analysis
HCI	Human Computer interaction
HCSE	Human Centered Software Engineering
HTA	Hierarchical Task Analysis
IDE	Integrated development environment
K-MAD	Kernel of Model for Activity Description
LOTOS	Language of Temporal Ordering Specification
LTS	Labeled Transition System
MAD*	Méthode Analytique de Description des taches
MDA	Model-Driven Architecture
MDD	Model-Driven Development
MB-UI	Model-based user interface
MUI	Multiple User Interfaces
OCL	Object Constraint Language
POMSET	Partial ordered multi set
POSET	Partial ordered set
RUP	Rational Unified Process
SE	Software engineering
SmE	Smart Environment
TAG	Task Action Grammar
TKS	Task Knowledge Structures
UI	User Interface
UCD	User Centered Design
VTMB	Visual Task Model Builder
WIMP	Windows Icons Menu Pointing Device

Chapter 1
Introduction

Interaction design is a complex task even for desktop systems. With the advent of miniaturization and seamless integration of devices into everyday life technology-enhanced physical spaces, so called Smart Environments (SmE(s)), are becoming possible. A SmE is a physical space in which technology is seamlessly integrated in order to assist the user in performing tasks to reach its goal more conveniently than without supportive technology. SmEs are not limited to a particular domain and therefore for almost all kind of physical places in which tasks are performed a SmE can be imagined in order to support the user. However, SmEs are limited to physical places and as such exclude some aspects which are relevant for ubiquitous and pervasive computing e.g., mobility, communication, and failures beyond the physical boundaries of the SmE.

The interaction design for such environments comprises a fundamentally higher complexity in several dimensions. In order to cope with such a complexity new methods need to be developed. The research field of Human Computer Interaction (HCI) has developed techniques for interaction design which are partially suitable for SmEs. However, they are not useful out of the box as the special constraints for SmEs are naturally not incorporated.

1.1 Problem Statement

HCI methods have become more and more mature in order to manage the complexity involved in developing interactive software systems. The methods developed range from entire development methodologies, requirements engineering techniques to specific methods based on models with corresponding tool support. Especially in the field of model-based user interface development (MB-UI) and Multiple User Interfaces (MUI) elaborate approaches exist [Luyten, 2004; Paternò, 1999; Seffah & Javahery, 2004; Vanderdonckt, 2008].

As the interaction with the software system is shifting from being explicit, usually involving desktop systems, to be more and more implicit, as it is the case in SmEs, those methods fail to incorporate the increased complexity. Several causes contribute to this complexity: SmEs are technical enhanced, physical environments where tasks are usually performed in a collaborative manner using tools and artifacts. Therefore the potential task performance is strongly interrelated to the environment's state and the group activity. In order to cope with such a complexity new methods need to be designed.

The research field of SmEs is dominated by technology driven approaches leaving out (to some extent) development methodologies, requirement elicitation and user needs. HCI methods can therefore offer different viewpoints on challenges in SmEs and additionally present solutions for these challenges.

Interaction design for SmEs has been tackled by two distinct research communities: First, there are researchers investigating how to develop explicit user interfaces (UI(s)) for SmEs. MB-UI development is a particular branch of that community. Research questions posed by UI development for SmEs are amongst others migratability, multiple modalities, suspendability, plasticity, location-awareness, platform independency, and composibility [Blumendorf et al., 2007; Demeure & Calvary, 2003; Luyten et al., 2003]. MB-UI development is able to partially solve some of those issues even though this naturally depends on the choice of approach and models involved. Second, the research field of implicit interaction examines interaction design based on gestures, movement and other behaviors of users which are not performed with the intention of interaction [Schmidt et al., 2005]. The various approaches supporting implicit interaction are mainly technically driven and no conceptual modeling is performed during development. Therefore, the following research hypothesis can be identified:

1. **Missing Integration of Explicit and Implicit Interaction.** The separate development of interaction in SmE is inconvenient. As both interaction techniques occur interleaved a coherent approach needs to be developed in order to achieve a usable interaction. Basing the interaction development of both types on the same process model and artifacts ensures better transitions of interaction and better combination of both interaction techniques at same time.

As model-based development has been successfully applied to explicit interaction, an integrated methodology may also be beneficial for the integration of both interaction techniques. The reasons for following a model-based approach are multifold: design is raised to a higher level of abstraction which enables conceptual modeling instead technology-driven design. Abstracting from concrete technologies allows for migrating a solution to another platform more easily. Design decisions are made at a conceptual level and thus better support forward and reverse engineering as well as cost, risk and time management. In order to employ a MB-UI development approach for explicit interaction appropriate models are needed.

Task analysis and modeling has been a vital research interest in HCI for decades. It has been successfully applied to numerous domains and application areas ranging from requirement elicitation to system operation. One particular application area of task modeling is MB-UI development in which task modeling is the first artifact to be created [Forbrig et al., 2003]. Various task driven approaches exist tackling explicit interaction [Luyten, 2004; Paternò, 1999; Vanderdonckt, 2008]. However, when examining the current development methodologies for implicit and explicit interaction for SmEs and applying the existing task modeling techniques to SmEs diverse limitations exist:

2. **Lack of Expressiveness.** Current task modeling techniques are not expressive enough in order to model tasks in SmEs adequately. Task models are often too abstract and miss important aspects of the domain of SmEs. In essence, the models do not incorporate the special constraints and concepts such as multiple users, location-awareness, and state

dependency. Moreover existing task modeling languages also lack the incorporation of interfaces to lower levels to continue design.

3. **Lack of Methodical Engineering.** SmEs are technology driven prototypes and usually not engineered. Such an approach implies the loss of some important features: reusability, consistency, traceability, cost and risk management [Kruchten, 2003; Sommerville, 2006; Vanderdonckt, 2008].

In this thesis a model-based approach for the interaction development in SmEs is proposed. More precisely, the Collaborative Task Modeling Language (CTML) is introduced in order to tackle the three issues named above (1.,2. and 3.) to improve the development of implicit and explicit interaction in SmEs. We attempt to bridge the gap between HCI and the research area of SmEs by introducing a task-based development methodology. A high level modeling approach is proposed which is able to specify the tasks in SmEs adequately in order to drive the development of explicit and implicit interaction. The task driven methodology introduced in this thesis makes use of refinement in order to guide the adaptations of CTML models which relies on a formal syntax and semantics. Having iteratively created a CTML model, transformations to artifacts used in explicit and implicit interaction can be derived (semi-) automatically. Interfaces to other artifacts are identified to continue design or derive a task model based on existing artifacts involved.

1.2 Scope, Aims and Contribution

1.2.1 Scope

The thesis attempts to bridge two worlds: SmEs and HCI task modeling. The first research area usually treats development as technical challenges whereas the latter takes into account user needs and the implications of the interaction presented by a system. The interaction in SmEs is complex to develop as implicit and explicit interaction are mingled at runtime. Nevertheless, the development of the interaction is usually underemphasized. Applying HCI task modeling to SmEs can be one approach to make interaction development more engineering-like. A process model needs to be established in order to create a structured procedure for interaction development.

However, the thesis does not claim that task models are appropriate to solve all issue in SmEs. In essence, we argue that they are suitable artifacts which can be discussed and refined based on user needs. When a proper task model has been defined new artifacts are derived that are used to further drive design (e.g., the dialog model in MB-UI) or operate the (sub) system of the SmEs (e.g., Hidden Markov model (HMM) for intention recognition).

The thesis is classified according to the methodological research framework given by Hevner *et al.* [2004]. The instantiated framework for the thesis is depicted in Figure 1-1. On the right hand side the environment the research is performed in is given which outlines the boundaries of research and defines the problem. On the right hand side the theories serving as foundation of the research in this thesis are listed. Those theories are applied in order to conduct the research in the center of the figure. In the remainder of the introduction Figure 1-1 serves as reference point in order to precisely define research objectives, contributions and research methods applied in this thesis.

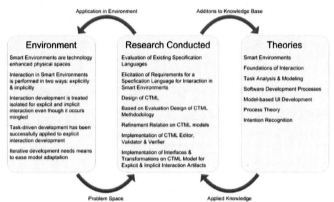

Figure 1-1 The Instantiated Research Framework according to [Hevner *et al.*, 2004]

1.2.2 Research Objectives

Based on the problem statement and the scope of the thesis we identified the following research objectives:

Iterative Development Methodology. The primary objective of this thesis is an integrated development methodology for the interaction in SmEs. Two core requirements can be identified: the incorporation of iterative design and the usage of tasks as building blocks for the methodology. The reason for both is to support a user-centered design process [Gulliksen *et al.*, 2005]. The development methodology based on tasks will serve as guidance during all stages of development and will give advice in which phases of the project what kind of activities are carried out. Depending on the stage of development, analysis, requirements or design, task modeling is performed (at different levels of abstraction). Due to the stepwise evolution of modeling artifacts in an iterative development methodology different refinement relations are needed to answer the question whether a certain adaptation of a model is still a valid implementation of its predecessor. In order to do so the modeling language to be developed implementing the methodology needs to be formally founded.

Enhancing Task Modeling. Task modeling for SmEs is to our knowledge an untackled research area in HCI. In the research field of SmEs languages exist for specifying the potential behavior of actors within such an environment. However those languages are mainly used for modeling system operations and have not been designed for user-centered design. HCI task models solve this issue as they are understandable by non-computer scientist (e.g., stakeholders, users) which fosters the capability for user-centered design. Classical task modeling languages are however not expressive enough to model tasks for SmEs adequately. Therefore several extensions need to be introduced in order to incorporate multi-user scenarios, location awareness and state-dependent task modeling.

Formal Foundation of Task Modeling. A superior expressiveness of a modeling language usually results in loss of understandability and increased ambiguity. This also applies to task modeling even though this is particular unfortunate as these are primary aspects of task modeling. To address this shortcoming, validation and verification algorithms are employed which base upon a formal syntax and semantics of CTML. Moreover, the semantic foundation is able to rule out ambiguities which fosters model sharing and cross platform implementations. In order to do so a suitable semantic model needs to be selected which captures the envisioned behavior best. Based on the formal foundation, a set of refinement relations are defined supporting the task modeler during all stages of development. More precisely, a flexible approach to refinement is needed that allows for defining which parts of a specification needs to be retained (and which can be dismissed) in the subsequent development steps.

Integration of Related Artifacts. Task modeling is not the only activity during interaction design. Requirement specifications may exist before task modeling is performed. In addition specifications may be derived based on task models. Therefore an integrated development methodology should advice the interaction designer how to transit from one specification to another. The task model can be either the transformation source or target. In order to integrate task modeling in software engineering practice interfaces to related artifacts need to be established. Therefore an elicitation approach needs to be developed which enables the designer to first derive an analysis task model. During the different phases this task model is adapted and refined. Eventually the created model needs to be transformed into a more detailed description which has to be supported by the development methodology as well.

Tool Support. To effectively make use of a modeling language suitable tool support needs to be provided. The functionality of such tools range from creation, manipulation, animation, validation and verification of models but also includes the support of the methodology defined in accordance with the modeling language. Moreover it is desirable to elicit early feedback through an integrated tool environment which presents the different functionalities of the tool in a homogenous manner.

1.2.3 Contributions

(1) **The Collaborative Task Modeling Language (CTML).** The modeling language presented in this thesis is characterized by its superior expressiveness with respect to its application domain. It extends CTT-like notations ([Paternò, 1999]) in several dimensions in order to support task modeling for SmEs. It inherently supports multi-user scenarios by a role-based task modeling approach and explicitly allows for modeling multi-user, device, location and state dependencies in a formal manner. A corresponding interpreter has been developed. More precisely, the modeling language is capable of specifying the interrelation of tasks of different actors within the environment on a role based level which enhances the cooperational aspect of the task modeling approach published by Mori *et al.* significantly [2002]. Preliminary results with regard to modeling cooperation have been published in [Wurdel *et al.*, 2008a; Wurdel *et al.*, 2008e]. An integration of location dependencies in task modeling has been described in [Wurdel, 2009] whereas the interplay of task modeling and device modeling has been proposed in

[Forbrig & Wurdel, 2010]. In [Wurdel *et al.*, 2008b] the bond of domain modeling and task modeling has been emphasized.

(2) **The CTML Development Approach.** The methodology in which CTML is embedded assumes a two-folded approach for task modeling. Either task modeling is performed in order to develop the explicit or the implicit interaction in a SmE. Both approaches naturally consist of a series of iteratively performed activities which not only involve task modeling but also include the following: analysis and requirement specification documents such as use cases, scenarios or questionnaires need to be integrated in order to bridge the gap between software engineers and interaction designer. As task modeling is also performed in different phases of development the development methodology gives advice how task modeling is supposed to be treated in each stage. In detail, the methodology defines the level of abstraction for performing task modeling and defines how transition from one development phase to another can be performed. In order to facilitate these transitions refinement relations have been defined to verify the validity of adaptations. However, simply creating a set of task models is insufficient. Eventually other artifacts need to be created. The development approach also covers the detailed design phase which employs other artifacts depending on the scope of development (explicit or implicit interaction). Preliminary results addressing the early stages of development have been published in [Wurdel & Forbrig, 2009] whereas [Wurdel *et al.*, 2008c] and [Wurdel *et al.*, 2008e] primary focus on the task modeling stages of development. Interfaces to lower level design artifacts have been proposed in [Wurdel *et al.*, 2007].

(3) **Formal Foundation and Refinement based on Meta Operators.** In order to manage complexity when using CTML formal methods are employed. To do so the syntax and semantics have been defined formally. The abstract syntax is defined using set theory whereas the semantic domain of choice is LTSs. This approach results in an interleaving semantics which in turn enables different comparison semantics for CTML specifications. The existing comparison semantics (such completed trace semantics) are well suited for task modeling but miss the flexibility which is needed to effectively use refinement. Especially when transiting between different development phases such general comparison semantics hamper the development and adaptation of models. Therefore an approach is proposed which makes use of interactively assigned meta operators to tasks in order to define which tasks need to be retained or can be dismissed in the subsequent model. Amongst others, we introduce the novel comparison semantics *mandatory scenario equivalence* and *mandatory scenario inclusion*. The defined refinement relations for CTML are used to drive the design of CTML models and therefore are the core instruments of the development methodology. The approach has been partially published in [Wurdel *et al.*, 2008d].

(4) **The CTML Editor, Validator and Verifier.** To effectively make use of CTML and its development methodology a tool suite integrated in the Eclipse IDE (integrated development environment) has been developed. First, there is the CTML editor which allows the task modeler to create and manipulate CTML specification graphically. Next, the

CTML validator can be used to interactively explore the created specification. Different visual modes have been developed to allow validation by animation. Moreover well-formedness criteria are checked to ease the design of CTML specifications. The refinement relations defined over CTML specifications are implemented by the CTML verifier. This tool takes two models as input and transforms both into LTSs which are then compared according to the interactively selected comparison semantics. The tool suite for CTML is integrated in the tools developed in our research group. Therefore the derivation of dialog models based on CTML models can be conveniently performed to further continue model-based UI (MB-UI) development. For implicit interaction hidden Markov models can automatically be created based on CTML specifications which are used to operate the intention recognition module of our experimental SmE (published in [Wurdel *et al.*, 2007]). The tool suite has been described in [Wurdel *et al.*, 2008e] and [Wurdel *et al.*, 2009].

1.3 Organization of the Thesis

The thesis is divided into two main parts. The first part reiterates through background information and related work which is sub-divided into three separate chapters:

In **Chapter 2** the basic terms of this thesis are clarified and the implications of interaction in SmEs are identified. Moreover the need for a structured engineering approach is claimed. Subsequently HCI and software engineering (SE) viewpoints are explained with respect to SmEs and task-driven development. Moreover in **Chapter 3** also existing task modeling approaches and languages are additionally assessed with respect to the scope of this thesis. The last chapter of the first part (**Chapter 4**) examines preexisting semantic domains, their application, their individual assets and drawbacks. Based on these explanations the semantic domain of choice for CTML is selected.

In the second part of the thesis the language and development approach of CTML are explained in detail. The requirements of an illustrating scenario are elicited on which the design of the language and its methodology are based on. **Chapter 5** introduces the usage scenario within the domain of SmEs, a technology-enhanced meeting room, and task models in order to illustrate the requirements for CTML. In **Chapter 6** the language is explained in detail. The chapter starts with an informal graphical description of the modeling elements and their semantics. Subsequently the formal abstract syntax and semantics based on LTSs are given. Moreover the refinement relations necessary to drive the design of CTML models are defined and described. In order to ease the understanding a running example accompanies the definitions. The development approach covering analysis, requirements and design is illustrated in **Chapter 7**. It is shown how a CTML model is best developed depending on the phase of development. Moreover it is shown which refinement relations are used during all stages of design in order to verify that defined requirements are truthfully transmitted to design and implemented accordingly.

Chapter 8 summarizes the thesis and highlights the major contributions of the thesis. In addition future research avenues are presented.

I. Smart Environments, Software Engineering, HCI and Formal Methods

Chapter 2
Smart Environments

2.1 Disambiguation

Before going into details about the research field of SmEs various related terms are examined and defined to build a common ground to start from. This is particular of importance as the research field of SmEs and similar research fields are rather young and do not provide a valid and sound basis.

2.1.1 Ubiquitous Computing

The term ubiquitous computing coined by Weiser describes the vision of a world where information can be accessed everywhere and at any time not by having a mobile device but by the existence of accessible devices in our surroundings which we are eventually not even aware of [1991]. In contrast to a virtual environment ubiquitous computing augments the reality with a vast amount of devices being connected via wireless network making a PDA unnecessary. Central to this vision is the omnipresence of small and cheap devices capable of delivering information services to ease everyday tasks and making information available at any place and any time. In order to integrate those devices into the surroundings they need to be physically small and network attached to cooperate seamlessly. Even though Weiser stresses that wireless networking is a major issue other challenges are posed by this paradigm (hard- and software compatibility, protocols, security, privacy) [1993]. Moreover with respect to HCI an innovative interaction paradigm is needed [Weiser, 1991]:

> "The most profound technologies are those that disappear. They weave themselves
> into the fabric of everyday life until they are indistinguishable from it."

In order to implement the so called invisible computer a new interaction paradigm needs to be developed from being explicit as it is the case in desktop environments to being more and more implicit. Implicit interaction is defined as an action which is not primarily performed to interact with a system but is used by the system as input or trigger [Schmidt, 2000]. In this vein gestures can become an interaction modality even though the user is not even aware of. Implicit interaction modalities add an enormous complexity in terms of development effort and rationale for interactive systems.

Originally not stated by Weiser but a very important point of a ubiquitous computing environment is context-awareness which is a prerequisite to implement implicit interaction. A system is called context-aware if its behavior is depending on continuously measured values characterizing the user or her preferences. The most often used source of context is location since it is by far the easiest one to measure and exhibits a high level of semantic information [Schmidt *et al.*, 1998]. Dey defines context as [Dey & Abowd, 2000]:

> *"... any information that can be used to characterize the situation of an entity."*

This definition shows the dilemma of a generally applicable definition of context. What constitutes to context information depends on the domain as well as the environment the system is installed in. If the system is developed to help elder people in performing everyday tasks in their home location is definitive a relevant context information. In contrast in office set up not necessarily location information are needed as the person might only move once in a while to get a coffee.

The concept of ubiquitous computing has already been implemented in experimental setups (e.g., [Bauer *et al.*, 2004; Cook *et al.*, 2009]) and is still a research field. However those prototypes show potential application fields and implications of a device augmented world. As devices become more integrated and cheaper they will make their way into everyday life in a sufficient manner to build reasonable ubiquitous computing environment.

2.1.2 Pervasive Computing

The vision of pervasive computing is also built upon the upcoming omnipresence of devices it has no substantial differences to ubiquitous computing. Throughout the remainder of the thesis ubiquitous computing is used as it is the older term [Ronzani, 2009].

2.1.3 Ambient Intelligence

Ubiquitous computing and pervasive computing are paradigms addressing primarily the technical challenges implicated by the omnipresence of devices. Taking for granted that networking issues are mainly solved and the omnipresence of interconnected device exists in small scenarios the need for services/ applications using those devices arises.

The research field of ambient intelligence (AmI) tackles this question. Originally defined as electronic environments being aware and responsive to users [Aarts *et al.*, 2002], new definitions emphasize the need for such a system to be "non-obtrusively integrated into everyday objects and environments" (ambient) and incorporate "specific forms of social interaction" (intelligence) [Aarts & de Ruyter, 2009]. By social interaction the authors mean the following characteristics of AmI applications:

- **Context-awareness.** As explained earlier, context-awareness describes the ability of a system to adapt its behavior according to the context of use which can be all relevant data according to the domain and user. When running a system over time it needs to adapt itself according to the users' habits and usage patterns in order to be supportive for the user.

- **Personalization.** Usually information services of ambient applications comprise personalized data. In order to be truly supportive this data can be taken into account. Based upon observation and queried data of the user, personalization can be implemented. In this vein AmI applications are able to react individualized according to the users' needs.

- **Proactiveness.** The most discussed characteristic of AmI applications is pro-activeness. It is understood as system actions performed without explicit interaction based upon observation. It is a fascinating idea to have a system being able to anticipate users' next action and perform it on behalf of the user (or a supportive task). Numerous proactive applications have been developed in the last years. However field studies document that users are often not comfortable when the system is acting autonomously without explicitly invoking an action [Koskinen *et al.*, 2006].

AmI needs to be unobtrusive and supportive. Whereas the first can be partly achieved by miniaturization and integration; both challenges can only be sufficiently tackled by focusing on the human needs. Actually the human needs and tasks are key objectives of such systems as they are supposed to serve the user. Therefore other requirements addressing the user needs can be stated:

- **Control.** As already briefly mentioned above users are not feeling comfortable when control is shifting from people to machine. Consequently developers need to bear in mind that AmI applications need to offer the opportunity to let the user control the system at least to a certain degree.

- **Correctness.** As long as the system delivers the correct services the user is fine but as soon as errors occur trust into the system ceases. Considering that proactive systems will always be incorrect in some cases mechanisms are needed to provide feedback to the users why the system performed a certain action. Additionally interfaces are needed to let users correct decisions made by the system.

- **Interfaces.** One lesson learned from mobile computing is that rendered UIs for desktop systems cannot just be scaled down to meet the requirements of a PDA or cell phone. The UI must be adapted substantially to meet the different contexts and device capabilities. Even though this raises the complexity of development it is still manageable. However for AmI applications the way how people will interact is not yet clear. Of course mobile devices will play an important role but other types of interfaces are interesting as well. In terms of explicit interaction tangible UIs are a candidate. They are physical objects belonging to the surroundings but used as control and representation of digital values which is totally new concept compared to display based UIs [Ullmer & Ishii, 2000]. There is no distinction between input and output device as tangible user interfaces comprise both. Hence they integrate seamlessly into the environment by being a part of them. An advantage of tangible UIs to ordinary GUIs is the bond of manipulated data and the interface itself. Therefore it is more intuitive to the user. An example of a tangible UI would be the control of a steerable projector with 3D objects whereas the rotation of the objects leads to the accordant rotation of the projector. By moving the focus can be adjusted.

- **Automation.** The reassignment of tasks from a human being to an automated system has been always discussed controversially. When this is performed explicitly the human is aware of the reassignment. In AmI application the reassignment may be performed silently and as such may not be anticipated or approved by the user which can lead to unsatisfying experience. A thorough analysis of users' behavior as well as users' need for automation is needed to avoid this pitfall. Research conducted in this area has been conducted by Sheridan [2002].

2.1.4 Smart Environments

According to Cook & Das a SmE (intelligent environment) is a physical place equipped with devices working to make the lives of the users more comfortable [2004]. As this is a generic definition they go into more detail and ground their definition upon the term *smart*. They state that such an environment should be able to acquire and apply knowledge autonomously about the users and the environment itself and to adapt to users' needs in order to improve their experience. What constitutes to an improvement depends on the type of environment, the individuals as well as the interaction facilities of the environment.

The concept of SmEs does not define on which level of abstraction "smartness" is implemented. Therefore a certain routing algorithm can constitute to a SmE as well as a certain sensor or interaction modality. It is even not clear whether the term smart really refers to intelligence as used for human beings but to just a new level of automation, user experience and usability. Cook & Das already state that SmEs try to make the user experience more comfortable which is not necessarily the case by the usage of artificial intelligence [2004].

Kirste refines the terms smartness in this context by the capability of an environment to react to the user's objectives and not to pure sensor data [2006]. To do so, according to Kirste, the environment needs knowledge about the user's point of view in the environment. This results in a conceptual framework with two source of information: sensor data and a prio knowledge used to interpret the sensor data resulting in appropriate solutions for the user. The definition of Kirste is therefore adopted in the remainder of the thesis.

In comparison to the provided definitions above it is to say that ubiquitous computing and AmI are both concepts to create a SmE. Providing a room with numerous devices realizing a certain value for the user can be a SmE implemented through ubiquitary presence of devices. However, having a set of devices in an environment being able to connect to the mobile devices of users implementing a service can be considered as SmE as well. Generally speaking the term which suits best to SmEs is AmI. Developing an AmI application for a physical environment results in a SmE. The characteristics of AmI can be straightforwardly applied to SmEs if they are bound to a limited physical space.

2.1.5 HCI Engineering

HCI is a multi disciplinary field involving, besides computer science, among others, psychology, organization studies, ergonomics, sociology, and engineering. However computer science is still the central discipline of HCI. The field HCI is working on can be characterized by the quote of Dix *et al.* [1997]:

> "... HCI involves the design, implementation and evaluation of interactive systems
> in the context of the user's task and work."

In order to design such a system sub processes addressing the software engineering life cycle need to be considered as well. Analysis and requirements engineering are important steps towards a valid design of an interactive system. The same applies for the implementation which involves coding as well, discussion, revision and high level design choices. The third part, according to Dix *et al.*, concerns the evaluation of an existing interactive system or of a prototype during design or implementation. The major topic of usability engineering and methods are belonging to this category.

Even though those activities highly correspond to software engineering practices a qualitative difference exists: design, implementation and evaluation are performed bearing in mind the user's task and natural work environment. This also includes studying the potential user(s) of the interactive system in accordance with their characteristics, capabilities and knowledge. Roughly speaking the idea of a task driven approach to create an interactive system relies on the hypothesis that the closer the interaction with the system is to the natural task performance the easier the user is willing to accept the developed system. On the one hand task analysis and modeling are central concepts to HCI as they help to incorporate the user's tasks into the development process; on the other hand HCI is much more than task analysis and modeling. Even though there is no unified theory of HCI there are commonly used techniques which help to improve the interaction varying from software development processes, requirements elicitation, design patterns, user involvement strategies to various evaluation techniques.

As a software engineer one is interested in the potential application areas during the software development process. This is when engineering comes into play. Engineering describes the structured way of achieving a design or artifact with respect to a certain criteria like quality, maintainability, traceability. According to this definition engineering the interaction means to apply HCI techniques to develop the interaction of the software system in a structured way. The criteria with respect to HCI can be, among others, usability, maintainability or soft criteria like appearance, low learning curve. Hence the development can be eased and less error-prone due to the structured way of developing.

Tool support can help in various ways to do so. In particular it helps to create, edit, manipulate, visualize, validate and verify certain artifacts. Moreover they can provide a basis for the implementation of a development process by making certain steps of the process supported by the tool. This becomes particularly important when artifacts become quite complex to understand and visualization techniques and verification algorithms are needed. In order to support an engineering process in HCI tools serve as a vehicle to reduce complexity, disburden the developer and foster development approaches.

The research field of MB-UI development serves as a good example of HCI engineering. UI design has been mostly treated as a creative process involving a UI designer creating the UI itself and a software engineer creating the functionality accessible via the UI. From HCI perspective this approach tackles the objective of creating the UI insufficiently. The HCI community agrees that a separate design process of the UI and the application core can easily fail because of a misleading UI being not appropriate for the developed functionality as well as the missing opportunity to create prototypes covering the UI and application core. The MB-UI process is able to solve those issues by integrating the user tasks in early stages of development. Hence prototypes of the UI can be created easily in accordance with the application core. The MB-UI process can also be considered as engineering method since it allows tracing design decisions, fosters maintenance, helps to improve usability, reduces complexity and allows for creation for UIs for multiple platforms. The various MB-UI tools (e.g., [Mori *et al.*, 2002; Reichart *et al.*, 2008; UsiXML, 2010]) for the creation, visualization and interpretation of models involved in creation of UIs in a model-based way are also a good example for the facilitation of a process through a tool chain.

2.2 Interacting with a Smart Environment

Generally speaking there are two ways of interaction within a SmE: implicitly and explicitly. This distinction was first discovered by Schmidt [2000]. Whereas explicit interaction is the standard concept since the invention of text-based interfaces, implicit interaction is a new paradigm developed in the research field of context-awareness in HCI. Although this distinction exists both paradigms are needed to implement a robust and usable system [Ju & Leifer, 2008]. Even current desktops systems involve explicit (e.g., using the mouse) and implicit interaction (e.g., starting the screensaver) even if it is rather simple.

Please note that there also other means for classifying SmEs. In [Shirehjini, 2007] a design space for SmE is proposed. Among others initiative is design decision for a SmE which is of interest here. Others are goal vs. functions based, modality or device selection. However such criteria play a minor role for the issues tackles in this thesis.

2.2.1 Explicit Interaction

As stated above explicit interaction is the common way of interacting with a software system. The concept is very simple: the system performs an action triggered by an explicit command of the user. The system changes its state accordingly to the performed action and provides feedback to the user who may in turn invoke another command resulting in an action.

According to Norman there are seven stages of actions how people do things and consequently interact with an interactive software system [2000]. Normans' model is depicted in Figure 2-1. The stages can be further classified to goal (1.), execution (2.-4.) and evaluation phase (5.-7.).

People start an action because they want to achieve a certain goal. According to Norman goals ("Dimming the light") are rather abstract and as such need to be concretized evolving into intentions ("Dimming the light by switch off lamp"). The steps 2.-4. create an action sequence implementing the intention ("Walk to the switch", "Press switch"). The next three steps are part of the evaluation phase. First, the new state of the world is perceived providing feedback to the prior executed actions. Second, the perceived state is interpreted according users' expectations and last evaluated with respect to the goal to be achieved. Even though those steps seem to be very rigid they are only a template where concrete procedure may fit into.

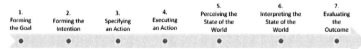

Figure 2-1 Norman's Model of Explicit Interaction

Certain steps can be dismissed whereas others might be iteratively executed. By defining these three phases (goal, execution and evaluation) two problems in HCI are identified: the gulf of execution and the gulf of evaluation. The first refers to the gap of available functions of a system and the available tasks from the user's point of view. The more the functions correspond to the tasks the more effective the interaction is. The later means the gap of presentation of the state of the device and the expectations from users' perspective. If the user perceives the presentation of the device state according to her expectations the gap is small and consequently the interaction effective. Hence the two gulfs can be kept small by delivering an appropriate UI as well as through the ability of users which can be trained. Certainly both approaches can be combined. However building the better UI is in most cases the reasonable option. This rather simple model is intuitive, easy to use and highlights primary issues for the development of interactive systems. Based upon that model Norman derives design aids to develop in a user-centered way resulting in a more usable system [2000].

After having investigated explicit interaction isolated it is now continued with the discussion of implicit interaction and development approaches implementing such an interaction technique.

2.2.2 Implicit Interaction

Due to its novelty implicit interaction has not been as thoroughly researched as explicit interaction. According to Schmidt *et al.* implicit human computer interaction is understood as [2005]:

> *...the interaction of a human with the environment and with artifacts which is aimed to accomplish a goal. Within this process the system acquires implicit input from the user and may present implicit output to the user...*

The predominant approach of considering implicit interaction only as a one-way approach which interprets actions of the users in order to assist is extended by Schmidt *et al.* because the reciprocity of input and output during interaction is considered. An implicit input is an action of the user which is not primarily performed in order to interact with the software system, SmE respectively, whereas an implicit output is a seamlessly integrated presentation of information to the user. The process of implicitly giving input to the software system can be conceptualized as layered model of intention recognition and strategy synthesis (e.g., turning on the light when a person enters the room, provisioning resources based on the predicted action). The seamless presentation of information is performed by embedding information presentation devices into the surroundings of the environment (e.g., LEDs, the cell phone, digital post-its). As embedded visualization of information is not in the scope of this thesis it will be left out from examination in the remainder.

In the following paragraphs existing conceptual framework addressing the development of implicit interaction are examined.

Goal-based Interaction

One particular design strategy in order to achieve implicit interaction is goal based interaction proposed by Heider and Kirste [2002]. In [Heider & Kirste, 2005] a layered model is suggested which employs formally defined goals. The model is based upon those goals to reduce complexity. On the highest level of abstraction the users' intention is analyzed which is directly mapped to a goal. Certainly a goal may be achieved by different actions sequences. The derivation and selection of action sequences is performed on the next level of abstraction: strategy planning. The resulting sequences of actions can be triggered to support the users' intention. The interface between both layers is the goal which is derived first and then achieved by a certain synthesized action sequence.

The model has only been validated for a technology enhanced meeting room and is therefore designed for this domain even though it seems to be prosperous to apply goal-based interaction to other types of SmEs and to a general case of interaction.

The Implicit Interaction Framework

A conceptual framework for the development of implicit interaction has been proposed by Ju *et al.* [2008; Ju & Leifer, 2008].

In Figure 2-2 the design space of implicit interaction according to Ju *et al.* is given [2008]. On the horizontal axis the initiative is depicted. This dimension defines the degree of automation and proactiveness the software system exhibits which matches the classification of Sheridan who proposed eight levels of automation and their implications [2002]. On the vertical axis attentional demand of the user in order to interact with the system is shown. The more the system is in the foreground the more attention is given by the user and is needed to use the system, and vice versa. The reason for defining such a design space is that the boundaries of implicit interaction are rather a continuum than a fixed set of properties. The first quadrant (Reactive, Foreground) is the design space where explicit interaction is used. The fourth quadrant (Proactive, Background) denotes the ideal case of an implicit interaction even though the degree of attentional demand and initiative may differ. Quadrant two and three are border cases as quadrant two (Proactive, Foreground) demand attention of the user while being proactive whereas quadrant three (Reactive, Background) needs explicit input but introduces automation to a certain degree.

The Implicit Interaction Framework classifies not only the design space for implicit interaction but also defines the boundaries of explicit and implicit interaction. Moreover due to its generality it is a domain independent model and can therefore be applied to any kind of SmE.

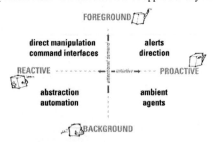

Figure 2-2 Implicit Interaction Framework by Ju et al. [2008]

However the generality of the approach is also a burden as only rather abstract guidance is given how to appropriately design implicit interaction. No artifacts and methods are proposed in order to develop interaction. Thus, the framework is useful for early stages of development in order to assess the envisioned way of interaction defining the degree of automation and attentional demand of the system under construction.

Contrariwise the novelty of the approach is the consideration of a transition of explicit to implicit interaction and an according continuous design space.

In order to fully cope with the different types of interaction in SmE a novel development approach is needed which takes into account both paradigms resulting in an integrated development methodology for the interaction in SmEs.

2.2.3 Explicit & Implicit Interaction

In [Kirste, 2006] a brief overview of existing prototypes of SmEs with respect to interaction is given. Kirste classifies the projects into three categories: implicit Interaction, explicit Interaction, and, explicit interaction with individual appliances. However the combination of all categories is actually the usual case. Here it is not distinguished between the different types of explicit interaction in contrast to Kirste.

Certainly simply applying the models from explicit interaction to implicit interaction is only with limited value. For example in Norman's model the user creates and executes an action sequence by herself which achieves the goal. In implicit interaction those actions are interpreted in order to derive the current intention which is used to trigger actions supporting the user in this current situation. To address this situation an adapted version of an interaction models is identified which is shown in Figure 2-3. The flow of events is very similar to Norman's original model but new steps are introduced comprising implicit interaction (A, B, and C). The new steps are not performed by the user but by the software system implementing the implicit interaction.

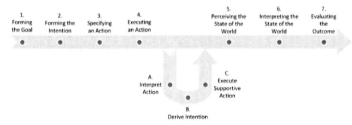

Figure 2-3 An Adapted Model of Interaction to incorporate Implicit Interaction

Only when the user executes an action implicit interaction is possible. What is considered as action to be interpreted depends naturally on the supported task and the level of automation to be envisioned [Ju & Leifer, 2008; Sheridan, 2002]. If such an action occurs it needs to be interpreted (A) in order to derive the current intention (B) of the user. Finally a mapping of the derived intention to a certain sequence of actions of the software system is performed. After the execution of the supportive tasks Norman's model of interaction is continued. However the perception, interpretation and evaluation of the result may need more work load as besides the executed action by the user also the supportive actions needs to be evaluated. The software developer of implicit interaction should bear that in mind. In certain cases the user may even be not able to perceive the current world state if the executed action sequence of the system performs invisible action from users' perspective or the gap between the last perceived state and state after the execution is just too big ("Gulf of Execution" and "Gulf of Evaluation" according to [Norman, 2000]).

Which technologies to be used in order to interpret actions, which actions to be interpreted as well as the same issues for the intention and supportive actions is not considered in this generic framework. To our knowledge a combined approach for the development of both interaction paradigms tackling the combination of explicit and implicit interaction has not been approached yet.

In the PhD thesis of Giersich it is stated that the ultimate goal is a pure implicit interaction [2009]:

> *"How can an ad-hoc smart environment optimally support a team of users in a meeting without explicit interaction?"*

However we believe that such an approach is counterproductive as there is always a transition between implicit interaction and explicit interaction. In fact the use of implicit interaction always implicates explicit interaction in the long run as users learn how the system reacts under certain conditions and interactions. In order to exemplify this fact the example of an automatic transmission of cars is consulted.

The idea of an automatic transmission is that the driver (user) of the car (system) does not need to care about which gear is appropriate at a certain speed. If the driver presses the gas pedal rather softly the car accelerates. However when pressing the gas pedal harder the transmission switches the gear in order to boost acceleration as the torsion is higher (as it is assumed that a high acceleration is needed). When passing a car the difference in speed of passing and passed car is crucial in order to reduce the distance needed to pass the car. Therefore a high acceleration is needed. Drivers using a manual transmission therefore switch the gear before starting the passing process which is not possible with an automatic transmission. When using an automatic transmission for the first time the passing process is performed by pressing the gas pedal hardly while passing the car. However switching the gear beforehand is much more desirable as it speeds up the passing process. Therefore some drivers of cars with an automatic transmission press the gas pedal hardly once before starting the passing process in order to force gear shifting to have a higher acceleration. Then they start the passing process. With respect to interaction a manual transmission is purely explicit. The user states what is needed by explicit interaction. Automatic transmission is partially implicit interaction as it is coded in the electronics of the system when gear shifting is performed. However this kind of interaction is not the best in all situations (e.g., passing a car). Therefore users derive a pattern how the system (e.g., the automatic transition) works and how it can be manipulated in order to suit their needs best. Pressing the gas pedal in order to make the transmission shift the gear (which has not been intended by the designer) is an explicit interaction.

This simple example already shows that users being in touch with a software system with implicit interaction tend to derive patterns about how the system works. Having formed a model about the system, the system is used with respect to that model. As the model is usually not complete implicit interaction may still occur but some former implicit interactions may become explicit. Therefore a combined approach is not only desired but mandatory in order to represent interaction SmEs adequately.

2.3 Smart Environments Prototypes

After having investigated the general interaction techniques applicable for SmEs more general examination about currently existing prototypes and their development are conducted.

2.3.1 Existing Prototypes

Industry and academia has produced numerous prototypes of SmEs. Naturally they differ in the field the research is conducted in which leads the development of the prototype. The most prominent projects accompanied by short abstracts are listed below:

- **Adaptive Home.** The aim of the project was the creation of a house which offers no additional UIs while being equipped with modern technology. The house is able to predict the behavior of its user by employing Artificial Neural Networks. Therefore the sequences of action to be executed are not hard wired but learned by the system. The software system ACHE (Adaptive Control of Home Environments) is used in order to adjust the light and ventilation of the environment. With respect to interaction only implicit interaction is used [Mozer, 1998; Mozer, 2004].

- **Aware Home.** Based on the findings of the Classroom 2000 project by Abowd a technology enhanced living environment was set up in order to design a living environment extensively making use of computing devices and services [1999]. The primary goal of the project was the assessment of potential supportive technologies in a home environment for elderly people and families. In order to do so different applications have been developed which can be found in [Kientz *et al.*, 2008]. With respect to technology localization tracking, image processing and machine learning techniques are used as building blocks to enable the development of the supportive software systems [Kientz *et al.*, 2008]. No statements are made about the interaction techniques used in the Aware Home. Based on the given information implicit interaction is assumed as sensing technology is employed. To which degree a combination of implicit and explicit interaction is used is not stated as well as development approaches for interaction in general are not tackled by the project.

- **EasyLiving.** Mircosofts initiative for the development of SmEs employs fixed rules in order to provide more comfortable experience. More precisely the predefined sequences of actions are triggered by conditions which need to hold in order to execute a certain sequence. With respect to interaction a combined approach of explicit and implicit interaction is envisioned even though explicit interaction is still an open issue [Brumitt *et al.*, 2000].

- **MavHome.** The application domain of this project is a technology enhanced home environment. In order to achieve this, a learning and prediction approach is followed [Das & Cook, 2005]. Based on predefined profiles representing common sets of sensor data and context information the future's context of the inhabitants of the environment are predicted. Moreover optimization of user goals can be achieved (energy consumption, manual interaction). With respect to interaction the authors' goal is to optimize the degree of manual (explicit) interaction. Therefore MavHome uses explicit as well as implicit interaction even though one of the major goals is implicit interaction. How interaction is developed is not stated.

- **Interactive Room.** The Interactive Workspaces project at the University of Stanford set up the Interactive Room (in short iRoom) as experimental infrastructure equipped with multiple stationary display which are able to communicate with mobile devices by means of a software system, so called iCrafter, in order to exchange information which can be used to control the displays, use an installed printing service in the environment or using a PDA as input device and the multiple displays of the environment as output devices [Ponnekanti *et al.*, 2002]. According to [Johanson *et al.*, 2002] iCrafter not only bridges the gap between different physical devices and their individual operating system but also generates UIs based on the available services in the surroundings. Therefore explicit interaction is the interaction type of choice in the iRoom.

- **Embassi.** The joint research project Embassi investigates new paradigms for the interaction with the technical infrastructure of the everyday life such as infotainment and home entertainment. In order to do so goal-based interaction is used (see Section 2.2.1) which employs speech, gestures and haptics. Those implicit interactions communicate goals to the system which in turn are achieved by means of assistance. Even though Embassi focuses on implicit interaction it is considered as important that explicit interaction still occurs. To which degree and how different interaction types are mingled is not part of the research in Embassi. Beside interaction also other research questions are tackled: dynamic composition of services, distribution of components forming an ad hoc ensemble which are not relevant for the thesis here [Kirste *et al.*, 2001].

- **Intelligent Room.** MIT's initiative to design intelligent spaces is the Intelligent Room project. In order to tackle common issues, such as heterogeneity, concurrency, distribution, etc., in SmEs a middleware, so called Metaglue, is proposed [Coen *et al.*, 1999]. During research several software systems and intelligent rooms basing on Metaglue have been developed which mainly focus on meeting scenarios. With respect to interaction explicit and implicit interaction components have been developed and evaluated but are developed isolated. For explicit interaction speech recognition and computer vision are used [Brooks, 1997].

- **Smart Office.** Another prototype focusing on work environments is the Smart Office project. It uses a location tracking system in order to derive the users' intention which is used to display potential useful information on a display. Contrary also explicit interaction via speech is used to control the Smart Office [Le Gal *et al.*, 2001].

The survey is to no extent comprehensive but gives an overview of existing projects and challenges in the domain of SmEs. Numerous other prototypes exist: The UMASS Intelligent Home Project [Lesser *et al.*, 1999], iDorm [Sharples *et al.*, 1999], Intelligent Classroom [Franklin & Hammond, 2001], OxyGen, Gaia [Christopher *et al.*, 2001], and Aura [Garlan *et al.*, 2002].

2.3.2 Current Challenges of Smart Environments

The challenges in SmEs with respect to feasibility are diverse. However explorative prototypes as shown before have produced rich showcases which exemplify the technical challenges in SmEs. Besides that, other challenges exist. Especially in the field of human factors proactive assistance is argued controversial. Therefore in this section still existing and recently discovered issues are examined. It is started with technical challenges which are investigated rather briefly. Subsequently, challenges with respect to the user are investigated more thoroughly which are important for the design of SmEs and interaction in particular. Finally it is shown that there are also research challenges with respect to method engineering.

Technical Challenges

An early survey about the encountered challenges while developing a SmE has been published by Coen *et al.* [1999]. In the paper seven properties of SmEs are stated and also tackled by the software system Metaglue. However those properties are partially not fundamental but provide the basis in order to introduce Metaglue. In [Kumar, 2009] numerous challenges for ubiquitous computing in general are investigated in a very low level manner resulting in a comprehensive survey of technical issues. Another more fundamental survey on challenges for ubiquitous computing has been published by Edward & Grinter which focuses on home environments [2001]. Based upon the named publications above a set of technical challenges has been distilled and are presented here briefly.

- **Distribution.** SmE are inherently distributed systems and therefore research questions related to this issue needs to be tackled. However distribution is a common challenge in various domains of Computer Science and has been researched thoroughly. With respect to quality criteria of the distributed components SmEs may have particular requirements (e.g., response time, reliability).

- **Heterogeneity and Interoperability.** Numerous components constitute a SmE. The devices are of different types (such as sensors, display, etc.) but are also created by different vendors. Therefore standardization and knowledge about the components of the SmE are crucial in order to enable interoperability on various level of abstraction (network layer, application layer).

- **Administration.** Ideally the components of a SmE administer themselves. To a certain degree autonomous configuration is feasible. However when it comes to hardware problem maintenance by people is necessary. For work environments this is not a problem but in home settings administration can be a crucial factor.

- **Dynamic Changes.** During operation of a SmE components may occur which constitute the SmE as long as they are within the physical boundaries of the SmE. Therefore SmEs are constantly changing with respect to the components they are consisting of. Moreover such an environment cannot be "switched off" or "restarted" in order to plug in a new device.

- **Inference in Situation of Ambiguity.** Due to the use of sensors and inference on the produced sensor data a certain degree of ambiguity is usually part of a SmE. The taken decisions by the systems are naturally error-prone. Therefore the implications of infe-rence should be bear in mind when implementing a SmE. It may be reasonable to use inference carefully. Moreover it should be analyzed to which degree the envisioned user is willing to accept non-determinism and potential wrong inferred intention of the user.

- **Consistency of Multimodal Adaptive UIs.** The general ability of a UI to adapt itself to the context of use while preserving usability is referred as plasticity [Sottet *et al.*, 2006]. Even though the idea of plasticity exists and MB-UI development is one approach to tackle it, it has not been reached yet. In SmEs the context of use is even more important than in typical scenarios of MB-UI as devices may appear and disappear. Moreover the modality of explicit interaction needs also to be taken into account. Besides GUIs, the user may interact via speech, touch, tangible UIs ([Ullmer & Ishii, 2000]) or any kind of combination. Combining plasticity and multi-modality with the characteristics of SmEs with respect to device heterogeneity consistency can hardly be assured.

Even though those bullets are vital research areas most of them do not tangent interaction in SmEs in particular (except for the last three). Human factors are much more important with respect to interaction and therefore are covered in the subsequent sub section.

Human Factors

As SmEs are physical spaces enriched with technology the impact of use on people is much higher than with ordinary desktop systems because they become part of the everyday life. Therefore the human factors of such applications are crucial to make them even usable and de-sirable for people. The vision of an autonomous working system sometimes scares people in-stead of seeing the potential benefits. Based upon the surveys and analytical insights given in [Hermann *et al.*, 2009; Langheinrich *et al.*, 2005] a set of essential factors concerning users are distilled:

- **Social Implications.** Currently computing systems in our surroundings can be easily switched off. However in the vision of Ubiquitous Computing the devices are even not visible anymore. With the devices the opportunities to switch them off disappear as well. Designers need to bear in mind that people may not want to live in a SmE each and every day. Moreover it might also be the case that a sub set of devices constituting the SmE is wanted to be switched off. Besides technology dependability, long term is-sues can also be disappearing of borders between human and machine, physical and cognitive involution, unnatural behavior, etc.

- **Privacy.** Several surveys ([Hong & Landay, 2004]) have shown that privacy manage-ment is the cornerstone of a SmE if personalized data is being processed during opera-tion. Even today privacy is becoming difficult to maintain with applications sharing personalized information. In SmEs due to their network capabilities and distribution an implicit handling of privacy is not adequate. Explicit concepts showing which data is being processed by which software system is needed in order to make people share their personalized data.

- **Control.** The reassignment of tasks from user to computing system exists since the en-tering of computers into work environments. Tasks that have been accomplished by the human are automated in order to ease the work (e.g., calculator). With respect to SmEs some new challenges are introduced. Task allocation can be dynamic meaning that depending on the current state of the SmE a task may be automated whereas under different circumstances (e.g., a certain device is not present) this is not possible. Such a dynamic allocation may also make users feel to be at the mercy of the computer system. Dedicated control mechanism can help to avoid this issue. Moreover the propagation of the current state of the system also helps to make users feel more comfortable as task allocation is traceable [Molich & Nielsen, 1990].

- **Decision Making by the System.** A related issue to the last one is the autarkic decision making of a computing system which may lead to an uncomfortable user experience. Transparency and traceability of decisions are necessary in order to provide the user with means to understand how and why the system decided in this way.

Development Processes

In their current state SmEs are research prototypes or as Kidd *et al.* state with respect to the Aware Home "Living Laboratories" [1999]. Prototypes are created incrementally from scratch based on the current needs and research focus. However in order to make SmEs enter everyday life method engineering is needed to provide a basis to develop SmEs well structured. More precisely as interaction is much more complex in SmEs analysis and requirements engineering addressing the interaction (UI requirements) are crucial to cope with the challenges elaborated above. The same applies for functional requirements. Especially the areas of integration of heterogeneous systems and devices, middleware, network infrastructure and others need to be examined beforehand. With respect to interaction a user-centered design approach seems to be suitable. The examination of different design processes and the selection of an appropriate one are given in Section 3.2.

2.3.3 The Human in the Loop

In the last sections existing prototypes of SmEs have been investigated with respect to technical challenges and human factors. These issues are very important in order to provide suitable means for interaction. What kind of interaction technique is useful in SmEs has been shown in Section 2.2. The given explanations lead to the conclusion that the crucial issues are user related. In order to develop suitable interaction techniques and a usable system the user has to be kept in the loop. This applies not only for the operation but also for the development of SmEs.

One way to achieve user involvement during development is user-centered design (UCD), human centered software engineering (HCSE) and agile methods. During operation explicit interaction can be used to integrate the user into decision making and to guide the system what kind of proactive assistance and implicit interaction is suitable in a certain situation. Explicit interaction needs to be dosed well. On the one hand, an overload of explicit interaction corrupts the disadvantages of SmEs as the user cannot focus on the current task but needs to interact. On the other hand too less explicit interaction may disregard the users' needs in this situation as implicit interaction always assumes the intention. Therefore a balanced interaction concept with respect to the user needs to be developed which can even shift during runtime as less explicit interaction is needed after long term use (or vice versa).

2.3.4 Perspectives on Smart Environments

This far it has been shown which prominent prototypes of SmEs exist and what kinds of challenges are involved during development. It has been stressed that human factors are extremely important to consider when developing supportive systems as the trust in such a system may cease as erroneous behavior occurs. Based upon the conducted survey in Section 2.3.1 two general perspectives on SmEs can be identified:

Smart Environments as Assistive Agent

The basic principle of this kind of approach is to use the metaphor of an autonomously acting agent which tries to assist the user while acting in a SmE. Woolridges defines an agent as [2002]:

> "An agent is a computer system that is situated in some environment, and that is capable of autonomous action in this environment in order to meet its delegated objectives."

For SmEs it is rather unclear whether to consider the entire SmE as an agent or such an environment as a multi agent system. Nevertheless, certain properties need to be present to classify a SmE as agent based system at all. According to [Russell & Norvig, 2003] an agent needs to perceive the environment through sensors and is able to perform actions on the environment through actuators. Applying this concept to SmEs the complete appliance of devices and computing resources serves as actuators and the user actions are interpreted by the agent as perception upon which it reacts. Agent-based systems have been characterized by numerous properties such as reactivity, social ability, rationality, learnability, etc. The actual property which is of most interest for SmEs is proactiveness. To which degree is an agent or agent-based system (in this case the SmE) able to react upon the actions of user and execute meaningful goal-directed behavior? Taking the perspective of a SmE as agent-based system this question is the actual research question to be answered. Such a perspective inherently incorporates the idea of implicit interaction.

Smart Environments as Complex Interactive System

From users' perspective a SmE is an appliance of numerous devices which have to be used in order to achieve a certain goal. The interaction with those devices constituting the SmE is complex as they are spatially distributed and have their individual capabilities and limitations with respect to in- and output, computing power, network access, etc. Such a user-centered perspective is mainly taken by approaches from HCI which claim that user focus deserves the highest interest. In this perspective a SmE is actually a more complex interactive system compared to desktop systems, MUI and context-aware applications (see Section 3.1) because of the special constraints a SmE has (e.g., spatial distribution, distributed interaction, proactiveness, etc.). In this vein autonomy is not a mandatory property as the SmEs purpose is user satisfaction. This does not need to be achieved by an intelligent, autonomic agent but also by predefined sequence of actions or hard-wired behavior of the system. This perspective does not make any claims with respect how the SmE is to be implemented (in contrast to the assistive agent) but emphasizes user satisfaction. Usability, natural task accomplishment, suitable interaction with respect to context of use and user characteristics are in line with this term.

Currently existing software engineering processes which will be examined in Section 3.2 integrate better with this perspective as the actual development process of the interactive systems is similar even though more complex. Moreover, explicit interaction as it is a commonly tackled field in software engineering is better supported by this perspective as implicit interaction.

Chapter 3
HCI Aspects

Having defined the terms and concepts involved in SmEs and the according interaction techniques it is now continued with an in-depth research of relevant HCI aspects in order to enhance the development of SmEs. First, it is shown that HCI is able to tackle the development of UIs for classic desktop application and MUIs. Then, it is exemplified why context-awareness adds additional complexity with respect to interaction development which is even exceeded by SmEs.

In the subsequent section different development processes are introduced which are relevant with respect to interaction development. Eventually MB-UI development is introduced in order to tackle explicit interaction for different types of applications. Furthermore it is exemplified why a suitable task modeling language is needed to provide means for MB-UI development for SmEs.

3.1 Dimensions of Complexity of Applications

The development of interactive applications is becoming more and more complex for several reasons. First UIs need to be more appealing in terms of functionality and usability as users employ systems more consciously nowadays. This applies for all types of applications even though this issue can be addressed for single platform applications, compared to the subsequent ones, easier. However the diversity of platforms in use for the very same interactive system raises the need for different UIs for the diverse capabilities and limitations of each platform still providing a consistent look and feel. This issue is mainly addressed by MUIs [Seffah & Javahery, 2004]. Certainly the development efforts for MUIs increase with the set of platforms. In order to develop an appropriate UI for a certain platform the context of use needs to be investigated [Gulliksen *et al.*, 2005].

Delivering the UI for different platforms is by far not sufficient as devices are mobile these days and rapid changes of context may occur. Therefore adaptation at runtime is consequently the next step and comprises new challenges. Context-awareness has been a research area since the 1990s (an overview of the roots can be found in [Dey & Abowd, 2000]) and investigates adaptation mechanisms for software systems with respect to continuously changing context of use [Schilit *et al.*, 1994].

It has been constantly discussed what constitutes context, how it is formalized best and how an application should make use of it. The range of context used in system design varies a lot. Exemplary the authors in [You *et al.*, 2009] use power consumption of sensor nodes as context for routing whereas in [Oliver & Flores-Mangas, 2006] the physiological state of the user is considered as context of use. Those examples already indicate that there is not yet a common agreed set of features to be considered as context for a particular domain. From our point of view that is one of the reasons why it is still cumbersome to implement a context-aware application as methodical knowledge of engineering as well as implementation frameworks for context-aware applications are still not comprehensive enough.

Beyond that, there is also the research field of implicit interaction in which interaction is taking place even the user is not aware of [Schmidt, 2000]. Implicit interaction is rooted in context-aware computing. Intelligent assistance [Boy & Gruber, 1990], SmE [Cook & Das, 2004] and ambient intelligence [Aarts *et al.*, 2002] are currently vital research areas in which implicit interaction is under investigation. To implement implicit interaction the context of use and the domain the user is confronted with are enormously important as actions may have a totally different semantics under a slightly different context or domain. Usually implicit interaction is accompanied, at least by a certain degree of, explicit interaction to synchronize the concurrently acting user and the executing system.

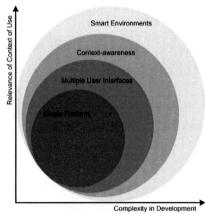

Figure 3-1 Complexity Chart for Application Types

The interaction paradigm used for SmEs differ vastly. Especially approaches in the HCI focus on explicit interaction in which UIs are generated dynamically. In [Blumendorf *et al.*, 2008] the authors propose an approach based on mobile devices whose UIs adapt according to the available services in the surroundings. Clerckx *et al.* follow a similar approach [2006]. Other related approaches can be found in [Duarte & Carri, 2006; Sottet *et al.*, 2008]. In the research community of SmEs, implicit interaction is the prevalent paradigm to reduce explicit interaction to a minimum. Goal-based interaction which has been investigated before is a representative of such an approach.

A classification of the prior named types of applications is illustrated by Figure 3-1. The chart shows the relation of the importance of context and the complexity of development for each type of application. The color denotes the amount of explicit interaction. The brighter the color the less interaction is necessary to use the application in an ideal case. This implies that even single platform applications and MUIs already support implicit interaction to a certain degree. This is actually the case as background processes may be started and assumptions about the users' habits are encoded in the system [Ju & Leifer, 2008]. The increasing complexity in development from single platform application to MUIs is due to the diverse platforms. The relevance of context increases because an application developed for MUIs is used in different contexts; one for each platform in the simplest case. The shift from MUIs to context-awareness is explained by the use of any kind of sensor to adapt the system accordingly. This applies for both axes as the sensors contribute to the context as well as to the complexity in development. Moving to SmEs context becomes even more influencing as explicit interaction is minimized resulting in implicit interaction based upon context. Certainly incorporating more context information and using them to provide proactive assistance adds a vast amount of complexity in development. For both, context-awareness and SmEs, adaptability plays also a major role for the complexity in development as systems of those kinds should adapt to users' needs accordingly.

In SmEs an additional fact comes into play. The interaction may be performed in spatially distributed way. Certain information might be provided by the user explicitly using personal or stationary devices, other information may be sensed and the output of the SmE can be visualized on device in the surroundings. The potential implications of such distribution for the user need to be investigated with respect to the usability and feasibility of the system for the envisioned users.

In Figure 3-1 only three dimensions (context of use, complexity in development and explicit interaction (by the color)) are depicted. Yet this chart can be easily extended to other dimensions:

- **Attentional Demand.** When interacting explicitly the users' attention is focused on the system. If systems disappear into the background and so do their interaction the attentional demand of the user is no longer bound to the system but to the actual goal [Ju & Leifer, 2008] which is one of the major objectives of context-aware systems and SmEs. Attentional demand can therefore be seen as an indicator for the quality of a context-aware system, SmE respectively.

- **Modality.** The usage of multiple modalities (gestures, voice, pointing) may result in an increased relevance of context and definitively adds new complexity in terms of development. Semantic unification of the multimodal application is of enormous interest to ensure a seamless integration of the different modalities [Oviatt, 1999]. Please note that some modalities are only available in context-aware computing and SmEs as sensors may be needed.

- **Initiative.** Who takes the initiative is highly related to the interaction paradigm of a system [Ju & Leifer, 2008]. If implicit interaction is prevalent the system may be more proactive then in explicit interaction. Proactiveness is a cornerstone to implement SmEs but should be used with care as users are frustrated easily by erroneous proactive behavior of systems.

- **Automation.** Initiative and attentional demand can be combined to scales of automation. In [Sheridan, 2002] the author investigates eight scales of automation. The scales start with no automation offered by the system and gradually allocates tasks to the system until the whole process is automated.

Again, those dimensions named above are only related to interaction. In fact, from system development viewpoint dimensions like system integration, network topology and others may be added as well.

Concluding, it is stated that the development of SmEs exceeds the development of all other types of applications named here. This applies for several types of dimensions but in particular for the interaction. Moreover the interaction techniques employed for SmEs comprise all others (see Figure 3-1) and shifts to implicit interaction even though explicit interaction is still used. The more implicit interaction is desired the more important the context of use becomes.

3.2 Software Engineering in HCI

One of the current issues of the development of SmEs is the lack of suitable and reliable process models for development (see Section 1.1 and Section 2.3.2). In order to improve the development a survey of relevant software engineering practices is given here. Moreover further investigations are presented with respect to interaction development and software engineering which serve as basis for the development methodology presented in this thesis in Chapter 7.

3.2.1 Classical Software Engineering Processes

A software engineering process embeds the low level activities, such as coding, testing, etc, involved in creating a software system into a higher context. In order to structure software development the various software development processes introduce phases where certain activities are performed. Those process models also define the sequence of low and high level activities as well as potential iteration cycles within a phase.

Before introducing process models relevant to HCI a brief overview of existing software engineering processes will be given:

- **Waterfall model.** In principle the model, first introduced by Royce [1987], consists of sequences of phases whereas the subsequent phase can only be started after the completion of the previous one. In detail the phases are requirements analysis, software design, implementation and testing, integration and operation. Each phase creates an output which is needed as input for the subsequent phase (e.g., requirements document as output of requirements analysis phase and input for design). During each phase problems may be discovered which lead to revision of documents defined previously. Thus iteration cycles are incorporated. However, more flexible approaches are needed incorporating early feedback and incremental delivery.

- **Iterative, incremental models.** As an extension to the waterfall model iterative, incremental models have emerged incorporating the delivery of prototypes and intermediate result to the customer even as productive system [Sommerville, 2006]. An increment is understood as a self-contained, deployable, tested piece of software. This kind of method allows for feedback of the stakeholder or user which can be incorporated in the next increment. The phases are mainly the same as in the waterfall model, but for each increment a whole iteration cycle s performed. This approach is much more flexible since it allows for packaging of requirements for each increment. Representatives of incremental models are the spiral model [Boehm, 1988] and the Rational Unified Process (RUP) [Larman, 2004] which is depicted in Figure 3-2.

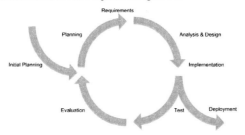

Figure 3-2 The Rational Unified Process [Kruchten, 2003]

- **Agile methods.** In recent years the need for more flexible approaches emerged in order to successfully complete rather smaller projects. Those methods are also incremental processes but with small iteration cycles to incorporate feedback faster. Agile methods try to reduce the overhead of plan-based development by concentrating on the programming of the actual system. The crucial advantage of agile methods is the incorporation of potential adaptations of requirements during the project life cycle. Even though there are different agile methods (Scrum [Schwaber & Beedle, 2001], XP [Beck, 2000], etc.) they all share common principles: customer involvement, incremental deployment, focus on people, made for change, refactoring and simplicity [Sommerville, 2006]. As those methods are made for smaller teams and projects they fail for long term projects and bigger teams.

3.2.2 Limitations according to HCI

As those process models are general software development processes they do not focus their activities on usability or the end user. Though, there are certain criteria making a process more or less suitable to incorporate usability and user-centeredness [Ferre *et al.*, 2004]. Due to the fact that the level of usability of the envisioned software system cannot be predicted in advance continuous usability evaluation is needed to revise certain design decisions. This can only be achieved by employing an iterative approach resulting in an artifact at the end of each iteration which can be evaluated according to qualitative and quantitative criteria [Dix *et al.*, 1997; Hackos & Redish, 1998]. However, an iterative approach only enables a user-centered process but does not assure a system to be usable. Besides this crucial requirement of a user-centered process, two others exist: user involvement and user understanding. Whereas the first means that the end user of the system should participate within all stages of development, at least to a certain degree, the latter stands for the analysis of the current user tasks and her context as well as the envisioned way of performing tasks while interacting with the software system. For both criteria HCI techniques exist covering all steps of development from requirement analysis to testing.

According to the three characteristics named above various HCI design processes have been proposed either as autarkic processes or as enhancement to existing software engineering processes examined above. In the next Section representatives of such processes are examined.

3.2.3 Human-Centered Software Engineering

According to Seffah *et al.* HCSE tries to bridge the gap of software engineering techniques and HCI [2005]. More precisely the integration of usability methods and software engineering is addressed. HCSE can be achieved by various techniques on different levels of abstraction. It can be implemented by guidelines spanning the entire software engineering lifecycle as well as by low level activities like early prototyping. The key issue to be addressed is how software systems can be developed fitting the user's needs. Usability engineering offers a lot of techniques being usable to improve exactly that issue but has rarely been adopted in most software engineering methods, and vice versa. Even if usability methods are considered in software engineering they are seldom used in every phase but the usability is assessed before deployment. Besides classical usability methods (such as expert evaluation, cognitive walkthrough, etc.) also certain methods from software engineering can be employed to provide the basis for a usable system.

The International Organization for Standardization (ISO) has addressed this issue by the standard 13407 "Human-centred design processes for interactive systems" [ISO, 1999]. It is stated that certain principles constitute the creation of a usable system: user involvement, an appropriate allocation of functions to human and machine, iterative development, multidisciplinary. Moreover, to establish such a development process, time needs to be dedicated to assess intermediate results and prototypes with the user. Other activities have to be performed to meet the requirements of a human-centered design process: analysis of the context of use of the software system under construction and assessment of the quality of the intermediate solutions with regard to the requirements and usability.

One principle that has been used successfully is user involvement. During the process of creating a software system the end users should be continuously integrated into the development progress. Certainly, the appropriate artifacts need to be presented which can be assessed by the users. Invaluable feedback should be integrated in the subsequent development steps. To do so, only an iterative development process is suitable as already stated above. User involvement is an interactive method which presents prototypes (vertical, horizontal, paper, etc.) to the user which are evaluated with regard to usability criteria (appropriateness, functionality, etc.).

3.2.4 User-Centered Design

In the same vein user-centered design (UCD) advocates an iterative approach to system design to enable feedback during the entire project lifecycle [Gulliksen & Goransson, 2001]. In contrast to HCSE, UCD is rather understood as a set of design guidelines or principles enabling to design a usable system. Naturally, such guidelines have an impact on the process model they are applied to, and therefore has to be adapted accordingly. Therefore HCSE can be understood as one way to perform UCD. Besides demanding an iterative process model, UCD can be applied to any development approach by supporting guidelines congruent to HCSE and further ones [Gulliksen *et al.*, 2005].

One of the major principles of UCD is the thorough analysis of current work situation of the user. This involves examining the domain of interest, the task the user is executing, the user itself and the surrounding of the user. Different techniques have been developed to support such an analysis. The domain can be analyzed with object-oriented analysis and design using objects and relations between those objects (or their generalization: classes) [Booch *et al.*, 2007].

Often the user is a rather abstract notion in development. Personas can help to make the later user more visible to the developer. The envisioned users are analyzed and a representative is modeled as persona [Cooper, 2004]. Yet there is no common agreed on technique to analyze and specify the environment the user is acting in.

In terms of analyzing the task world of the user task analysis has been applied successfully over decades. Moreover task analysis does not try to study tasks isolated but also considers the working artifacts, the surroundings and users of the system [Hackos & Redish, 1998]. Advocates of UCD claim that a system suits the user better if the task world of the user has been analyzed and based on that a system is developed. Therefore, different methodologies exist proposing to use a task-driven approach to system development. The most relevant ones are examined in the subsequent section.

3.3 Task-Driven Development Methodologies

Interaction design has been tackled of diverse research communities employing different techniques. Task-based approaches have been successful due to the incorporation of the task world of the user. By doing so the gap between the normal way tasks are executed and the way tasks are to be executed using the envisioned software system under construction can be kept close. This is important as users are able to map their normal way of task execution to the new computerized way. Figure 3-3 shows the basic idea of task-based processes to interaction development. The ordinary way tasks are performed are depicted on the left hand side. The user applies the knowledge about the tasks and the domain in order to get the work done and achieve the goal. After having deployed the new software system the tasks and the domain are still existent (even though adapted) but being encapsulated by the system. Now the user interacts with the system in order to work in her domain. Therefore an interaction based on the task world of the user leads to a more consistent and appropriate interaction.

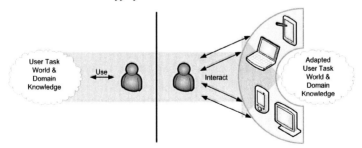

Figure 3-3 The Idea of Task-based Processes

Task-driven approaches can be classified into two categories: task modeling as documentation of requirements and task modeling as specification mechanism. In the first category task modeling is used as knowledge transmission tool for software designer and user/customer in order to present intermediate solutions to the user/customer. In accordance with the principles of HCSE and UCD this approach is highly beneficial as task models can be already considered as first prototypes. Thus iterative development is facilitated. Moreover those created models can, after several iteration cycles, serve as requirement documents in order to start design.

3.3.1 Analysis, Requirements Engineering & Design Techniques

Collaborative Interactive Applications Methodology (CIAM) is a representative of this kind of approach [Molina *et al.*, 2008]. It is conceived to design groupware UIs based on a set of graphical notations (among task models). It makes use of modeling approaches from HCI, software engineering and computer supported cooperative work (CSCW). CIAM relies on several stages of modeling (Sociogram Development, Inter-Action Modeling, Responsibilities Modeling, Work-in group Tasks Modeling and Interaction Modeling). As the names already indicate the social and organizational structure as well as the group tasks are modeled in the first stages. In the subsequent phases the focus shifts from group to role perspective. First, roles and their responsibilities are specified. Next, group tasks are gradually refined by role-based tasks defining collaboration and cooperation. Last for each identified (groupware) task an interaction model is created which use Concur Task Tree (CTT) as notation. CIAM is an elegant high level modeling approach which focuses on the dependencies involved when developing groupware application. Unfortunately the authors do not make any statements whether principles of UCD are supported within the development methodology. Moreover, tool support for diverse proposed models does not exist as well as no execution semantics of the high level models is defined. Thus, created models can only serve as requirement specification documents with limited value because they have to be reimplemented using an executable language to construct the envisioned system [Selic, 2003].

In the same vein as the approach mentioned before Penichet *et al.* investigate how the development of groupware applications can be improved by thoroughly performing analysis, requirements engineering and eventually design [2009]. The approach primarily focuses on analysis and requirement gathering for UIs for groupware systems and therefore offers a dedicated metamodel in order to adequately represent the analysis and requirements models. In order to do so, the special constraints of groupware applications are taken into account resulting in novel models and diagrams emphasizing the interaction involved in groupware. In order to perform structural analysis of the system under construction class diagrams ([UML, 2010]) and a novel type of diagram, the organizational structure diagram, is introduced. An example taken from [Penichet *et al.*, 2009] is depicted in Figure 3-4.

According to the TOUCHE process, which is the development methodology defined by Penichet, an organizational structure diagram specifies the organizational units relevant with respect to the groupware system to be developed. The entities involved are decomposed into groups, roles, users and system components (e.g., in Figure 3-4 the whole system is decomposed into internal and external groups and system agent responsible for notifying, etc.). The decomposition in this kind of diagram is continued until a user or a system agent has been reached.

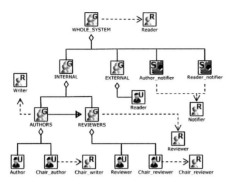

Figure 3-4 Organizational Structure Diagram from [Penichet *et al.*, 2009]

During analysis not only decomposition of organizations are modeled but also other relationships can be defined. More precisely, the *play* relationship which connects an actor, agent or group and a role in order to define that the entity is fulfilling this role (e.g., Chair_author and Chair_writer). Next, the hierarchy relationship exists defining a dependency between certain entities (e.g., Authors and Reviewers). However the name and semantics of this type of relationship is rather unclear. Having analyzed the organizational unit within the domain in order to elicit the UI requirements for the groupware application a more fine-grained model is needed specifying not only structural properties but taking also into account behavior. Different models are proposed to enable and capture the behavioral analysis of groupware systems. First, Cooperative Concur Task Trees (CCTT) are used to model user and system interaction by means of temporal ordering of tasks of different actors and system (CCTT is explained in detail in Section 3.4.3). Second, so called Co-interaction diagrams are used in order to model interactions of users among each others. For each envisioned usage scenario a Co-interaction diagram is modeled. It sets into relation previously defined actors and agents of the system by means of tasks. Basically it is defined which entities of the organizational structure diagram cooperate by means of tasks described in the CCTT models.

TOUCHE which is also described in [Penichet *et al.*, 2008; Penichet *et al.*, 2010] offers analysis models and a process for groupware systems. It furthermore focuses on the requirements elicitation before development has been started. The models are suitable and rich for analysis but fail when used for design as they are not executable and therefore cannot be interactively explored. With respect to SmEs several relevant entities are missing (e.g., modeling of location, devices).

3.3.2 Task-Based Specification Methodologies

This kind of approaches employs task models as specification mechanism which are interpreted by a software system to create the interactive system. Usually an interpreter is employed to either derive a lower level model or the specification is interpreted at runtime to tailor the UI dynamically [Vanderdonckt, 2008]. New challenges are thereby introduced (machine independent semantics, machine readable format, deadlocks of distributed execution, etc.). Basically the approaches have the objective of building UIs in a model-based manner.

In the same vein as the Model-Driven Architecture (MDA) [MDA, 2010] tackles the question whether the development of the application core can be eased (in terms of time, budget, maintenance, etc.) by the usage of declarative models, refinement of models and transformations, MB-UI development is concerned with the development of UIs. The idea of a model-driven (or model-based) approach is to reduce complexity by having a model for each viewpoint on the system on an arbitrary level of abstraction and transformations relating those models. Models are adapted and transformed until an appropriate level of abstraction is reached which serves as executable model. In the MDA a set of models has been established being the de facto standard: computation independent model, platform independent model, platform specific model. As the names already suggest those model are used on different levels of abstraction. During each transformation additional aspects are taken into account (e.g., platform). Such an evolution can also be noticed for MB-UI development.

In particular MB-UI development is a major research area in HCI focusing on engineering the interaction for different types of applications by techniques adopted from MDA. Various development methodologies for interactive systems based on tasks exist: TERESA [Paternò et al., 2008], UsiXML [Limbourg et al., 2005], UC-TM [Sinnig, 2009], MASP [Feuerstack & Blumendorf, 2007] and Dygimes [Luyten, 2004]. Naturally, they differ in level of abstraction, used notation, focus and procedure. However over the years consent about the general rationale of MB-UI process has emerged [Paternò et al., 2008; Vanderdonckt, 2008].

Figure 3-5 shows the rationale of the general MB-UI process. It mainly consists of four steps. Starting with task and domain analysis a conceptual model of the task world of the user is retrieved. In HCI, it is commonly agreed upon that task modeling is a good starting point for MB-UI design [Forbrig et al., 2003]. Software enables the user to achieve a goal by the execution of tasks. Those tasks need to be presented in a UI which shows the relation of a UI and a corresponding task model. Task-based approaches argue that the closer the UI corresponds to the natural way a goal is achieved the better the user perceives the UI.

After that the tasks are specified with regard to the envisioned software system under construction, an abstract UI (AUI) description is created. In the next phase AUI components may be replaced by concrete ones, so called concrete UI (CUI). For MUIs an abstract UI is used to derive a concrete UI for each platform. So, AUIs are platform independent whereas CUIs are not. In the last step the final UI is generated into a specific technology. Design adaptations might be needed to fine-tune the final UI (beautification) [Vanderdonckt, 2008].

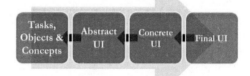

Figure 3-5 Basic Model-based UI Process

MB-UI design is not a straightforward process which is indicated by the smaller arrows from right to left in Figure 3-5. It is an iterative design process driven by evaluation and feedback. This can be achieved by prototyping on each level of abstraction within the development life-cycle. In order to support an iterative process model adaptations need to be inherently supported by the involved artifacts, the tool support and the process model itself.

With respect to the AUI a standard notation has not been yet identified. Dialog modeling is one technique to derive the first abstract canonical prototype. Tasks are grouped into dialogs and transitions of dialogs are defined by means of task execution [Reichart *et al.*, 2004]. A related approach has been published by Traetteberg in which data flow of dialogs is emphasized [2008]. In UsiXML the AUI consists of different containers on various levels of abstractions which eventually consist of abstract controls. A tree of containers is created whose leafs are controls. Tasks are assigned to containers and the enabled task set is used to drive the flow of the UIs [Montero & López-Jaquero, 2008]. This approach has been originally proposed Luyten [2004].

The CUI is typically expressed by a UI markup language such as UsiXML(USer Interface eX-tensible Markup Language), UIML (User interface markup language), XUL (XML User Inter-face Language), etc. [Vanderdonckt *et al.*, 2004]. Concrete UI elements are mapped to AUI elements (e.g., a selection control is replaced by a combo box). Depending on the envisioned modality the mapping can be of different complexity. For GUIs the mapping process is quite straightforward whereas for voice interfaces the mapping is much more complicated.

TERESA in its current version supports the previously depicted process with special regards to multimodal interaction on the abstraction level of abstract and concrete UIs [Paternò *et al.*, 2008].

In the same vein UsiXML approaches MB-UI development but also takes into account the con-text of use considered as the platform, devices and users of the system [Limbourg *et al.*, 2005]. Both methodologies support multi-path development meaning that the software designer may start on any level of abstraction which is very practical especially in early stages of develop-ment. In [Limbourg *et al.*, 2005] those paths are further concretized by explicit path steps: reifi-cation, abstraction and translation. Reification defines the transformation of a model to lower level model in MB-UI chain in Figure 3-5. Abstraction is the complementary transformation. Translation defines the process of translating a model for a certain context of use (e.g., desktop environment) to another one (e.g., mobile setting).

However, recently the task concepts and their tool support has been enhanced by FlowiXML [Garcia *et al.*, 2008]. In this work task modeling is studied in context of workflow modeling. More precisely extensions to task modeling have been introduced to combine high level workflow modeling and task modeling for workflow items as necessary. Workflows are mod-eled by means of adapted Petri-nets. Task modeling comes into play by further defining transi-tions using extended CTT models as described before. The rationale of this approach is based on the assumption that task models highlight the user' point of view on the system much better than a process model [García *et al.*, 2008b]. Unfortunately there are no statements how such a combined modeling approach of workflows and task models suits with UsiXML. Still this approach overcomes the limits of CTT task modeling to incorporate modeling of distributed actions of different users. In FlowiXML workflows are used to specify the casual dependencies of tasks of different users, in FlowiXML called *workers*, from different *organizational units*. This is definitely an enhancement of CTT and CCTT in terms of expressiveness. Moreover such an approach bridges the gap of two worlds: business process modeling and task modeling which have been mostly considered separately. Beside the modeling facilities FlowiXML also offers modeling elicitation methods and tools. Task identification criteria are introduced in [García *et al.*, 2008a] and an appropriate tool is shipped with FlowiXML. A precise classification of tasks becomes indispensable especially if tasks are considered in the context of workflow modeling as there are also processes and workflows involved. A distinction of tasks, processes and workflows is necessary to keep the level of abstraction consistent on each layer while modeling. Another elicitation tool offered by FlowiXML uses text-based scenarios to elicit modeling entities in the text.

As FlowiXML employs Petri-nets for workflow modeling and CTT as task modeling language semantics can be defined. However, to our knowledge such an interpreter (e.g., a workflow management system or task model interpreter) is not included in FlowiXML. This is actually unfortunate as animation has been proven as an excellent validation tool. Moreover, an interpreter may also be used at runtime to govern the information and control flow. Without an interpreter transformations are necessary to derive executable models. Without interpreter or transformation models are limited to be requirements artifacts or documentations.

In his PhD thesis Sinnig proposed a development process for interactive applications bridging the gap of software engineering and UI development [2009]. It is based on use cases and task models which are in each domain the prevalent requirement specification mechanism. More precisely he states that use cases specifying the functional requirements and task model specifying the UI requirement should be developed in accordance. This approach does not advocate MB-UI design itself but the development approach can be used to enhance MB-UI design.

The design of UIs has been considered as an interactive process involving design iterations and discussion. As a result of such a process a design solution, a UI, is created. However there are scenarios where a UI cannot be created at design time but needs to be tailored at runtime. Luyten proposed an approach based on task models to derive a UI for versatile devices in his PhD thesis [2004]. This approach analyzes the task model and calculates the enabled task sets ([Paternò, 1999]) in order to group tasks in dialogs appropriately. More precisely tasks of an enabled task set are grouped into one dialog. To derive an abstract UI UIML fragments are attached to tasks. UIML is a device independent interface description language based on XML [Constantinos, 2000]. In essence, in Dygimes only task models with UIML fragments are specified. At runtime those extended task models are interpreted and a UI is generated dynamically. Moreover Dygimes supports context-sensitive task models to incorporate different contexts of use at runtime but does not incorporate means for multi modalities.

The MASP (Multi-Access Service Platform) has been developed by several PhD students at the DAI-Labor in Berlin [Blumendorf, 2009; Feuerstack, 2009]. The aim of this project is to employ UI models, like the task model, abstract UI model, etc., to automatically generate UIs for SmEs. Moreover explicit layout modeling is performed to create more appealing UIs [Feuerstack *et al.*, 2008]. The approach relies on the basic model-based process but the final UI is not created at design time but is generated at runtime [Feuerstack, 2009]. Depending on the current context of use at runtime an appropriate UI is derived based on the model defined at design time. Therefore a context-sensitve UI can be created.

3.4 Existing Approaches to Task Modeling

Almost each prior investigated methodology introduces its customized version of a task model. Even though nowadays a set of features can be found in almost each task modeling language those concepts are often extended. In this section it is clarified why task analysis and task modeling is beneficial for the design of interactive systems and what kind of modeling languages exist. More precisely it is started with task analysis which is not bound to any modeling language but provides means to elicit a valid task description from a certain problem domain.

3.4.1 Task Analysis

The application domains for task analysis are not limited to the development of interactive systems but includes training, development, assessment of mental workload, performance and error prediction just to name a few [Hackos & Redish, 1998]. The overall goal of such an analysis is to enable designers to understand the user's work situation which can be of any kind (e.g., work, leisure) in order to improve design (e.g., training plan). According to Johnson:

> "...the role for the task analysis is to provide an idealized, normative model..."

of the tasks users carry out to achieve goals in a particular domain [1992]. With regard to interactive system development task analysis is important to elicit UI requirements (which are usually not captured by functional requirements) and detect potential usability flaws. UI requirements detectable via task analysis are in turn function allocation (to user or system), logical decomposition of dialogs, consistent ordering of tasks and appropriateness of a UI for a certain user [Dix *et al.*, 1997; Kirwan & Ainsworth, 1992].

Task analysis is not primary performed when a new system is to be developed but during all phases of development even maintenance. More precisely task analysis cannot be performed from scratch as it needs some situation which is under investigation (e.g., a legacy system a user is working with, the work situation without a software system). The feasibility of an analysis of the user and her tasks is rather limited if the circumstances of the user during task execution are omitted. Thus task analysis is not only about tasks but also about user goals (why is somebody performing a certain task?), the user itself (who is executing a certain task?) and the environment (where is somebody executing a certain task?). Such a holistic understanding is necessary to provide a valid view on the task world of the user.

To perform task analysis different techniques have proved its value over time. The easiest one which is also used in domain-driven design [Evans, 2003] is establishing a vocabulary of tasks (task inventory according to [Hackos & Redish, 1998]). As users naturally tend to decompose tasks into more simply ones task descriptions are usually hierarchically arranged. Besides the pure tasks a user analysis needs to be performed reflecting the skills and capabilities of stereotypical users. Different concepts to do so exist. Either the different levels of capabilities with respect to the system are analyzed or the domain specific users are taken into account. Whereas the first results in users like "novice", "beginner" or "expert" the latter leads to roles existing in the domain ("editor" and "author" in book writing). Moreover task specifications should naturally reflect such a classification of users. In order to develop analysis documents truly reflecting the way tasks are performed direct interacting with the users is invaluable. Therefore visiting the user and discussing the way the user is performing the task can be very helpful to gain understanding as assumptions are often misleading or just wrong. Interviews, questionnaires, card sorting or thinking aloud are techniques which can be applied during a site visit [Johnson, 1992].

Recently proposed task analysis techniques focus on groupware applications. As coordinative task accomplishment comprises much more complexity analysis techniques need to adapt accordingly. In [Penichet *et al.*, 2008] a conceptual framework is proposed which clearly distinguishes between different types of groupware tasks. Even though such a distinction seems to be beneficial no statements about the implications of the different types of tasks are given. As a pure analysis method no new modeling technique is introduced to effectively make use of the fine-grained classification of tasks.

3.4.2 From Task Analysis to Task Modeling

The result of task analysis should be an artifact specifying the tasks the different users are currently performing. However when a system is build the task world actually changes as tasks are reallocated, new tasks may be introduced and others are obsolete. Therefore there is also an envisioned way tasks are performed using the software system under construction. Thus there is a gap between the tasks the users are currently performing in their work environment and the work situation after a new system has been introduced. One of the reasons why users may not accept a certain system can be the divergence of these two models. This issue is known in the HCI and has been taken into account by task analysis methods and MB-UI processes. Van der Veer and van Welie distinguish between those two task models and emphasized their importance as the analysis model comprises the knowledge of the user about the current work situation whereas the envisioned task model specifies the refined task situation in accordance with technology. The second is usually designed by an expert of the system under construction and the user (as the knowledge of the users is integrated) [2000]. In the same Wilson *et al.* distinguish between those two types of models but further state that restructuring the tasks should not only be supported by the methodology and task analysis technique but also by the tool support [1993].

Figure 3-6 depicts the evolution of a task model for the development of interactive systems. It is started with the first version of the model of the current work situation. This model is iteratively refined by discussion with the users. Once this model is of sufficient quality (Task model 1.4 in Figure 3-6) the envisioned work situation is derived. The first version of this model (2.1) is naturally based on the last version (1.4) of the current task situation but incorporates the envisioned support of technology for the task execution.

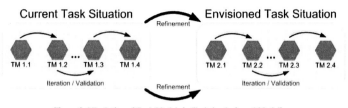

Figure 3-6 Evolution of Task Models in Task Analysis and Modeling

Task model 2.1 is usually created by an expert of the system under construction who knows best the capabilities of automation, reallocation of functions etc. Certainly this model needs adjustment to meet the requirements of the user which is achieved by iterative validation with the user (denoted by 2.2, 2.3 and 2.4). The eventually created task model (2.4) can therefore be considered as contract between user and interaction designer in terms of interaction for the system under construction. Again, the task model cannot be regarded as isolated but needs naturally to be defined in accordance with the domain and user model [Dittmar & Forbrig, 1999].

As each (intermediate) task model may be discussed with the user an understandable notation is necessary to enable iterative task analysis and modeling. Therefore the notation and its tool support have a great impact on the UI design. In the next section common approaches are examined with regard to origin, expressiveness, application domain and other criteria.

3.4.3 Task Modeling

In the last decades several languages have been created to specify tasks and their interrelation with respect to the application domain. This section provides an overview of current research of relevant modeling languages and motivates the need for the developed language CTML.

In essence, task modeling languages can be classified according to their origins [Limbourg & Vanderdonckt, 2003; Pontico *et al.*, 2007]:

Cognitive psychology. Task modeling is understood as vehicle to transmit knowledge about how users interact with machines or software. Task analysis identifies cognitive processes during interaction and task structures. In addition assessment of work load, performance, task allocation and usability can be performed. Representatives of task modeling languages of this type are Hierarchical Task Analysis (HTA) [Annett & Duncan, 1967], Task Knowledge Structures (TKS) [Johnson, 1992], Goals Operators Methods Selection Rules (GOMS) [Card *et al.*, 1983], Task Action Grammar (TAG) [Payne & Green, 1986], Méthode Analytique de Description (MAD*) [Scapin & Pierret-Goldbreich, 1989].

Software Engineering. Task models are used as specification mechanism in various stages of software engineering. Task analysis can be used in early stages to elicit requirements which in turn may be specified by means of task models [Hackos & Redish, 1998; Reichart *et al.*, 2004] as it the case in MB-UI development. As already hinted in the last sections, task models may also be used at runtime which requires a machine readable format and precisely defined semantics especially for remote systems. Therefore some task modeling language (CTT [Paternò, 1999], TaoSpec [Dittmar & Forbrig, 2003]) can be traced back to process algebras such as CSP [Hoare, 1978]. In addition, domain specific extensions may be introduced to incorporate the special constraints and concepts of the domain of interest [Bomsdorf, 2007; Giersich *et al.*, 2007; Sinnig *et al.*, 2007; Wurdel *et al.*, 2009].

Ethnography. Ethnography studies, among others, the interacting of humans through empirical studies. Different methods are employed to gather the data such as interviews or observation. Task modeling can be another source of data as task models can be discussed with the humans under observation. Groupware Task Analysis (GTA) [van der Veer *et al.*, 1996] is one representative of this type of task model.

After classifying the task modeling approaches based on their origins it is now continued with a detail examination of most relevant ones. Among the most popular task modeling languages are GOMS [Card *et al.*, 1983], HTA [Annett & Duncan, 1967], TKS [Johnson, 1992], and CTT [Paternò, 1999]. Even though all notations differ in terms of presentation, level of formality and expressiveness, they assume the following common tenet: tasks are performed to achieve a certain goal. Moreover, complex tasks are decomposed into more basic tasks until an atomic level has been reached.

Within the domain of HCI, CTT is the most popular notation, as it contains the richest set of temporal operators and it is supported by a tool, CTTE [Mori *et al.*, 2002], which facilitates the creation, visualization and sharing of task models.

Abstraction   User   Application   Interaction   Cooperative

Figure 3-7 Task Types in CTT and CCTT

Tasks are arranged hierarchically, with more complex tasks decomposed into simpler sub-tasks. CTT distinguishes between several task types, which are represented by the icon representing the task node. There are abstract tasks, which are further decomposable into combinations of the other task types including interaction, application and user tasks (see Figure 3-7 for an overview of the available task types). The task type denotes the responsibility of execution (human, machine, interaction, cooperation with human). CTT includes a set of binary (enabling, choice, order independence, concurrency, disabling, suspend/resume) and unary operators (optional, iteration). The former are used to temporally link sibling tasks at the same level of decomposition whereas the latter are used to identify optional and iterative (unbounded iteration and n-times iteration) tasks (see Table 6-2 for accurate descriptions of the semantics of the identical operators used in CTML). A comprehensive overview on CTT can be found in [Paternò, 1999]. An example of CTT model is given in Figure 3-8 which shows how a presenter may give a talk. The abstract root task "Give Presentation" is decomposed into four children tasks. The tasks on the second level of abstraction are connected with the enabling operator ($\gg$) in order to specify that one task has to be performed before the other can start (e.g., "Present" can only be performed after having executed "Configure Equipment").

An exception to this is "Leave Room" as it can be performed at any time due to the deactivation operator ([>) resulting in a prematurely abortion of the currently running task. "Configure Equipment" is furthermore consisting of the tasks "Start Projector", "Start Laptop" and "Connect Laptop & Projector".

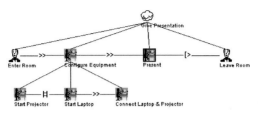

Figure 3-8 CTT Model for "Give Presentation"

Those basic tasks are connected with the orderindependence (|=|) and enabling operator. The orderindependence operator defines the sequential execution of the tasks in arbitrary order meaning that once one of the tasks is started the other has to wait for the first one to terminate. Tasks which are not further decomposed are actions and considered as atomic. They represent the smallest entity of execution (e.g., Start Projector).

In the following paragraphs the concepts of hierarchical decomposition and temporal operators to restrict the task execution order are referred to CTT-like notation as those concepts are used in most task modeling approaches.

HTA being one of the first attempts to task modeling decomposes tasks until an atomic unit is reached [Annett & Duncan, 1967]. Instead of temporal operators so called plans are used to restrict the execution order of tasks. Plans are informal descriptions of conditions of task execution on the same level of abstraction. They are very powerful but are not interpretable by a tool. In Figure 3-9 the running example of "Give Presentation" is specified by means of HTA. Boxes represent tasks and lines denoted hierarchical decomposition. Plans are annotated in order to comment the intended temporal order.

GOMS has been developed to assess the time needed to achieve a certain goal. Therefore in GOMS goals are decomposed until a goal can be achieve by operators [Card *et al.*, 1983]. Methods specify how operators are combined and selection rules define which methods to use under certain circumstances. MAD is a CTT-like notation but actions are attached to atomic tasks which define how to perform the atomic task (e.g., the atomic task *get a drink* is implemented by *go to the bar tender*). This formalism is very similar to CTT.

Figure 3-9 HTA Example of "Give Presentation"

In order to support the spsecification of collaborative (multi-user) interactive systems, CTT has been extended to CCTT (Cooperative ConcurTaskTrees) [Mori *et al.*, 2002]. Similar to the cooperative task modeling language presented in this thesis, CCTT uses a role-based approach. A CCTT specification consists of multiple task trees. One task tree for each involved user role and one task tree that acts as a "coordinator" and specifies the collaboration and global interaction

45

between involved user roles. An example for the formalism is given in Figure 3-10. The role task models for "Presenter" and "Listener" are given on top, on the lower right hand side respectively. The model specifying the coordination of the individual tasks is depicted on the lower left hand side. For each action in the coordinator task model a counterpart in the role specific task model has to be defined which is denoted by the dotted lines in Figure 3-8. In essence, the coordinator task specification adds additional execution constraints to the individual task models. In the given example it is specified that "Wait for Questions" of the role "Presenter" needs to be performed before the "Listener" is allowed to perform "Ask Question". After that "Answer Question" of the role "Presenter" can eventually be executed.

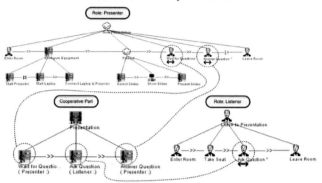

Figure 3-10 Cooperative CTT Model for "Presentation"

The main shortcoming of CCTT is that the language does not provide means to model several actors simultaneously fulfilling the same role as well as that an actor is assumed to fulfill only one role within a CCTT specification (strict one to one mapping of actors and roles).

Groupware Task Analysis (GTA) developed by van der Veer *et al.* primarily focuses on analysis and modeling of multi user task achievement [1996]. The approach bridges two worlds, HCI and CSCW (Computer supported Cooperative Work), by applying techniques from both areas. More precisely classical task analysis and modeling techniques from HCI and groupware analysis from CSCW are used. The authors embed task modeling into a higher level context by also considering roles, work, objects and agents as entities relevant for task modeling. The task model uses the common set of features ([Welie *et al.*, 1998]) explained before but actions are employed as top level elements in a dialect of UAN (User Action Noation) diagrams which is used as low level notation determining the dialog structure [van der Veer & van Welie, 2000]. Moreover, in contrast to CTT and similar notations each task is assigned a goal even on lower levels of abstractions. Artifacts and tools necessary to accomplish a task (by manipulation or creation) are modeled by means of UML class diagrams. On the higher level of abstraction roles describe stereotypical users and their tasks to be performed. Agents play one or more roles and a role can be played by several agents. An agent is not necessarily a user as it may also be the system. The situatedness of actions is addressed by events and triggers. Whereas the first defines the circumstances when an event occurs, the latter indicates the task relevant for the event. The model entities are represented in GTA by different representations: task tree, workflow model and object model. The first is the way tasks are represented in HCI. The workflow model classifies tasks with respect to time, order and roles. In GTA a so called "variation of UML Activity diagram" is used which uses swim lanes to collocate tasks of the same role and control flow to order tasks accordingly. Moreover a goal lane is added to represent which goal is currently being worked on. GTA is the richest approach in HCI for task analysis and modeling for groupware applications as it does not only cover a modeling language but also a lightweight process, means for evaluation and usability engineering. Moreover tool support for model creation and documentation is offered. From our point of view the approach only lacks formality and executability. As modeling distributed actions becomes quite complex validation and verification analysis of GTA is important to ensure consistency. Currently this issue has not been addressed yet. A formal basis would also allow for model interpretation and which would in turn facilitate prototyping which is even considered as highly important by the authors [van der Veer & van Welie, 2000]. Interestingly in the very same paper the authors also suggest to incorporate the physical layout of the working environment to complete the task specifications. However this issue is not tackled in GTA.

Bomsdorf [2007] as well as Klug and Kangasharju [2005] introduced an extension to task models where a task is not regarded as an atomic entity (like in CTT) but has a complex lifecycle, modeled by a so-called task state machine. Bomsdorf defines a task by a state chart to trigger additional events as the specification is more fine-grained. Hence in this vein also external events which may occur in web based interfaces (closing the browser) can be handled. Klug and Kangasharju use a state chart based approach to define temporal operators with information exchange more precisely. The former approach does not consider tasks being not enabled (initiated) whereas the latter does not consider abortion or skipping of tasks.

Tasks are always performed within a certain context or environment and hence their interplay with the environment should be taken into account. This issue was first tackled by Bierre *et al.* [1999a]. The authors proposed to model the execution environment in accordance with the task specification. The environment captures the domain entities which are manipulated, created or needed for the performance of a certain task. Based upon a CTT-like notation conditions can be defined over the object world state. A task in the Visual Task Model Builder is only executable if its preconditions are fulfilled. Moreover through performance of a task objects may also be created, manipulated, destroyed or assigned to a variable. The language is supported by a tool incorporating editing of all entities and interpreting the model for interactive validation. The approach is very rich and offers a very robust and usable tool. Modeling of the domain is performed by object-oriented design with limited expressiveness (no multivalued associations).

The interplay of object and task modeling has not only been tackled by Biere *et al.* In [Caffiau *et al.*, 2008] an overview on that issue is given. In essence, most task modeling languages consider objects as noteworthy but are used informally as properties, relationships (like "uses") or as preconditions to perform a task. Rarely objects are used to constrain the task execution (and in turn task execution may manipulate objects) in order to construct more realistic task models being usable for MB-UI development and to generate early prototypes.

TaOSpec [Dittmar & Forbrig, 2003] is one of the few. In the same vein as the Visual Task Model Builder, TaoSpec allows for modeling task specifications with binding to the execution environment. Unfortunately the approach by Dittmar and Forbrig is not very well integrated with standard software engineering models as a new concept for domain modeling is introduced. With respect to expressiveness and modeling of realistic scenarios TaOSpec is a major contribution in the domain of task modeling.

Kernel of Model for Activity Description (K-MAD) is a task modeling language based on MAD* which explicitly advocates the use of objects in preconditions and postconditions of tasks [Caffiau *et al.*, 2008]. Moreover termination conditions of iterations can be defined over objects. Objects are modeled in very restricted object-oriented fashion. So called "abstract objects" are classes whereas "concrete objects" represent objects being instances of classes. Sets, lists and stacks of abstract objects can also be specified. Inheritance, associations and methods are not considered in the approach which limits the approach to pure records or structs. K-MADe is the tool facilitating the use of the language which is equipped with editors for all entities of the language as well as a simulator which allows for rapid feedback cycles. K-MAD enhances the previously presented approaches in terms of integration of domain modeling.

AMBOSS is a task modeling environment dedicated to modeling of safety critical systems (e.g., medicine, aviation) [Giese *et al.*, 2008]. In contrast to most prior examined languages the objective of AMBOSS is not MB-UI development but modeling of work of actors within their environment. It is a CTT-like notation offering some novel extensions addressing the challenges of the domain it is used for. Thus an AMBOSS task model does not specify an idealized way of task performance with respect to safety criticalness but explicitly models risks and assurance. Exemplary barriers can be specified representing conditions need to hold at simulation time in order to prevent harm or damage to humans or material. Cooperation is modeled in AMBOSS by a role assignment to tasks (including machines). Therefore no task type similar to CTT exists as this information is already specified by the role. In contrast to CCTT not for each role a task tree is defined but a single monolithic task model specifies the task execution of all actors which may result in complex specifications which are difficult to manage. Formal preconditions are incorporated by AMBOSS addressing barriers as mentioned earlier (a task is only executable if its barrier holds) and message flows. In AMBOSS message flows can be specified between arbitrary tasks. At simulation time the receiving task can only be executed if the message has already been sent. This concept is actually very powerful as it allows for defining complex dependencies between tasks of different levels of abstractions. Object modeling is also supported by AMBOSS but is restricted to concrete objects. Those objects are very similar to resources in workflow modeling [Russell *et al.*, 2005]. Preconditions cannot be defined directly addressing object states. As AMBOSS is designed to specify how people perform work within physical environments spatial information are from interest because an actor may be needed to be co-located with a certain object to perform a task. Therefore location modeling has been integrated using a logical hierarchical model of locations. For each task it can be defined where it needs to be performed. However it is unclear how such information is taken into account during simulation. AMBOSS is the first approach which integrates location modeling, object modeling and task modeling. Hence, it is one of the few approaches dedicated to the specification of work situation in physical environments.

Besides the pure task modeling concepts some approaches present the tasks and their dependencies (such as context of use, platform, user handicaps, etc.) explicitly in one model. Representatives of such approaches are [Vanderdonckt *et al.*, 2008] and [Luyten *et al.*, 2006]. Whereas the former approach defines an extensive meta-model as UML class diagram in order to incorporate the different factors constituting the relevant context of use, the latter uses ontologies to define complex dependencies between tasks and their execution environment.

3.5 Specification Mechanisms for Implicit Interaction

In the following paragraphs vital research areas concerned with the model-based development of implicit interaction are investigated. The conducted examination especially focuses on the capability of specifying on a high level of abstraction as the model-based approach for implicit interaction should start with such a description (in order to benefit from model-based development).

The current research activities in the field of implicit interaction can be categorized into model-free and model-based approaches. The first infers the intention without explicit models of the envisioned implicit interaction (which is actually the behavior of interest of a human in the SmE) whereas the later relies on models specifying the envisioned behavior of the user. In this thesis model-free approach for implicit interaction are out of scope as the thesis explicitly proposes modeling to boost the quality of the system under construction. Moreover, the developed system exhibits higher quality and integrates much better with principles of UCD and HCSE as human needs are considered within the development explicitly when following an iterative model-based approach.

For the model-based development of implicit interaction different approaches exist. They are not as well-defined as MB-UI development due to novelty of the research area which has been started with the definition of Schmidt [2000]. Basically the question to be answered is whether one can infer the intention of the user which is expressed by implicit interactions (e.g., gestures). On a lower level of abstraction probabilistic models are used for intention recognition which explicitly makes use of observations and hidden states as the intention of the user can only be determined by the observed behavior. Artifacts such as the Hidden Marko Model (HMM) or more general Dynamic Bayesian Networks are used. Therefore research activities how to use such models are excluded in this explanation here (low level models for explicit interaction have not been reiterated either).

In general, two major research avenues can be identified for model-based development of implicit interaction. Either the model is created in a top-down approach (as it is the case while task modeling) or atomic actions are designed individually and are composed as needed which is a bottom-up approach. The subsequent paragraphs comprise examinations about representatives of the previously named categories of high-level description formalism being transformable to probabilistic models such as the HMM. After having investigated the existing approaches they are assessed with respect to task modeling.

In [Kiefer & Stein, 2008] context-free grammars are proposed in order to specify potential intention in accordance with the individual behavior of the user expressing the intention. Therefore non-terminals are intentions and terminals represent behavior. From perspective of user modeling this distinction is rather unclear as also complex behavior may constitute an intention. To achieve location-awareness production rule of the grammar are annotated with region (or locations). Only when a user is at an annotated region the production rule can be applied. In order to create a parsing tree terminals are further defined by certain sensor data. In the given example of Kiefer & Stein GPS data is used. The approach seems to be fruitful and prosperous especially with respect to the close bond of intention and behavior. However from our point of view the major shortcoming of the approach is the missing generality. As explained above intentions may also be defined by complex behavior (non-terminals) which is not an intention. Another major shortcoming is the missing of means to specify concurrent behavior which is fundamentally to truly reflect users adequately. More precisely, this is a general shortcoming of context-free grammars.

In the same vein probabilistic context-free grammars are used. Actually introduced by Charniak for natural language processing they can also be employed to parse potential intentions to infer behavior of people [1997]. They extend ordinary grammars by adding a function which assigns each production rule a probability. Such an extension allows assigning a probability to each word, sentence respectively, of the grammar.

[Burghardt & Kirste, 2008] proposed a novel approach to integrate a priori knowledge into intention analysis. Instead of starting with high-level activities and gradual refine them a bottom-up approach is taken. Atomic actions are specified by means of Planning Domain Definition Language (PDDL) which can be composed into sequences of actions representing the potential execution sequences valid in the current state. By calculating the valid sequences the set of actions of the user in the current states can be derived representing the intention. As the actions are independent new actions can easily be added at runtime. This allows for coping with dynamism in SmEs. However the shortcoming of this approach is that such a modeling approach in not intuitive. From our perspective gradual refinement and decomposition of high level activities into more basic ones is natural to humans and should therefore be supported by the modeling languages used to drive the design of implicit interaction.

3.6 Other Relevant Background Work

After having reviewed task-driven development approaches, task modeling languages and development approaches for explicit and implicit interaction it is continued with further relevant work which does not match the former categories.

According to [Garrido & Gea, 2002], the most important aspects for the development of interactive systems for collaborative environments are user groups, roles and tasks. In their approach, groups and roles are modeled using state charts whereas the definition of a task is specified by activity diagrams. As semantic domain Petri nets [Petri, 1962] have been chosen which allow the animation of the models as well as the verification of properties. The behavioral specification of this approach is sound but lacks the integration with the domain model which is an important aspect to consider when developing those systems. A development methodology has not been defined.

Workflow systems have been a focus of research over decades. Distribution of work in time and space are inherently factors of such systems. Traditionally workflows do not model cooperation by several workflows and glue them by preconditions and effects but by a monolithic workflow whose activities are allocated to different actors in the system. Therefore cooperation is modeled by sequence flow, allocation and message flow [White, 2004]. However in the Business Process Modeling Language (BPMN) no means for explicit cooperation exist. To visualize activities of different participants pools and swimlanes are used.

A pool is a container for process which involves cooperation. It can be either subdivided into swinlanes representing activities of one participant or can be considered as atomic containing the activities of the process. In Figure 3-11 an example of BPMN specification is given which is taken from the BPMN specification [BPMN, 2010]. *Financial Institution* and *Supplier* are pools. Moreover *Supplier* is subdivided into *Sales* and *Distribution* specified as swimlanes. Swimlanes are atomic and cannot be further decomposed. Activities belonging to the participant are arranged within its swimlane. Cooperation is modeled by sequence flow (e.g., *Process Order* of *Sales* and *Pack Goods* of *Distribution*) or by message flow (*Authorize Payment* of *Sales* and *Credit Card Authorization* of *Financial Distribution*). Pools and swimlanes rather structure a workflow properly than model cooperation as the actual dependencies between the activities are modeled by sequence and message flow. The expressiveness of such a modeling approach is powerful even though some limitations exist. It is not clear how to model cooperation of multiple participants with the same activities (e.g., multiple *Sales* participants) and no precise execution semantics for BPMN is given even though the Business Process Execution Language (BPEL) exists. The transformation of BPMN specifications into BPEL (and technological specific BPEL extensions like BPEL4WS) is defined by an informal mapping which has rather the form of a proposal than a semantic definition [Ouyang *et al.*, 2006; White, 2004].

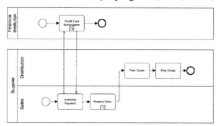

Figure 3-11 Pools and Swimlanes in BPMN from [BPMN, 2010]

Dynamic composition is another current challenge of workflow specification and web services (which are the state of the art implementation mechanism of workflows). Similar languages to BPMN have therefore been designed. The semantic web as a formalism to enhance syntactical interface matching to a semantic level is one approach to do so (e.g., DAML-S is one representative [Paolucci & Sycara, 2003]). Such approaches are certainly feasible for SmEs which has been exemplified in [Reisse *et al.*, 2008]. Yet the existing approaches focus on modeling device capabilities and software services. The special constraints of human behavior modeling as tackled here are not taken into account.

The ambient calculus developed by Cardelli and Gordon is used to specify processes with respect to mobility [1998]. More precisely, process algebra is used to specify the diverse computing resources. The special concept *ambients* is used to denote a certain boundary of execution. Ambients can be moved to represent the mobility of a certain process. In this vein the computing resources are modeled in accordance with the relevant topology of the system. Even though the approach is sound with respect to formality only the boundary of execution of a process is considered. A suitable language also needs to incorporate other facts but the ambient of a process, activity respectively.

In the area of safety critical applications and UIs human behavior modeling is also relevant. In [Basnyat *et al.*, 2007] an approach is discussed which employs Petri-nets as language for specifying the potential behavior of the user. In essence, the system and user model is specified as Petri-nets. Moreover barriers are defined which represent threshold to avoid erroneous states. Having defined the entire behavior by means of Petri-nets formal analysis of the model with its barriers can be performed.

3.7 Conclusion

Different types of applications comprise different complexity with respect to interaction development. In this chapter it has been shown what constitutes the complexity for each of the examined types, such as single platform, MUIs, context-aware applications and SmEs. In order to tackle the most complex type of application, namely SmEs, common approaches from the HCI and MB-UI are introduced which are from our point of view highly beneficial to investigate and to enhance. In order to do so task modeling has been investigated in-depth as the task model is the starting point for MB-UI development and is also suitable for implicit interaction which has not been researched thoroughly in HCI.

Furthermore the rationale and basic idea of task-driven approaches have been illuminated which relies on the hypothesis that a system is more appropriate if the work processes are kept as close as possible to the previously existing work processes. Therefore analysis task models are designed which are in turn enhanced to introduce the system under construction.

As a task model is usually an idealized normative description ([Johnson, 1992]) about the real world task performance certain facts are omitted. Even though this is in the nature of abstraction also important issues are sometimes not considered. Naturally this is due to the domain a task modeling language has been developed in. None of the languages presented in the last section have been designed in order to model tasks in SmEs. Therefore certain relevant facets are disregarded and application domains of task modeling are missed. Based on the existing ones new concepts need to be introduced in order to cope with the complexity in SmEs.

Chapter 4
Semantic Domains

In this chapter of the thesis the potential foundations of the semantics of CTML are discussed. In the first part the advantages of assigning formal semantics to a language are highlighted. Subsequently an evaluation of existing semantic domains is conducted which serves as guidance for selecting an appropriate semantic domain for CTML. Finally the notion of refinement with respect to the semantic domains is introduced and different approaches for refinement are formally defined and exemplified.

4.1 Introduction & Illustration

In software engineering it is well-known that the earlier an error is detected the less it costs to eliminate it. Prominent example of that finding is the 1:10:100 rule which states that costs of fixing problems rise exponentially with project progress [Oleson *et al.*, 2009]. Therefore the assessment of quality properties of a certain model is of high interest. In some cases the erroneous execution cannot even be rolled back (e.g., air traffic, nuclear power plants). Within such projects it is mandatory and not optional that the software system holds certain quality thresholds.

In order to assess the quality of a model an unambiguous semantics must be defined. It not only rules out any confusion about meaning it can also serve as reference point to define refinement relation between two specifications. Sharing of artifacts between different tools can only be performed if semantics are defined in a technology independent format in order to avoid misunderstanding. Tools for creation, editing, exploration and operation also rely on the semantics assigned as usually different tools are created which need to share the same model. Further reasons for formal syntax and semantics can be found in the subsequent paragraphs.

Managing Complexity

As development progresses models can become quite complex. In order to oversee the created artifacts different means need to be provided. Not only formal methods can be employed for that but also visualization of structural properties based on the formal syntax (e.g., dependence graphs). Modularization is another tool based on the syntax to do so. However when it comes to behavior syntax is useless. Semantics can be another source of information to oversee issues created during the development process.

Validation

Another reason to assign semantics is the opportunity to enable validation algorithms. This concept is often referred to as "Validation by Animation" and describes an interactive walkthrough using a tool [Hallerstede *et al.*, 2010]. Modeling mistakes can be found by animating the model several times to gain insights of the model. Validation can be performed using different configurations highlighting the current focus of evaluation. It is a complementary tool to verification.

Verification

Validation is a good tool to improve models as the behavior of the model is interactively explored. Therefore validation is a kind of testing because a model is tested with respect to different inputs by the user. However validation has its limitations or as Dijkstra states [1972]:

> "Program testing can be used to show the presence of bugs, but never to show their absence!"

The aim of verification is to proof properties for a certain model. Therefore algorithms based on formal methods are necessary. Basically verification algorithms answer the question whether a certain model exhibits a desired property. One of the most prominent examples is deadlock analysis. Informally a deadlock during execution occurs if no action is executable in a certain non-final state. The property of interest is deadlock freedom describing the fact that a certain model cannot deadlock. Other properties of interest depending on the domain are liveness and safety [Magee & Kramer, 2000].

The feasibility of verification algorithms strongly depends on the selected semantic foundation. If the model used to define the semantics is not able to capture the case of a deadlock a corresponding analysis cannot be performed. Contrary if the semantics of the model are too expressive the models cannot be verified as algorithms do not exist.

Refinement

In modern software engineering, the development lifecycle is divided into a series of iterations. With each iteration a set of disciplines and associated activities are performed while the resulting artifacts are incrementally perfected and refined. In order to assess that the enhanced version is a valid adaptation of its origin appropriate refinement relations are needed. Such relations can be based on structural and behavioral properties of a model. What constitute a valid refinement depends on the model, the domain the model is used in, the designer as well as the phase of the project. A comprehensive overview of refinement relations is given in Section 4.5.

4.2 Evaluation of Semantic Domains

In the following sections an introduction about potential formal semantic domains, accompanied with examples, is given. Moreover the differences of each are given in order to select an appropriate semantics for CTML.

Task models are belonging to the class of scenario-based specifications meaning that a task model specifies a set of "runs" by means of traces or scenarios. Scenario-based specifications has been proven successful for the specification of requirements by means of different techniques ([Uchitel *et al.*, 2004]) such as use cases, message sequence charts and state charts [UML, 2010]. A scenario refers to a successful run through the specification which can be easily understood even by non computer scientists. There is also the term scenario-based design by [Carroll, 1995] proposing to drive the development of the system by scenarios. However, in [Carroll, 1995] the term scenario is used in a much more informal sense even though the meanings are very similar. The design method is based on concrete scenario to transmit knowledge from stakeholder to developer and vice versa.

There are two semantic domains for scenario-based specifications: truly concurrent semantics (non-interleaving semantics) and interleaving semantics. Both are models for the specification of concurrent behavior. Whereas the former is based on the assumption that actions are truly distributed and parallel execution is inherently occurring, the latter eliminates true concurrent behavior by the nondeterministic choice of the sequentialization of parallel actions [Cleaveland & Smolka, 1996]. Exemplary, true concurrent behavior is the usage of multiple processors for several processes while a sequentialization of several processes on one processor results in an interleaved execution. Followers of interleaving semantics argue that their model is a suitable abstraction whereas advocates of non-interleaving semantics say that their model is more accurate and realistic [Marr, 2007].

A basic example of the difference of both types of semantics can be shown by the processes $ab[] ba$ and $a \parallel b$. The first one specifies that either the sequence of a and b or the sequence of b and a is executed. The latter specification describes the concurrent execution of a and b. One can easily see that the traces and scenarios of the two are equal (scenarios: $\{\langle a, b \rangle, \langle b, a \rangle\}$), please note that if two processes are scenario equivalent they are also trace equivalent). Those specifications cannot be distinguished by interleaving semantics. In contrast, non-interleaving semantics is able to recognize the difference as it is examined which events can occur simultaneously. In the first example no action can be performed at the same time whereas in the latter a and b may be performed simultaneous.

In what follows, representatives of approaches for the definition of interleaving and non-interleaving semantics are examined. An overview of different semantic definitions is given which enables a deliberate selection of an appropriate definition of the semantics of CTML.

4.2.1 Interleaving Semantics

Interleaving models are characterized by the property that there is a total order (being a binary, antisymmetric, transitive, total relation) of events meaning that for each arbitrary pair of events one can say which happened before [Garg, 2002]. Thus the run of a system is defined by a sequence of events in the interleaving model. Simultaneous occurring events cannot happen as all events are only interleaved.

The theory of processes has been examined for decades and is well understood. A process can be anything of interest (e.g., an algorithm, a vending machine [Hoare, 1978], a network protocol [Fokkink, 2000], etc.) The reason for specifying something as a process is mainly verification of certain properties like correctness, congruence, deadlock and lifelock freedom [Cleaveland & Smolka, 1996; Roscoe, 1997]. The basic idea is that systems are consisting of an arbitrary number of processes running concurrently exchanging data and synchronizing their actions. As those systems become quite complex mechanisms are needed to prove certain desired properties. Process theory offers a wide range of mathematically founded languages (such as Communicating Sequential Processes (CSP) [Hoare, 1978], Calculus of Communicating Systems (CCS) [Milner, 1980] and Algebra of Communicating Processes (ACP) [Baeten & Weijland, 1990]) offering analysis of processes and algorithms to prove congruence of processes. Different means have been proposed to define the semantics of process algebras. In [Roscoe, 1997] three different ways are examined for CSP. First, operational semantics via deduction rules and Labeled Transition Systems (LTS(s)) is proposed. Process terms are interpreted via inference rules to determine the actions a certain process enables. More precisely, a process has a certain action if and only if that is deducible based on the given inference rules. For each CSP operator a set of corresponding inference rules exists. These rules can be used to map a process term to a LTS based on action relations. An action relation defines that a certain process P can evolve into the process Q by the action a [van Glabbeek, 1990]. A LTS is a graph in which vertexes represent states and links represent state changes triggered by (invisible or observable) actions. In the corresponding LTS the processes P, Q are mapped to a LTS state whereas a is mapped to a LTS transition between the corresponding states of P and Q. By virtue of this approach the whole state space of a process is explored by means of a LTS which represents the entire semantics of the process. Model analysis and verification algorithms are performed on the deduced LTS. Several tools to do so exist. FDR (Failures Divergence Refinement) presented in [Roscoe, 1997] not only allows for comparing behavioral relations but also enables users to perform refinement checks and deadlock analysis. Hence it makes use of partial order reduction [Peled, 1993] to reduce the state space to be explored in order to accelerate the checks. The LTS analyzer by [Magee & Kramer, 2000] allows for validation and verification of LTS based models. Validation is achieved by animation whereas deadlock analysis and certain safety properties such as progress are verified. As comparison semantics the authors state that from their point of view strong equivalence and weak equivalence are useful being synonyms of simulation semantics (with invisible actions and without invisible actions).

As hinted above there are also other instruments for defining interleaving semantics for processes. Denotational semantics by means of traces, scenarios, failure and divergences can be defined. Basically a mapping of process terms to traces, respectively scenarios, failure and divergences, is defined. Even though denotational semantics is drastically different from operational semantics congruence can be proofed [Roscoe, 1997]. Semantics has also been defined in terms of axioms defining the semantics of process terms [Bergstra & Klop, 1990]. This approach is called algebraic semantics.

Different extensions for process algebras have been introduced. There are timed process algebras [Reed & Roscoe, 1986], stochastic process algebras [Herzog, 1990] and priority process algebras [Cleaveland et al., 2000].

LOTOS (Language of Temporal Ordering Specification), standardized in [ISO, 1989], is a formal description language for distribute systems [Bolognesi & Brinksma, 1987] which is based on process algebras and as such is not more expressive. The basic concepts are similar even though the concrete syntax differs to most process algebras. Equivalent to process algebras an operational semantics is defined by virtue of LTS. Over the years several interpreters and model checkers have been implemented to facilitate the use of LOTOS [Garavel & Hautbois, 1993; Jeong et al., 1997; Logrippo et al., 1988]. They include validation, specification comparison by means of bisimulation and code generation.

4.2.2 Non- Interleaving Semantics

Interleaving semantics is characterized by a total order of all events. However for truly concurrent systems this might not hold. By giving up the total order of events and defining a partial order true concurrency can be introduced [Pratt, 1986]. In contrast to a total order, a partial order (being a binary, reflexive, antisymmetric, transitive relation) defines that not all pairs of events need to be comparable. Intuitively one would call the relation *precedes*. Elements that neither precedes the other are allowed to occur simultaneous.

The most common approach to non-interleaving semantics are Petri-nets [Petri, 1962]. Petri-nets are bipartite graph structures in which vertexes are either places or transitions which in turn are connected by directed edges. Places are used to store token(s) which represent the state of the system at a time. The distribution of tokens over a Petri-net is called *marking*. The operational semantics of a Petri-net net is defined by firing rules. For a Petri-net a transition is *enabled* if and only if all input places (places directly connected with the transition as destination) exhibit enough tokens (the amount of tokens to enable a transition can be modeled). If a transition *fires* the tokens of the input places are consumed and new tokens (the amount of tokens to be placed can be modeled) are placed on the output places (places directly connected with the transition as origin). The firing of a transition is considered as atomic action and is as such non-interruptible. Please note that if a transition is enabled does not imply that it fires since if a Petri-net contains several enabled transition only one fires. Concurrent behavior can be modeled by having a transition with more than one subsequent place. If such a transition fires each place is supplied and the subsequent transitions may fire independent of each other. By applying this model true concurrency is not yet formally introduced. A more rigorous semantic definition is needed to do so. The most common way of giving meaning to Petri-nets are partial order sets (POSETs) [Pratt, 1986]. Due to its popularity Petri-nets have been extended in numerous ways. One can classify the extensions into two categories: convenience and semantic extensions. Extensions belonging to the first category are only for reasons of convenience (e.g., colored Petri-nets [Jensen, 1987], hierarchical Petri-nets [Huber et al., 1991]) and can be transformed into semantically equal basic Petri-nets. In contrast, the latter adds real value to the expressiveness of Petri-nets (e.g., timed Petri-nets [Ramchandani, 1974]) which allows for modeling more complex scenarios but also may prohibit the potential automated analysis of the net. Verification algorithms for basic Petri-nets include amongst others reachability of a certain marking, boundedness or liveness (see [Murata, 1989] for a comprehensive overview).

Partial ordered sets (POSETs) are one formalism to assign truly concurrent semantics to Petri-nets and other models of concurrent behavior [Pratt, 1986]. Basically a POSET defines a potential run through the system (as sequences do for interleaving semantics) whereas a set of POSETs (as set of sequences do for interleaving semantics) define the entire behavior of the system. Other models for non-interleaving semantics are trace theory [Mazurkiewicz, 1977] and event structures [Winskel, 1980].

4.3 Other Relevant Semantics

Even though the two given semantic domains are suitable for scenario-based specifications also other relevant definitions of semantics can be applied for task modeling. One major drawback of the interleaving and non interleaving semantics is the limitation of considering only actions as relevant for the semantics. The actual state of the system is implicitly encoded in the order, partial order respectively, of events. A representative of state-based foundations of semantics is Temporal Logic of Actions [Lamport, 1994]. Temporal formulas specify the system on which reasoning should be applied. Properties such as liveness, safety, fairness can be proven for a certain specified system (set of formulas).

4.4 Semantics for Task Specifications

Formal task specifications have their semantic origins in process algebras. CTT the most common notation for basic task models adopted its operators from LOTOS ([Paternò & Santoro, 2001]). CTT offers similar but yet not identical operators as LOTOS. The semantics of CTT are defined by a set of inference rules (one for each operator) eventually translating a CTT expression into a LTS (an operational interleaving semantics). The translation of CTT to LTS is not comprehensive and misses several aspects like successful termination and some operators.

User Action Notation (UAN), another task notation, has been successfully translated into process terms in [MacColl & Carrington, 2000]. The approach aims on defining system components based on formal task models to start a rigorous development approach taking into account user needs expressed by task models. System development is driven by the derived CSP specification and used for development, testing and verification purposes. However the authors do not make clear how UAN and CSP are used in the development lifecycle of interactive systems. Moreover the described translation is rather informal.

Van den Bergh and Coninx [2007] translate entire task expressions into state charts. As a result a generic state machine is created for leaf tasks as well as for complex task expressions. Transitions are used to implement temporal operators by connecting the corresponding task state charts appropriately. The approach lacks of formality as the transformation is only described informally and no automatic transformation algorithm has been developed. Therefore the feasibility stays unclear.

Sinnig proposed a formal unification of task models and use cases [2009]. In order to do so he translates an extended CTT like notation into nondeterministic finite state machines and set of partial order sets. Whereas the first defines an interleaving semantics the second supports truly concurrent behavior. In the defined development methodology the different semantic domains are used as needed to define suitable refinement relationships depending on the phase of software creation (requirements and design). In the same vein as proposed in [Wurdel *et al.*, 2008d] Sinnig defines structural and behavioral refinement for task models (Sinnig also proposes refinement of use cases which is not in the scope of the thesis). In more detail, during requirements engineering Sinnig only allows to refine a task model by scenario inclusion but with the constraint of only restricting user choices. It is argued that restricting user choices lead to more intuitive and less error-prone ways of executing tasks. Moreover the restriction of system choices is forbidden as it would contradict to the functional requirement defined in terms of use cases serving as foundation for the task model. When moving from requirements to design the refinement relation becomes more rigid. Scenario equivalence is demanded. The same applies for refinement on the level of design. Structural refinement is allowed in every phase of development. The approach of Sinnig is comprehensive in terms of software engineering and formality. However shortcomings exist. Such strict refinement relations may hamper the development of task models. A more customizable refinement relation as proposed in [Wurdel *et al.*, 2008d] seems to be more suitable to meet the requirements of an iterative, incremental software engineering process.

4.5 Refinement

As stated earlier refinement relations are of interest in order to integrate model adaptations into the software engineering lifecycle. They need to be tailored with respect to the semantic foundations of the modeling language and the domain of interest. Especially the usage of the modeling language in practice influences the criteria constituting a suitable refinement relation. Different refinement relations may be defined in order to allow a flexible approach depending on the state of software engineering and the current quality criteria.

The term refinement has been used in a rather wide manner. Therefore this section will examine the term and highlight differences in interpretation. Moreover it is shown that the different examined refinement relations exhibit a certain relation (being a lattice) which can be used to rule out a set of inappropriate refinement relations with respect to the domain of application here.

Refinement between two specifications has been investigated for decades and definitions have been proposed for various models [Brinksma *et al.*, 1995; Khendek *et al.*, 2001; Sinnig, 2009]. Except for Sinnig, to our knowledge a generically applicable notion of refinement has never been defined for task models. The approach of Sinnig who introduced refinement on task models and use cases with its assets and drawbacks has been investigated in the previous section.

The distinction between truly concurrent and interleaving semantic models is naturally important for the definition of refinement as the behavioral properties of a model (which are captured by the semantic domain) are compared during refinement analysis. Therefore the defined refinement relations of each semantic domain are fundamentally different.

For interleaving semantics various refinement and equivalence criteria have been defined. Among the most popular ones are trace-, testing- and bisimulation equivalence [Bergstra, 2001]. They are all based on LTS. Therefore LTS are defined formally:

Definition 4-1 (LTS -Labeled Transition System): A Labeled Transition System (LTS) is defined by the quadruple $\langle Q, \mathcal{A}ct, \rightarrow, q_0 \rangle$:

1. Q is the set of numerable states.
2. $\mathcal{A}ct$ defines the finite set of actions.
3. $\rightarrow \subseteq (Q \times \mathcal{A}ct \times Q)$ is the action relation.
4. $q_0 \in Q$ is the initial state.

Intuitively the action relation defines the states in which a certain action is executable and to which states the execution is leading.

Definition 4-2 ($\checkmark$ -Tick): In order to denote a successful termination of a process the special symbol $\checkmark$ is used. The set of actions with $\checkmark$ is denoted by $\mathcal{A}ct^\checkmark = \mathcal{A}ct \cup \{\checkmark\}$. $\checkmark$ cannot be added explicitly to the alphabet of actions.

Definition 4-3 (τ -Tau): In order to denote an invisible action the special symbol τ is used. The set of actions with τ is denoted by $\mathcal{A}ct^\tau = \mathcal{A}ct \cup \{\tau\}$. τ is never part of the observations of a LTS and cannot be added explicitly to the alphabet of actions.

The set of actions with $\checkmark$ and τ is consequently denoted by $\mathcal{A}ct^{\checkmark,\tau}$. Moreover $\mathcal{A}ct^*$ denotes the set of finite sequence over $\mathcal{A}ct$. The set of all LTS satisfying the prior given definition of a LTS is denoted by $\mathbb{L}$.

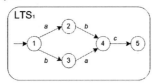

Figure 4-1 Example LTS

Figure 4-1 depicts an example of a LTS with $Q = \{1, 2, 3, 4, 5\}$, $q_0 = 1$, $\mathcal{A}ct = \{a, b, c\}$, and $\rightarrow = \{(1, a, 2), (1, b, 3), (2, b, 4), (3, a, 4), (4, c, 5)\}$.

Definition 4-4 (Set of $initials$): Let p be an arbitrary LTS ($p \in \mathbb{L}$) and q be an arbitrary state of p ($q \in Q$) then the set of enabled actions of q are:

$$initials(q) = \{a \in \mathcal{A}ct | \exists x \in Q : (q, a, x) \in \rightarrow\}$$

Please note that in the prior definition $q \in Q$. One can easily define the initials of a LTS with $p \in \mathbb{L}$ and q_0 the initial state of p by:

$$initials(p) = \{a \in \mathcal{A}ct | \exists x \in Q : (q_0, a, x) \in \rightarrow\}$$

An abbreviated notation for $(q, a, p) \in \rightarrow$ is $q \xrightarrow{a} p$ (if $a \in \mathcal{A}ct^*$ the cascading executing of the sequence is intended). This notation is preferred throughout the thesis. Thus the prior given definition can be abbreviated by:

$$initials(q) = \left\{ a \in \mathcal{A}ct \mid \exists x \in Q: q \xrightarrow{a} x \right\}$$

The initials of LTS_1 depicted in Figure 4-1 are the action a and b:

$$initials(LTS_1) = \{a, b\}$$

Furthermore the initials of the state 2 is the set $\{b\}$.

$$initials(2) = \{b\}$$

Definition 4-5 (Set of $refusals$): Let p be an arbitrary LTS ($p \in \mathbb{L}$) and q be an arbitrary state of p ($q \in Q$) then the set of refusals of q are:

$$refusals(q) = \{X \subseteq \mathcal{A}ct \mid intials(q) \cap X = \emptyset\}$$

The set of refusals of a LTS in a certain state denotes all sub sets of actions which do not contain any of the enabled action in the current state q. Due to the finiteness of $\mathcal{A}ct$ X is finite as well.

By defining a binary relation over the set of equivalences which can be paraphrased as "is equal to or coarser than" a lattice is created over the different equivalences [van Glabbeek, 1990].

Definition 4-6 ($\preccurlyeq$ -"Is Equal To or Coarser Then" Relation over Interleaving Semantics): Let the semantics S form an equivalence relation $=_S$ on LTSs $\mathbb{L}$ and let S and T be semantics over LTSs $\mathbb{L}$. Then we write $S \preccurlyeq_\mathbb{L} T$ to denote that T includes all criteria of S to define the semantics. To be more precise:

$$S \preccurlyeq_\mathbb{L} T \Leftrightarrow \forall u, v \in \mathbb{L}: u =_T v \Rightarrow u =_S v$$

In order to generalize this relation on all existing LTS it is written:

$$S \preccurlyeq T \Leftrightarrow \forall \mathbb{L} \, S \leq_\mathbb{L} T$$

It has been proven that the existing different equivalences on LTSs form a partial order with the prior defined operator $\preccurlyeq$. An abstract of this partial order is depicted in Figure 4-2. It illustrates the coarsest grained semantics (traces) as well as the most fined grained semantics for LTSs (bisimulation). Several others are omitted being in between the shown ones denoted by horizontal doted lines.

In the subsequent paragraphs four of the eleven semantics are examined more in detail (trace, completed trace, failure, and bisimulation semantics). This will not only show the difference of each but will also serve as basis to define a suitable equivalence semantics for the task specification language in this thesis.

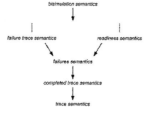

Figure 4-2 Excerpt of Partial Orders of Interleaving Semantics

Definition 4-7 ($=_T-$ Trace Equivalence): Trace equivalence is the weakest known equivalence on LTSs. The LTSs are trace equivalent if two LTSs produce the same set of traces:

$$u =_T v \Leftrightarrow traces(u) = traces(v), with\ u, v \in \mathbb{L}$$

The set of traces of a LTS u can be defined by:

$$traces(u) = \left\{ t \in \mathcal{A}ct^* | \exists q \in Q : q_0 \xrightarrow{t} q \right\}$$

This definition states that each valid sequence of actions starting from the initial state is a trace of p. Please note that the empty sequence is always included in the set of traces. For the given example LTS in Figure 4-1 the set of traces are:

$$traces(LTS_1) = \{\langle\ \rangle, \langle a \rangle, \langle b \rangle, \langle a, b \rangle, \langle b, a \rangle, \langle a, b, c \rangle, \langle b, a, c \rangle\}$$

A trace equivalent LTS to LTS_1 is given in Figure 4-3 because $traces(LTS_1) = traces(LTS_2)$. Therefore $LTS_1 =_T LTS_2$ applies.

This example shows already that trace semantics (and the other equivalences to some extent as well) does not investigate the structure of the LTS itself but only the observable behavior of the LTS. Trace semantics define what a LTS is able to do but do not say what they have to do. In order to overcome this limitation more comprehensive semantics exist. Depending on the way complete trace semantics is defined it is possible to determine what a LTS needs to do in order to terminate successfully. This approach is followed here.

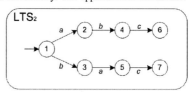

Figure 4-3 Trace Equivalent LTS

Definition 4-8 ($=_{CT}-$ Completed Trace Equivalence): Two LTS u and v are completed trace equivalent iff:

$$u =_{CT} v \Leftrightarrow completedtraces(u) = completedtraces(v)$$

The set of completed traces of the LTS u is defined as follows ($\wedge$ denotes the concatenation operator of sequences):

$$completedtraces(u) = \left\{ t \in \mathcal{A}ct^* | \exists q \in Q : q_0 \xrightarrow{s} q, s = \langle t \wedge \checkmark \rangle \right\}$$

Two LTS are therefore completed trace equivalent if the set of successful terminated traces are equal. Completed trace semantics has also been defined without the restriction of successful termination. However it is claimed that the approach here is more comprehensive. In order to give an example the LTSs need to be extended to mark successful termination (see Figure 4-4). The completed traces of the given models:

$$completedtraces(LTS_1') = \{\langle a, b, c \rangle, \langle b, a, c \rangle\}$$

$$completedtraces(LTS_3') = \{\langle a, b, c \rangle\}$$

Therefore $LTS_1^\checkmark$ and $LTS_3^\checkmark$ are not completed trace equivalent ($LTS_1^\checkmark \neq_{CT} LTS_3^\checkmark$). Without introducing the restriction of successful termination these models would indeed be completed trace equivalent.

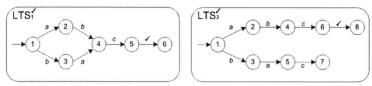

Figure 4-4 Extended Examples with Successful Termination

As $=_T \leqslant =_{CT}$ (see Figure 4-2) every two LTS being completed trace semantics equivalent are also trace equivalent [van Glabbeek, 1990]. Contrary there are LTSs which are not distinguishable by trace semantics but by complete trace semantics (e.g., $LTS_1^\checkmark =_T LTS_3^\checkmark$ and $LTS_1^\checkmark \neq_{CT} LTS_3^\checkmark$).

Both introduced semantics examine a LTS from the perspective what the LTS is able to do. On the first glance this approach seems to be comprehensive. However one can also investigate what the LTS cannot accept as input in a certain state. This approach is followed by failure semantics which was proposed by Brookes *et al.* [1984]. In the partial order of semantics it is the subsequent of completed trace semantics and makes therefore less identifications than completed trace semantics (identifying less LTSs as equal).

Definition 4-9 ($=_F$– Failure Equivalence): Two LTSs u and v are failure equivalent iff:

$$u =_F v \Leftrightarrow failures(u) = failures(v)$$

The set of failure of a LTS is defined as (with $\mathcal{P}$ denoting the power set of a set):

$$failures(u) = \left\{(t,X) \in \mathcal{Act}^* \times \mathcal{P}(\mathcal{Act}) | \exists q \in Q: q_0 \xrightarrow{t} q \wedge X \in refusals(q)\right\}$$

In contrast to the previously investigated semantics the set of failures contains pairs of action sequences and arbitrary sub sets of actions. The first element of a failure pair denotes the current trace under investigation whereas the other element state which actions are not accepted as input after having executed the trace. The set of failure pairs are all failure pairs of a LTS. More in detail for each trace all sets of refusals are recorded.

$LTS_4^\checkmark$ and $LTS_5^\checkmark$ shown in Figure 4-5 are completed trace equivalent ($LTS_4^\checkmark =_{CT} LTS_5^\checkmark$) because:

$$completedtraces(LTS_4^\checkmark) = completedtraces(LTS_5^\checkmark) = \{\langle a,b,\checkmark\rangle, \langle a,c,\checkmark\rangle\}$$

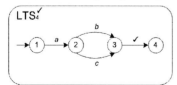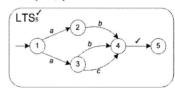

Figure 4-5 Non Failure Equivalent LTSs

However calculating the set of failure of both LTSs reveals that those two LTS are not failure equivalent ($LTS_4' \neq_\mathcal{F} LTS_5'$) as they have different sets of failure pairs:

$$failures\left(LTS_4'\right) = \{(\langle\ \rangle, X) \mid X \in \mathcal{P}(\{b,c\})\} \cup$$
$$\{(\langle a \rangle, \emptyset), (\langle a \rangle, \{a\})\} \cup$$
$$\{(\langle a, b \rangle, X) \mid X \in \mathcal{P}(\{a,b,c\})\} \cup$$
$$\{(\langle a, c \rangle, X) \mid X \in \mathcal{P}(\{a,b,c\})\}$$
$$failures\left(LTS_5'\right) = \{(\langle\ \rangle, X) \mid X \in \mathcal{P}(\{b,c\})\} \cup$$
$$\{(\langle a \rangle, \emptyset), (\langle a \rangle, \{a\})(\langle a \rangle, \{c\}), (\langle a \rangle, \{a,c\})\} \cup \{(\langle a \rangle, \emptyset), (\langle a \rangle, \{a\})\} \cup$$
$$\{(\langle a, b \rangle, X) \mid X \in \mathcal{P}(\{a,b,c\})\} \cup$$
$$\{(\langle a, c \rangle, X) \mid X \in \mathcal{P}(\{a,b,c\})\}$$

The failure pairs for the traces $\langle\ \rangle$, $\langle a, b \rangle$ and $\langle a, c \rangle$ are equal but having executed the trace $\langle a \rangle$ LTS_4' only prohibits to execute a (resulting in the failure pairs $(\langle a \rangle, \emptyset)$ and $(\langle a \rangle, \{a\})$) whereas LTS_5' due to its non determinism refuses a and/or c depending which way through the LTS is taken. The corresponding failure pairs are therefore $(\langle a \rangle, \emptyset), (\langle a \rangle, \{a\})(\langle a \rangle, \{c\}), (\langle a \rangle, \{a,c\})$.

As $=_{\mathcal{CT}} \preccurlyeq =_\mathcal{F}$ (see Figure 4-2) every two LTS being failure equivalent are also completed trace equivalent [van Glabbeek, 1990]. Contrary there are LTSs which are not distinguishable by completed trace semantics but by failure semantics (e.g., $LTS_4' =_{\mathcal{CT}} LTS_5'$ and $LTS_4' \neq_\mathcal{F} LTS_5'$).

After having defined the coarsest-grained semantics for LTSs it is now continued with the finest one. The reason to introduce this semantics is to show to what extent one can distinguish between LTSs. In the semantic domain of LTSs there is no semantics making less identifications of LTSs. Moreover bisimulation comprises all other semantics as it is the maximum element of the partial order $\preccurlyeq$.

Definition 4-10 ($=_\mathcal{B}$ – **Bisimulation Equivalence**): Two LTSs p and q are bisimulation equivalent iff there exists a bisimulation $\leftrightarrow_B$ with $p_0 \leftrightarrow_B q_0$ (p_0 and q_0 are the initial state of p, q respectively).

Let Q_x be the set of states of LTS x then the relation $\leftrightarrow_B$ satisfies the following constraints with $a \in \mathcal{Act}, p_1, p_2 \in Q_p, q_1, q_2 \in Q_q$:

1. If $p_1 \leftrightarrow_B q_1$ and $p_1 \xrightarrow{a} p_2$, then $\exists q_2 \colon q_1 \xrightarrow{a} q_2$ and $p_2 \leftrightarrow_B q_2$

2. If $p_1 \leftrightarrow_B q_1$ and $q_1 \xrightarrow{a} q_2$, then $\exists p_2 \colon p_1 \xrightarrow{a} p_2$ and $p_2 \leftrightarrow_B q_2$

In order to exemplify the interpretation of $\leftrightarrow_B$ (and consequently $=_B$) an extended example of Roscoe is consulted which is shown in Figure 4-6 [1997]. The dotted lines show bisimular states of the LTSs (e.g., $A \leftrightarrow_B X, B \leftrightarrow_B Y, C \leftrightarrow_B Y$). Following the first rule if $A \leftrightarrow_B X$ and one can transit to B via action a, then Y must be reachable by the same action and $B \leftrightarrow_B Y$ has to hold. The second rule states the same symmetrically for the LTS q. In order to proof that the given LTSs are bisimulation equivalent ($=_B$) the initial states need to be bisimular which implies that all reachable states need to be included in the bisimulation relation $\leftrightarrow_B$. As this is the case here those LTSs are bisimular ($LTS_6 =_B LTS_7$).

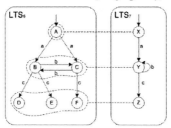

Figure 4-6 Bisimulation Example

The previously examined semantics have individual assets and drawbacks with respect to the application domain. In order to decide for or dismiss a certain equivalence the application domain needs to be taken into account. Naturally this is task modeling in the context of model-based development for explicit and implicit interaction here. The relation of these different refinement equivalences and task modeling is examined in Section 6.5.

The relation $\leqslant$ defines that certain equivalence are finer than others meaning that if two LTSs equivalent in certain semantics they are also equivalent in all coarser semantics. Hence it is shown that $=_T \leqslant =_{CT} \leqslant =_F \leqslant \cdots \leqslant =_B$ [van Glabbeek, 1990].

Trace semantics only states what a LTS can produce. There is no notion of deadlock or successful termination as all potential sequences of actions are captured independent of their further behavior in the LTS. Thus rather soft constraints are defined. Completed trace semantics is able to detect deadlocks and also states what a LTS needs to do (in order to terminate successfully) which is a stronger constraint than trace semantics. Failure semantics not only defines what a LTS needs to produce but also examine a LTS with respect to what it cannot produce. This is a different approach to assign semantics to LTSs then before. For each path taken through the LTS the sets of refusals are specified. Thus it is specified which actions are not possible in a certain state in the LTS (more precisely which sets and sub sets of actions). Therefore the constraints are extended with respect to the refused actions in a certain state. Several semantics are finer then failure semantics and coarser then bisimulation. Bisimulation is the finest grained semantics. In order that two LTSs are bisimular the nodes of each LTS are assigned to equivalence classes. Moreover there is a bijective mapping of equivalence classes from the first to the second LTSs equivalence classes. Then for each transition connecting a source state with a target state the corresponding equivalence classes must be reached in the second LTS via the action assigned to the transition (and vice versa). The only equivalence which is finer then bisimulation is graph isomorphism (in addition to bisimulation nodes are mapped by a bijective function).

In the last paragraphs different semantic equivalences have been introduced. However sometimes strict equivalence is not desired but behavioral inclusion or extension may also be of interest. Taken the example of model-based development for an adapted version of an artifact not only the previously defined behavior may be desired but also some new features are added on purpose. Strict equivalence is counterproductive in this case but behavioral extension may be appropriate. In the same vein a specialization of an artifact supporting only a sub set of features of the previously resulting in a restriction can be defined. In this case inclusion may be desired. Therefore the given definitions can be extended to inclusion and extension for several types of semantics equivalences.

Definition 4-11 ($\subseteq_S$ - Restriction, Extension of LTS regarding Semantics S): The LTS p restricts the LTS q, the LTS q extends the LTS p respectively with regard to semantic S iff:

$$p \subseteq_S q$$

This definition can then be applied to the concrete semantics such as trace, completed trace semantics or failure semantics. A LTS q extends a LTS p with respect to trace semantics iff:

$$p \subseteq_T q \Leftrightarrow traces(p) \subseteq traces(q), with\ p, q \in \mathbb{L}$$

The same can be defined analogously for completed trace semantics and failure semantics. Whether strict equivalence, inclusion or restriction is appropriate for a certain model depends, again, on the application domain and the stage of development in a process.

The proposed semantics are all based on interleaving semantics. The characteristics of true concurrency have been examined in Section 4.2.2. For this type of semantics the necessity of refinement exists for the same reasons as for interleaving semantics. However as it is shown in this thesis true concurrency is not of interest for the task modeling language presented here. The reasons for that are given in Section 6.3 and 6.4.

In general when examining a model one can distinguish between structural and behavioral properties in order to define equivalences or refinement relations. The prior given definitions of refinement are only based on the observable behavior of the models. The structural properties of a model may also constitute a proper refinement relation. With regard to LTSs actions may be typed and not allowed to be adapted during refinement just to name a simple example. Moreover as LTSs serve usually as semantic foundation and not as source specification structural properties can be checked on a higher level of abstraction.

The definition of refinement for a specific model is a complex task as the usage of the model in practice and the application domain needs to be taken into account. However even the general notion of refinement still offers some challenges which are presented in the following paragraphs.

Actions are considered as atomic units in interleaving and non-interleaving semantics. However if an actions in a source model is further refined in a sub specification (replaced by a complex expression) so called *action refinement* is performed [van Glabbeek & Goltz, 2000]. The stepwise development of a system or model was already advocated by Wirth with the term of *stepwise refinement* [1971]. With the advent of iterative, incremental development processes such a case is even more common. Especially in interleaving semantics action refinement cannot be defined properly or as Pratt states [1986]:

> "*A serious difficulty with the interleaving model is that exactly what is interleaved depends on which events of a process one takes to be atomic.*"

More precisely in [van Glabbeek & Goltz, 2000] a canonical example is given in which two bisimlar processes are given which are not even trace equivalent after a simple action refinement. In contrast in partial order sets which is a representative of truly concurrent behavior action refinement can be introduced while preserving the existing equivalence relation [van Glabbeek & Goltz, 2000].

4.6 Conclusion

In this chapter formal semantics with respect to task specifications have been investigated. More precisely, it has been started with explanations about the reasons for assigning formal semantics to models. Next, two different semantic domains have been evaluated with respect to their suitability for task modeling. Subsequently, existing approaches to assign semantics to task models have been examined. Based on that survey and the evaluation before interleaving semantics seems to be very fruitful to investigate as the refinement relations researched in the subsequent section are suitable for task specifications.

With regard to refinement different comparison semantics have been reiterated. Moreover it has also been shown that two specifications cannot only be compared by means of the comparison semantics but also by the type of refinement (equivalence, restriction, and extension). The refinement relations for CTML are defined and explained in Section 6.5.

II. Applying HCI Task Modeling to Smart Environments

Chapter 5
Bridging the Gap: HCI Task Modeling and Smart Environments

Having reiterated through relevant background information it is now continued with the in-depth examination of interaction design and the reasons for following a task-driven approach in this thesis. The complexity of SmEs with respect to interaction design is exemplified by a scenario which is, first, used as vehicle to distill the requirements of the task modeling language and, second, consulted as running example in the remainder of the thesis. During this chapter the experimental infrastructure in our university is introduced as well.

5.1 Interaction Development for Smart Environments

Interaction design is usually developed in accordance with the functional components of the system and is therefore driven by the functional requirements. According to [Heider, 2009] the functional components of a SmE are implemented using different approaches (for reasons of brevity explanations are omitted, see [Heider, 2009] for details):

- Custom-tailored by the software designer.
- Plan recognition.
- Learning by observation.
- Matchmaking.

These are the basic approaches in order to implement functional components of a SmE. However no statements about the interaction technique (and its development) are made. The interaction is naturally influenced by the implementation of the functional components even though it is not dependent. Therefore explicit and implicit interaction can be used in each type of approach for developing proactive assistance. This fact is also stressed by Kirste who therefore divides the development into two distinct layers: intention recognition and strategy planning [2006].

Whereas the first refers to implicit interaction, the latter is one approach to implement the strategy synthesis of the SmE (Ad hoc composition of services). In Figure 5-1 on the left hand side the principle of goal-based interaction of Kirste is depicted. Based on the users' behavior the intention of the user is derived (more precisely it is tried to do so as this is quite a complex task). Each intention is mapped to a set of goals which are then examined in order to generate a valid action sequence to satisfy the goals. Those actions are eventually assigned to (and executed by) devices in the environment.

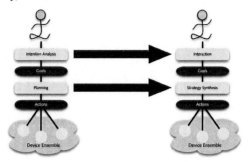

Figure 5-1 Goal-based Interaction [Kirste, 2006] and Extended Framework for Interaction

Even though this principle has been defined in order to achieve implicit interaction and ad hoc service composition it can be validly adapted to a general framework which divides a SmE into two distinct categories: Interaction and Strategy Synthesis. How interaction is implemented, following an explicit, implicit or combined approach, in a concrete SmE depends on the envisioned behavior of the system. Usually a combined approach is preferred. This also applies for Strategy Synthesis as different approaches can be used in order to implement proactive assistance with either interaction technique. The adapted layered model is depicted on the right hand side of Figure 5-1.

Such architecture is excellent for interaction design as it is independent of the Strategy Synthesis and as such can be tackled independently. As explicit and implicit interaction are usually used combined a holistic interaction development approach should incorporate both paradigms as well as should be founded on the same artifacts in order to assure consistency between both interaction techniques. This is important if the user of a SmE changes the interaction technique during runtime which is not necessarily an intended process.

The research community of MB-UI development investigates the challenge of an engineering approach to UI development for decades [Molina, 2004] which has been shown in Section 3.3.2. Diverse approaches have been highlighted tackling explicit interaction in SmEs based on MB-UI [Blumendorf, 2009; Luyten *et al.*, 2006; Paternò *et al.*, 2008]. The approaches validate the general rationale of explicit interaction for SmEs based on a task-driven approach using model-based development. The advantages of such an approach are:

- **Advantages of model-based engineering.** Such as separation of concerns, multiple viewpoints, high level decision making, short turnaround cycles, technology independence, roundtrip engineering, declarative models and transformations, etc.

- **Incorporation of task world of the user.** As already shown in Figure 3-3 focusing on tasks of the users helps to incorporate their real needs. Task models are the prevalent tool for specifying UI requirements as they are understandable, expressive and describe tasks on a high level of abstraction.

- **Gradual refinement.** Declarative models, such as the task model, can be incrementally enhanced. However not only on the same level of abstraction gradual refinement is desired but also between the different modeling stages. The existing MB-UI chain is therefore a reference point for UI development.

As stated before interaction development needs to be founded on the same artifacts independent of the type of interaction to withstand switches of interaction (from explicit to implicit interaction, and vice versa) at runtime and provide a consistent interaction. As explicit interaction for SmEs is currently developed by MB-UI which is started by task modeling it is investigated whether task models are an appropriate tool to start development of implicit interaction as well in order to ground both interaction techniques on the same artifact.

Despite the employment of task models within the interaction development process it has to be assessed whether the currently existing task modeling languages are able to cope with the complexity of SmEs. Therefore it is now continued with an example of a SmE which has been set up within our Graduate School MuSAMA (Multimodal Smart Appliance Ensembles for Mobile Applications)[1] at the University of Rostock. After that an envisioned scenario of use is given in order to distill the requirements with respect to task modeling to adequately represent task structures in SmEs.

5.1.1 An Example "The SmartLab"

In order to exemplify existing research questions and evaluate developed concepts an experimental infrastructure is very helpful. In our Graduate School we are in the fortune situation of having a technology enhanced environment which enables us to test the developed concepts in concrete settings. In Figure 5-2 the SmartLab while being used is shown. It is a multi display environment with currently nine projectors and six projection surfaces installed. It has been designed to serve as technology enhanced meeting environment to support people during knowledge work.

Figure 5-2 Experimental Infrastructure of MuSAMA: "SmartLab"

---

[1] http://www.musama.de/

The research conducted in order to deliver the envisioned support is ranging amongst other from network infrastructure, localization algorithms based on Bluetooth and RFID to interaction development and usability evaluation.

Even though the experimental infrastructure defines a particular domain of interest and the scenarios based upon such infrastructure, we claim the methods developed in this thesis can also be applied to other SmEs (e.g., home entertainment, elderly care). This fact is evidenced by projects at the University of Rostock addressing assistive technologies for elderly care. Other assistive applications and other types SmEs are also closely coupled to the task the user is executing (or will execute). Therefore, the approach is also feasible for other types of SmEs. Within the conducted research especially elderly care task performance has been also analyzed and modeled by means of the developed language presented in this thesis. The results are promising.

5.1.2 Requirements for Task Modeling in Smart Environments

The given task modeling languages examined in Section 3.4 have been designed in order to support task modeling in a certain domain and for a special purpose (e.g., MB-UI development for groupware applications). With respect to SmEs no dedicated language exists. In order to assess the languages a scenario is introduced which highlights the requirements for task modeling.

An Illustrating Scenario

The characteristics of task modeling in SmEs are exmplefied best by a scenario which is also used in as running example throughout the remainder of the thesis. It will not only highlight the complexity of task modeling in SmEs but will also serve as means to elicit requirements for a task modeling language in an intuitive manner. Even though SmEs are not limited to function rooms but they are one prominent example in which assistance is appreciated.

More specifically the running example is a "Conference Session" in a technology enhanced meeting room. The challenges of such scenarios are multi-layered. On each level of abstraction research challenges can be identified. To emphasize the challenges with respect to task modeling an appropriate scenario has been chosen. It can be paraphrased as follows:

> *The session chair Dr. Sheldon Cooper introduces himself and defines the topic of the session. Afterward he gives the floor to the first speaker, Dr. Leonard Hofstadter, who enters the presentation area and sets up the equipment. The laptop switches to presentation mode and the speaker starts with the talk. A presentation device is used to switch back and forth between the slides. During the presentation the audience accesses additional information related to the talk using personal devices. After finishing the talk the chairman asks for questions from the plenum which are answered by the speaker. Eventually the chairman closes the talk and announces the next one. Subsequent talks are given in the same manner until the chairman encourages an open discussion, wraps up the session and finally closes it.*

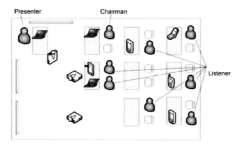

Figure 5-3 Visual Representation of the Illustrating Scenario "Conference Session"

In Figure 5-3 a visual representation in bird's eye view of the scenario is given. It shows the relevant entities from task modeling perspective. The scenario includes multiple actors (Dr. Cooper, each presenter and the listeners), whose behavior is characterized by the role they are fulfilling (chairman, listener, presenter). More in detail tasks are performed with regard to the role the actor is fulfilling. However they are not undertaken isolated but in accordance with other attendees meaning the actors need to synchronize their actions. During the paper presentations the role of the actors is not fixed but fluent. In this particular scenario an actor is a listener first (listening to a presentation), then becomes a presenter (presenting his/her own paper) and eventually after finishing the presentation goes back to being a listener again.

Moreover the location of an actor strongly influences the tasks the actor is able to perform as devices may need to be present in the near surroundings or predefined zones (presentation area for a presenter). Hence stationary and personal devices assist the actors during their task performance. Laptops are used to store slides or mobile devices may be employed in order to access information during the presentation and a stationary projector is utilized to show the slides. Besides those functional properties static properties of devices may be relevant. The network adapters or in- and output capabilities of a device may be relevant in order to model tasks in such a scenario appropriately.

The domain also needs to be taken into account. Tasks may only be executable if certain objects of the domain are in a desired state or present at all. Domain objects can be either virtual (e.g., slides) or physical (e.g., switch, pen). Moreover the execution of tasks may also manipulate a certain device or domain object. Moreover due to the execution of tasks the location of actors may also change.

Besides those rather obvious facts also other relevant characteristics can be identified. Amongst others there is cognitive load, stress level, etc. Presenting a paper in front of an audience is a stressful task to accomplish. Another fact which is necessary to consider is the organizational structure of the attendees of the session which actually influences the cognitive load of the attendees (e.g., giving a lecture in front of students is less stressful than defending a project against external reviewers). Also the ambient noise level, temperature, light conditions, and other physical properties of the environment can influence how tasks are performed.

Based upon the scenario and the last paragraphs a set of requirements that are particular for a specification framework for SmEs can be distilled. However, also some properties are left out. Cognitive load and stress level are very hard to formulize adequately and therefore are not included in the formal specification language in this thesis. Contrary, physical properties can be modeled quite easily (continuous values need to be discretized) but are not considered as major influencing factors of the task performance. We have summarized the requirements into the following distinct three categories which in turn are further subcategorized.

Modeling Approach

The modeling approach relies on a user-centered design methodology and therefore proposes the use of tasks as central building blocks of the modeling language. Due to this perspective the user needs can be incorporated better which fosters the user satisfaction during the use of the developed system. The following two subcategories have been identified:

(1) **Task-Based Specification.** The concept of a "Task" is central to SmEs. Typically various actors collaborate and interact with each other by sharing, synchronizing on, and triggering common and related tasks respectively. Therefore, we believe that a specification framework for collaborative environments should be built around the concept of a task. It should furthermore intrinsically support well-known task related concepts such as decomposition into subtasks and temporal ordering. Such an approach is also necessary to allow high-level modeling using a top-down approach which is intuitive for human behavior modeling.

(2) **Modeling Cooperation.** SmEs are inherently multi user systems. Naturally the task performance of individuals is influenced by others. In order to model collaborative work, synchronization constructs to coordinate task performance are needed. Examples of such constructs are preconditions and effects. The former denotes additional constraints defined over the state of the SmE whereas the latter defines state modifications as a result of task execution.

Context Modeling

The context of use as set of influencing external factors has not only been discussed in the research field of context-aware applications but also in UCD and HCSE (see ISO 13407 [ISO, 1999]). The definitions of context are manifold as already explained in Section 3.1. For CTML we found the following subcategories of context expedient and relevant to consider for task specification method for SmEs:

(3) **Location Modeling.** To be able to model tasks performed in physical environments location modeling and its integration into task modeling is an important feature to be supported. This feature allows for building location aware computing based on a task-driven approach. Van der Veer and van Welie already emphasized that the physical layout of environment in which tasks are performed needs to be considered [2000]. However GTA which is the task specification technique of the authors does not incorporate that feature. Additionally, in recent years available location tracking systems using different technologies such as GPS, RFID, Bluetooth or Ultra Wideband have become sufficiently precise. Therefore, the location of an actor is not only

very relevant but also quite easy to measure which is a key requirement when using the approach in real world settings.

(4) **Device Modeling.** The functional and static properties of devices and even their presence in a SmE are relevant to adequately represent the tasks performable by the users. In HCI, and consequently in task modeling, devices have been rather considered as platforms for UIs. In SmEs a wider context is necessary as tasks also depend on the functional state of devices (e.g., the projector has to be switched on to present slides). Moreover the present devices and their functionalities are not only relevant for the executability of the tasks but also influence to which degree assistance can be provided as the assistive technology needs a platform and computing power. Actually dynamic reassignment of human task to system tasks is mainly based on the present devices in a SmE.

(5) **Domain Modeling.** The interplay of objects and tasks are commonly known and considered as important. Several approaches have been proposed in order to combine both descriptions (see Section 3.4.3). Those approaches are considered as important and need to be adopted by a task modeling language dedicated to SmEs. Moreover there are also approaches in the research field of ubiquitous computing in which the importance of objects for tasks is emphasized and taken into account. For example, in [Bellotti *et al.*, 2008] a framework is proposed which enables software developers to use RFID sensors to detect objects in the near surroundings without caring about RFID hardware and sensor evaluation.

Means of Engineering

The pure modeling concepts are by far not sufficient. In order to allow an engineering approach which relies on a structured way of modeling and evaluation other requirements can be derived. Such means for engineering can guide the software developer how to make effectively use of the language, rule out any ambiguities, assure consistency throughout the use of the modeling language and provide interfaces to other modeling languages, code respectively. With respect to SmEs the following criteria are of main interest and should be supported by a task modeling language.

(6) **Development Methodology.** Software engineering is a process of a set of iteratively performed activities and not an isolated modeling step. Therefore low level activities such as creating a model need to be embedded into a higher level context. Such a process model not only guides the software developer which model is created on which level of abstraction but also provides interfaces to other models and helps to transits between different phases of the process model.

(7) **Formal Syntax and Semantics.** In order to make effective use of the task specification language formally defined syntax and semantics are needed. The underlying formal model will not only rule out ambiguities but also serve as a reference point for the definition of a refinement relation between two specifications. It is also an obvious precondition for sophisticated tool support.

(8) **Support for Refinement.** In general, software development consists of a series of transformations in which models (or code) are iteratively refined. Modeling collaborative environments is no exception to this rule. Often a coarse-grained, even incomplete specification is successively transformed into more complete fine-grained specifications. With each transformation step it is important to ensure that the resulting model is a valid refinement of the base specification.

(9) **Tool Support.** Another key requirement for a formal specification framework is tool support that assists developers in handling collaborative task specifications. In particular tools can facilitate the actual specification of the collaborative model, perform automated refinement checks, simulate/animate the specification, and allow derivation of other models/code. Most desirable is an integrated tool environment (CASE Tool) which allows for accessing the above named functionalities in a coherent manner.

None of the examined languages in Section 3.4 supports all features named above. More precisely location modeling and integration in task modeling, behavioral device modeling, and refinement are not supported by any of the languages. Moreover CCTT only supports very limited capabilities of modeling cooperation of actors.

All categories are addressed in the task modeling language, CTML, presented in this thesis in order to support explicit and implicit interaction development. Moreover to effectively make use of the language a methodology is proposed covering all major phases of software engineering in order to develop the interaction of a SmE in an integrated manner.

Besides being able to specify tasks in SmEs in a natural manner explicit and implicit interaction is the domain of interest and must therefore be supported via the task modeling language.

5.1.3 Task Structures of Interaction

The difference of implicit and explicit interaction has been exemplified in Section 2.2. An interesting issue to investigate is the impact of the interaction type on the task structure of the user interacting. Generally it can be stated that explicit interactions (e.g., GUIs) are more rigid in the execution order of tasks. If a certain GUI element is not visible or enabled it cannot be pressed in order to trigger a function. On the other hand during implicit interaction user action cannot be prevented. If the user wants to perform an action she can do it. This obvious result has a direct impact on the design of task models for both interaction types as the enabled task set in each task execution step divergent from explicit to implicit interaction (and vice versa). This finding can be further explained by considering the enabled task set according to the definition in [Paternò, 1999]:

> *"An enabled task set is a set of tasks that are logically enabled to start their performance during the same period of time"*

A task model may define multiple enabled task sets and one task may belong to several enabled task sets.

For explicit interaction the task models are more rigid as actions can be forbidden due to the interface. Therefore fewer tasks are enabled simultaneously. In general, the cardinality of the enabled task set for explicit interaction is smaller than for implicit interaction. Due to this, the cardinality of the set of enabled task sets which are defined by the structure of the task model is higher as each task needs to belong to at least one enabled task set.

Besides the difference in the set of enabled task sets another difference can be identified. When specifying tasks for implicit interaction the set of actions (atomic task) is rather small compared to task models for explicit interaction. Our finding during modeling is that the atoms of task models for implicit interaction are reoccurring. Typical reoccurring atoms are *move to* and *take*. With respect to our experimental infrastructure, presented in Section 5.1.1, also *sit* and *present* are typical atomic tasks. Naturally, in task models for explicit interaction atoms are also reoccurring but in HCI there is still an ongoing discussion whether tasks such as pressing a button or click events are really tasks or facts that should be specified on the level of dialog modeling.

Another insight which has turned out through ongoing modeling in practice is that the task structures in task models for explicit interaction are much deeper compared to those of implicit interaction. Task models designed for being used as input for MB-UI development easily span over five or six levels of abstractions whereas in implicit interaction the depth of three is usually not exceeded. The reason for this difference is from our point of view twofold. In implicit interaction the work processes cannot be specified as precise as for explicit interaction as the user cannot be prevented from executing an action if she wants to. Because of that it is not practical to specify the task model in a very detailed manner. Another issue which needs to be taken into account is that the work processes in SmEs do not need to implement certain business rules or accomplish the goal in the manner as specified. For example, in safety critical applications the UI has to assure that a certain goal is reached in the different ways it has been designed. The same applies for other systems. A fully specified model is therefore mandatory to ensure consistency and traceability. Currently, such criteria are not relevant for implicit interaction in SmE.

Based on the given explanations it is hypothesized that four main differences in the structure of task models for explicit and implicit interaction development exist:

1. **Number of Concurrent Enabled Tasks.** In implicit interaction more tasks need to be enabled concurrently in order to represent the task execution in physical environment adequately as the user cannot be hindered from executing a certain task.

2. **Number of Enabled Task Sets.** Due to the first bullet the number of sets of concurrently enabled tasks is much higher in task model for implicit interaction.

3. **Number of Actions.** The set of atomic tasks in task models for implicit interaction is smaller compared to task models used to specify explicit interaction as actions are usually more often reoccurring.

4. **Depth of the Task Models.** Task models for implicit interaction usually do not span over three levels of abstractions. In MB-UI development the task models easily exceed this level. Basically this is due to the precision needed in explicit interaction

and the ambiguity in the design of task models in implicit interaction which makes it impractical to further refinement certain actions.

The results of the properties above are mainly that task models for implicit interaction are less precise and define much more scenarios than task models for explicit interaction in which the course of actions are much more structured.

5.1.4 Feasibility of Task Modeling

Task analysis and task modeling has been successfully applied to ordinary GUI systems for decades. Due to the application of these methods the developed UIs can be improved and suit the needs of the user better. For GUIs and explicit interaction in general the task model is a valid description as the explicit performance of a certain action is part of the model. Moreover GUIs are somehow limited in their way tasks can be performed (e.g., if a button is not displayed it cannot be pressed). Due to the limited possibilities of deciding for or against a certain task (the user cannot select an invisible/not enabled action) this approach is feasible. Therefore, a complete description of the tasks the user is able to perform with the UI is feasible in general. However, when moving from explicit interaction to implicit interaction the question is raised whether task modeling is still a good vehicle to specify the diverse actions a user can perform to interact implicitly. The main difference between explicit and implicit interaction with respect to task modeling is that (most) actions performed by the user within a physical environment cannot be prohibited by the SmE (e.g., going in front of the audience) even though it contradicts to the specified interaction model. The user can select any task even if it is not meaningful and not anticipated by the designer. In explicit interaction such inconsistent actions (from designer perspective) can be avoided. This new degree of freedom in task execution needs to be taken into account not only by the modeling language but also by the interpretation what the task model actually specifies. In explicit interaction the task model specifies all potential ways a task is performed and a goal is achieved. Due to the freedom of behavior such a view is not valid in implicit interaction. In contrast to explicit interaction an open world assumption is needed which means with respect to task modeling that there can also be other ways of achieving the goal. The completeness of task modeling as specification mechanism can be regarded as an unrealistic assumption. By dismissing the assumption the task model becomes a pattern of behavior which represents the intended way tasks are executed under the current circumstances. In practice such an approach means that the user can be assisted as long as she sticks to the defined pattern of behavior. For certain situations and configurations of the SmEs different task models can be designed or selected at runtime. Therefore a task model can only be a blueprint for achieving a goal and not a complete description. This is not necessarily a drawback. Not yet specified ways of achieving a goal can be observed and traced in order to integrate them into the task model during the next development cycle. In this vein the artifact is gradually improved by the observed behavior of the user which is the most natural way a task is performed. Therefore task models for implicit interaction are considered as behavioral patterns of the user within a SmE and not as complete descriptions of the performable actions.

5.2 Explicit Interaction with Task Models

The MB-UI development process has been proven as successful even for SmEs [Feuerstack & Blumendorf, 2007; Feuerstack *et al.*, 2008; Luyten, 2004]. The maturity of MB-UI development is based upon a set of identified and commonly agreed on models and transformation which allows for gradually adding information in order to eventually generate the final UI. In the research community of HCI the set of models has been identified over years. The basic MB-UI process is depicted in Figure 3-5 in Chapter 3. This process model is also valid for SmEs even though that due to unforeseen configurations and situations the UI may need to be generated automatically or adapted based on the given situation. In Section 3.3 examples of such approaches have been explained.

Based on the given example we claim that the MB-UI chain is working well for such dynamic systems and should therefore be continued in the same manner. Therefore the process given in Figure 3-5 is also used in this thesis to driven the explicit interaction process.

5.3 Implicit Interaction with Task Models

It has already been clarified why MB-UI development is the method of choice for explicit interaction. It is assumed that implicit interaction can also be tackled by a model-driven approach via task models (the assumption is actually strengthened by [Giersich *et al.*, 2007]). If that assumption holds an integrated methodology for interaction development in SmEs can be derived.

With respect to Section 3.5 task modeling is the most appropriate modeling formalism as it combines several advantages:

- **Focus on User.** When modeling tasks the developer focuses on the way tasks are performed by the user and not how the system needs to be developed. Such a viewpoint enables the developer to focus on the user instead of specifying already the interaction. Especially for implicit interaction the natural behavior of users needs to be reflected in order to avoid unnatural behavior.

- **Top-Down Approach.** People tend to decompose complex tasks into smaller one. In order to model tasks adequately this concept should be supported. This will not only help the developer in modeling tasks but will also be more natural for the user being integrated in the development process according to a UCD process.

- **Temporal and Causal Modeling.** Modeling temporal ordering of tasks is common in existing task modeling languages. However in the task modeling language presented here also dependencies based on the current world state are considered. Such a combined approach allows for modeling tasks more easily and can be used as preferred.

- **Modeling of Concurrency.** Modeling of multiple users and concurrent behavior of individuals is crucial. A modeling language which is not able to cope with concurrency is not purposeful. Moreover synchronization constructs needs to be offered by the modeling language because parallel activities need to be synchronized.

Based upon these bullets CTML has been designed as modeling language for activities in SmEs. The created models can be used for intention recognition and therefore for implicit interaction.

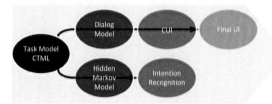

Figure 5-4 The Envisioned Process of Interaction Development

The combined development process and the involved artifacts are depicted in Figure 5-4. It implements the requirements of a common artifact for the interaction development in general. Moreover it relies on a model-based approach. Therefore gradual refinement and separation of concerns are supported. How explicit (on the top of Figure 5-4) and implicit (on the bottom of Figure 5-4) interaction development is performed in detail is explained in Section 7.4.

5.4 Conclusion

In this chapter it has been shown that the functional components of a SmE can be either accessed using implicit or explicit interaction. Therefore the development framework of Kirste is extended to both kinds of interaction. Based upon that extended framework it is argued that both interaction paradigms need to be tackled by the same artifacts in order to support smooth transitions between the interaction types and assure consistency during the whole interaction process. An artifact suitable for interaction design in SmEs is the task model. For explicit interaction it has been used for decades in HCI and certain research projects have shown the feasibility of task-driven approach for UI design in SmEs [Feuerstack & Blumendorf, 2007; Feuerstack *et al.*, 2008; Luyten, 2004]. The same applies partially for implicit interaction. In [Giersich *et al.*, 2007] and [Wurdel *et al.*, 2007] task models have been used for intention recognition which is one of the most fundamental components in a SmE. The advantages of task modeling for both interaction paradigms have also been compiled and a model-driven approach has been advocated.

To be able to follow a model-driven approach based on task models a suitable task modeling language is needed. An illustrating scenario based on the experimental infrastructure of the university has been consulted to show the complexity and relevant entities with respect to task modeling. The scenario is used to distill a set of requirements for a task modeling language suitable for SmEs. In the last part of the chapter implicit and explicit interaction are investigated with respect to interaction design based on task modeling.

Chapter 6
Modeling Tasks for Smart Environments – CTML

After having shown why task modeling is of high interest for interaction development of SmEs and having identified the requirements for task modeling useful for SmEs it is now continued with the detailed specification of the task modeling language of this thesis. More precisely the language addresses each of the named requirements in Section 5.1.2 explicitly.

During this chapter not only the modeling elements and their purpose are highlighted but also the design decisions during the development of the language are underpinned by related work and explanations.

In order to foster understanding an overview of the modeling elements, their purpose, their relation to other modeling elements and related approaches in various research fields is given. Subsequently, the formal syntax and semantics is explained. Based upon that, various appropriate refinement relations on CTML models are introduced. In the end of this chapter the tool support for CTML is described which help to create, edit and validate specifications.

6.1 Overview of Syntax, Semantics and Design Rationale

In this section we present the collaborative task modeling language (CTML). We first describe the syntax of CTML, explain its design rationale and provide an example. Then we present the semantics of collaborative task expressions and collaborative task models.

The design of CTML is based on four fundamental assumptions:

1. **Role-based Modeling.** In limited and well-defined domains the behavior of an actor can be approximated through her role [Constantine & Lockwood, 1999; Penichet *et al.*, 2009].

2. **Hierarchal Decomposition and Temporal Ordering.** The behavior of each role can be adequately expressed by an associated collaborative task expression.

3. **Causal Modeling.** The execution of tasks may depend on the current state of the environment (defined as the accumulation of the states of all available objects) and in turn may lead to a state modification.

4. **Individual and Team Modeling.** The execution of task of individual users may contribute to a higher level team task.

Based on these assumptions we define a collaborative task model in a two-folded manner:

- **Cooperation Model.** Specifies the structural and behavior properties of the model.

- **Configuration(s).** Holds runtime information (like initial state, assignment) and simulation/animation configurations.

For each Cooperation Model several Configurations may exist in order to describe different situations in which the model is used.

6.1.1 Cooperation Model

Figure 6-1 shows a schematic sketch of a cooperation model. Elements in the inner blue circle show modeling entities of the cooperation model (post fixed with "-1") whereas diagrams outside of the blue circle show specifications realizing the corresponding entities (post fixed with "-2").

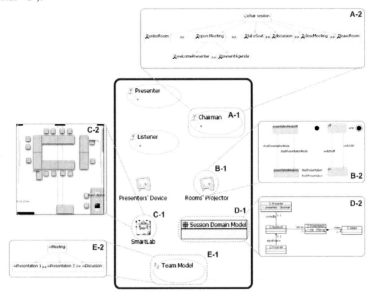

Figure 6-1 Schematic Cooperation Model for Meeting Scenario

On a higher level of abstraction the cooperation model specifies the entities relevant to task modeling in SmEs. Therefore roles (e.g., A-1), devices (e.g., B-1), a location model (C-1), a domain model (D-1) and a team model (E-1) can be specified. Roles categorize users of the same kind in terms of capability, responsibility, experience and limitations according to the domain. Thus roles are abstractions of actors sharing the same characteristics. Role modeling is a common concept in software engineering ([Constantine & Lockwood, 1999; Larman, 2004]) to reduce complexity and build systems for diverse users. What constitutes to a certain role and distinguishes it from another one relates to the system and development approach. In [Larman, 2004] it is stated that a user is not limited to one role at a time and role switching is often taking place. In CTML the role concept is employed to define the pool of actions of a user by means of task expressions. In task analysis and modeling this approach is quite common but is usually restricted to a one-to-many relation of role and user [Molina *et al.*, 2008; Mori *et al.*, 2002]. However this is a rather rigorous constraint. In the domain of SmEs it is frequently the case that an actor changes her role at runtime and that one role is being performed by several actor simultaneously (being a many to many relation of role and user). The role concept implemented in CTML incorporates this case. Moreover a user cannot only perform roles concurrently but also other relations such as choice, orderindependence, enabling, disabling and suspend/resume are considered (adapted from temporal operators) which allows for modeling more realistic scenarios. In the example in Figure 6-1, a meeting scenario, the roles are *Presenter*, *Listener* and *Chairman*. They represent the different types of stereotypical behavior in the meeting scenario.

In CTML the potential action a user is able to perform is determined by her role(s). More precisely a role is associated with a collaborative task expression (A-2 in Figure 6-1). which is visually represented by a task tree in a CTT-like notation [Paternò, 1999]. Tasks are arranged hierarchically defining a tree structure. Atomic tasks, non refined tasks, are referred as actions. In addition tasks on the same level of abstraction can be connected via temporal operators defining the temporal order of task execution. The precise semantics of those operators are explained in Table 6-1.

N-Ary Operators $(t_1, t_2, ..., t_n)$	
Choice ([])	Only one operand task is executed
Order Independence (|=|)	Operand tasks are executed in any order with no interleaving of subtasks
Concurrent (|||)	Interleaved execution of operand tasks and their subtasks
Enabling (>>)	Operand tasks are executed sequentially
Binary Operators (t_l, t_r)	
Disabling ([>)	Execution of t_l is aborted as soon as t_r is started
Suspend/Resume (|>)	At any time the execution of t_l may be interrupted by t_r. After t_r has finished its execution t_l resumes.
Unary Operators (t)	
Iteration (t*)	Repetitive execution of t
Optional ([t])	Execution of t is optional

Table 6-1 Semantics of CTML Operators

Each task is attributed with a (unique) identifier, a set of precondition and a set of effects. Preconditions add additional execution constraints to a task as a task may only be performed if its precondition is satisfied. An effect denotes a state change of the system or environment as a result of a task execution. Both, preconditions and effects are needed to model collaboration and synchronization across collaborative task expressions. They also denote the binding to the devices, location and domain.

An exemplary task tree (informally the term *tree* is used here even though the abstract syntax is defined by an expression) is shown in Figure 6-2. It shows how a chairman may chair a session at a conference. First she enters the room, followed by an introduction. After doing so she manages the individual talks of each presenter. However she may also interrupt the presenter while supervising the talk. Optionally she opens a discussion for each talk. After having listened to all talks the session is closed. Finally she leaves the room. Please note that the symbol ⊞ denotes that a task which is further refined but whose children are currently not visible. Thus *Introduce Session* and *Close Session* are not atomic.

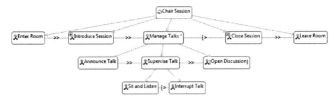

Figure 6-2 Task Tree for Chairman at a Conference

In CTML, devices (e.g., B-1) represent types of devices relevant to the task performance of users in the SmE. In HCI device modeling has been mostly performed to model platforms on which tasks are executed [Mori *et al.*, 2002]. In this vein physical and technical properties are used to characterize the devices. This approach is suitable when the task execution need to be constrained by a property of the device or a task need to be assigned to a certain device (e.g., a task needs a certain display size or input capability). However in some situations it is also useful to model the behavioral properties of devices. Especially when tasks are executed by the user themselves and not hosted on a device but the device is still relevant for the task execution (which is uncommon in MB-UI) only static properties are insufficient. There is also the distinction between tools and artifacts (even though more in the field of domain modeling). Whereas tools are supporting certain tasks in changing an object, artifacts are objects to be changed by the task performance [Forbrig *et al.*, 2003]. Thus behavioral specifications are expedient for tools as it would formalize the process of changing an artifact but the notion of behavioral specification is not tackled in this field. Behavioral models of devices are relevant for SmEs (e.g., taking the example of Figure 6-1: the projector needs to be connected to the presenters' notebook and the notebook needs to be in presentation mode).

CTML allows structural and behavioral specifications of devices. Basically it can be specified whether a device type has or has not certain technical features (like wireless network, touchpad or display) which can also be parameterized (e.g., display size and resolution). Additionally, name/value pairs can be specified to characterize the device types adequately.

Behavioral specifications are achieved by means of state machines (B-2). Basically each device specification is characterized by a finite state machine in order to model the functions and states necessary (e.g., the function "Switch to presentation mode" and the state "Presentation mode").

The importance of location information for task execution in physical environments as SmEs is obvious. For both, explicit and implicit interaction, location information is relevant. Explicit interaction can only be performed with immediate proximity to the UI and implicit interaction is based on context information such as location information. Even though location information is a very selective type of context information but it is, compared to other types of context, easy to measure and model. In CTML one can specify a location model (C-1 and C-2) which allows for modeling local geometrical locations.

The device model captures the behavioral and structural properties of electronic objects exhibiting a well defined behavior in the environment. However there are also virtual objects (e.g., slides on a notebook) and physical objects which are not devices (e.g., whiteboard and pen). In order to be able to capture those obviously important aspects for task performance a domain model has been introduced. It captures domain specific concepts and objects as well as associates them to each other. Moreover the existing roles can also be related to domain objects (e.g., a presenter brings her slides on her notebook"). The distinction between device and domain objects is done by its activeness. A passive device is modeled as domain objects whereas an entity which exhibits a certain well-defined behavior is modeled by a device specification. Nevertheless devices are a sub set of the domain objects as they contribute to the concepts of the domain and may support task performance. Thus in CTML devices can be additionally modeled as objects of the domain if the dedicated domain model does not capture all important aspects relevant to the domain (e.g., the relation of the device to other domain objects by means of associations). As the domain model serves also as vocabulary ("visual dictionary" [Larman, 2004]) for the software developer, user and stakeholder the implied redundancy of modeling a device in the domain model and device model is not a problem as a comprehensive model of the objects involved in the domain helps to foster understanding. The domain model (D-1 and D-2 in Figure 6-1) is represented using an UML class diagram ([UML, 2010]) as this is the de facto standard for domain modeling in industry and known to software developers [Constantine & Lockwood, 1999; Larman, 2004]. In software engineering there is a clear differentiation between a conceptual domain model and a data model even though they share information and are often treated as the same. A domain model captures concepts and their relations whereas a data model specifies persistent data for implementation. In CTML data modeling is not of interest since CTML is used in early stages of software engineering and persistence is not an aspect.

Individual task performance in multi user environments is usually coordinated by a higher level plan. Perhaps certain tasks of actors can only be started after the execution of tasks of others. This kind of cooperation is necessary to be described and needs to be considered for task modeling. Additionally certain task state configurations may constitute to a higher level state. In CTML this is called team state. The corresponding model is the team model (E-1 and E-2 in Figure 6-1) which is basically a task model consisting of tasks of a certain type which in turn are defined by statements when a certain team task is being activated and completed. Details on that issue are discussed in Section 6.1.4.

In the following Section the runtime information necessary to instantiate a Cooperation Model are exaplined

6.1.2 Configuration

Besides the cooperation model a CTML specification also contains one or more configurations providing essential runtime information for the cooperation model. A configuration represents necessary information for a concrete situation. This allows for testing different settings for the same cooperation model without much effort by defining different configurations.

As the cooperation model relies on a role-based specification actors operating in the environment need to be defined in accordance with a corresponding actor-role mapping. More precisely an actor may fulfill more than one role concurrently and a role may be assigned to different actors simultaneously (many-to-many relation). Moreover not only concurrent role fulfilling is allowed but also all other temporal operators defined in CTML are implemented (see Table 6-1). None of currently existing task modeling supports this assumption even though this is a common case in SmEs. Taking the example of the "Conference Session" one can imagine the case of an actor presenting a paper in front of the audience but also listening to other presentations afterward. Therefore the simultaneous (or more precisely ordered) performance of more than one role is an important feature of the language as it also allows separating roles from another since they are assembled at runtime. Thus modularization and separation of concerns are achieved. Additionally some properties for actors are defined (e.g., initial position in the environment).

On the left hand side of Figure 6-3 an example Configuration for the schematic Cooperation Model in Figure 6-1 is depicted. Not all before mentioned information have visual counterparts but the actor-role mapping is represented by blue arrows. More precisely it is specified that *Leonard* only acts as *Presenter* whereas *Penny* fulfills the role *Presenter* and *Listener* simultaneously. *Sheldon* acts as *Chairman*. The precise assignment of temporal operators for an actor fulfilling more than one role is performed in a dialog which is shown on the right hand side. Currently it is specified that *Penny* first acts as *Presenter* and afterward as *Listener*.

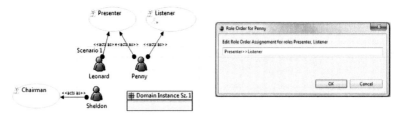

Figure 6-3 Configuration "Scenario 1" for Cooperation Model "Conference Session"

As the domain model is defined using a UML class diagram an object diagram is needed to define the initial state of the domain objects when starting an animation, simulation respectively ("Domain Instance Sz.1" in Figure 6-3). The object diagram is a visual representation of the objects which needs to be valid with respect to the defined domain model in the cooperation model. A detailed description of domain modeling and the object diagram is given in Section 6.1.7.

A configuration can be considered as a concrete scenario under which the cooperation model is tested or used. However sometimes one might test only certain features of the model. Therefore simulation modes have been introduced to vary the models to be considered during animation and simulation. A certain simulation type defines whether a model (e.g., location or domain model) is considered during runtime. This also implies whether a precondition or/and an effect defined over the model is considered at runtime. The modes can be freely combined. The following modes exist:

- **Task Mode.** By enabling this mode precondition and effects defined over the task model are being considered during runtime. Thus additional execution constraints limited to the role based task expression are enabled.

- **Task Cooperation Mode.** In contrast to the task mode the task cooperation mode is used for preconditions and effects defined over other role based task expressions. This mode enables means for modeling cooperation and synchronization between different roles.

- **Device Mode.** A cooperation model can have a set of device models which can be used to enrich the task expressions by preconditions and effects. Whether those device models are considered during runtime is defined by this mode.

- **Location Mode.** In the same vein as the device mode the location mode defines whether the location model and correspondingly defined preconditions and effects are to be considered at runtime.

- **Domain Mode.** This mode specifies whether the domain model is considered at runtime. Accordingly this also applies for preconditions and effects defined over the domain model.

By the usage of those modes certain features of a CTML specification can be tested and validated in a more flexible manner.

The concept of explicit defined goals has been rarely tackled in task modeling languages even though user goals are considered in various HCI and task analysis methods [Dix *et al.*, 1997; Hackos & Redish, 1998; Kirwan & Ainsworth, 1992]. Kirwan and Ainsworth define goals as [1992]:

"desired states of systems under control or supervision"

which is a common definition of the term. Goals are treated usually as informal descriptions and as such cannot be interpreted and evaluated during runtime. Especially when taken into account that implicit interaction can be implemented through explicit formal goals this concept becomes interesting for CTML. There are two ways of specifying a goal in CTML:

- **State based Goals.** Tasks are performed to reach a certain goal which is defined by a certain state of the system. Therefore CTML allows for defining goals by means of expressions over the domain model, device model and location model as those define the state of the SmE. State based goals correspond to the definition of goals from literature.

- **Task based Goals.** The execution of a task changes the state of the system and may lead to the achievement of a certain goal. Therefore, tasks are rather means to achieve goals than defining a goal. However the goal of cooperative task performance can be easily specified through a set of tasks to be performed. One can consider the state of the SmE not only by the union of state of the devices, objects and location but also by the task state of each actor. Task based goals are a valid and easy to use method. This approach is rather pragmatic and may be substituted by a state based goal based on the effect of the task of the task based goal.

Goals define a state in which the performance of tasks is successfully finished. Once the goal is reached no other tasks can be executed anymore. This also applies for multi user specifications. More precisely when an actor executes a task reaching the goal defined in the currently applied Configuration not only the actors' task performance is finished but also the task performance of all other actors is successfully terminated. This implements the hypothesis of a common high level goal of all actors which CTML relies on. Obviously there are cases in which this hypothesis does not hold. As goals are an optional feature the concept can be omitted.

Explicit goals are useful in different ways. In terms of expressiveness of the language they help to define a successful run in an easy to use manner. Especially for cooperative task performance where the envisioned goal is difficult to specify by means of the state of an object task based goals offer a simple solution. Another application of explicit goal description for CTML is deadlock analysis which will be explained in Section 6.6. Please note that the concept of goals is not defined formally for CTML and is used in a pragmatic way.

6.1.3 Semantics

In the last section a brief description of the syntax of CTML has been given. To complete the overview the intuitive semantics follows in this section. Please note that this section does not provide a rigorous semantic definition (which is given in 6.4) but aims to foster the understanding of the rationale of CTML specification. To do so a bottom up approach is employed. First the semantics of a single task expression is defined. Based upon that, the semantics of a composed task expression for each actor can be defined accordingly. Eventually, the semantics of the complete CTML animation/simulation based on the prior explanations is described.

The execution order of the tasks of a single collaborative task expression (e.g., Figure 6-2) is determined by the following three criteria: (1) The defined temporal operators (see Table 6-1), (2) the task-subtasks decomposition, and (3) the preconditions defined for each task.

In order to illustrate the interplay of all three criteria, let us consider the lifecycle of a task. As depicted in Figure 6-4 each task starts in the state *disabled*. Upon receiving the message "enable" a task moves from state *disabled* to *enabled*. If, and when, an "enable" message is sent depends on the super-ordinate temporal operator as well as the task state of the sibling tasks. Table 6-1 gives an intuitive definition of the semantics of all temporal operators defined in CTML. Upon receive of message "start" an enabled task starts executing by transiting into state *running*, given that its precondition is satisfied. In state *running* the task executes its predefined effect (denoted by "do/effect") which becomes externally visible. A successful run of the task is denoted by the "end" transition to state *completed*.

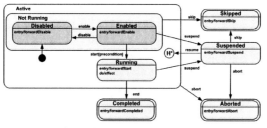

Figure 6-4 Task Life Cycle as State Chart

At any time a task may be prematurely aborted, as a result of the disabling operator (see Table 1 for details). A task that is enabled, or already running can be suspended upon receive of the "suspend" message. Once a task is suspended it returns back to its previous state when it receives "resume".

As long as a task is not started, it can be skipped, which is either due to an optional (unary []), iterative (*) or choice ([]) operator. Additionally a task may be skipped when a super-ordinate task becomes skipped or disabled. Note that each state of the task state chart is equipped with so called entry actions whose purpose is to notify the state charts of sub- and super-ordinate tasks of state changes. This implements an update mechanism to assure synchronization between all state charts. Table 6-2 summarizes the semantics of task states.

State	Symbol	Semantics
Disabled	⊗	Initial state of a task. It is waiting to become enabled.
Enabled	◉ or ◎	The task is waiting to start its execution. The first symbol denotes the ordinary case: the assigned preconditions are fulfilled and the task can be activated. The latter denotes that one or more preconditions are currently not satisfied and the task cannot be started (implemented by a guard in Figure 6-4).
Running	◉	The task is currently under execution. It has been started but the execution is not yet finished.
Suspended	⓪	The task has been suspended. Keeps waiting until it is resumed.
Completed	◎	The task has been executed successfully (Final State).
Skipped	◎	Execution of the task has been skipped (Final State).
Aborted	◎	Prematurely abortion of task (Final State).

Table 6-2 Task States, Symbols and Semantics

In CTML, not only each task but also each temporal operator is represented by a state chart which formally implements the semantics given in Table 6-1.

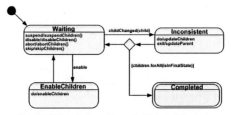

Figure 6-5 Generic State Chart of a Temporal Operator

In Figure 6-5 the generic state chart for a temporal operator is given. It starts in state *waiting* in which messages from superordinate state charts are dispatched to its children. An exception to this rule is the "enable" message which triggers a state transition to state *enableChildren* in which the set of subordinate task state charts are enabled according to the semantics of the operator (e.g., in case of the choice operator ([]) each child becomes *enabled* whereas in case of the enabling operator (≫) only the first child becomes *enabled*). Figure 6-5 also portrays how the operator state chart handles a temporally *inconsistent* state which is due to a state change of a child. Depending on the current state of the changing child the state chart implements the semantics of each temporal operator (e.g., if a child task of the choice operator is executed all other children become *skipped*, whereas if a child task of an enabling operator is executed the next sibling task becomes *enabled*). The operator state chart changes its state to *completed*, if, and only if, all children state charts are in a final state. Otherwise it returns to the state *waiting*.

By mapping each task and operator to a state chart a network of communicating state charts is created, where operator state charts mediate messages between task state charts of adjacent levels of abstraction.

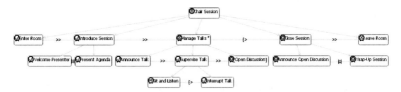

Figure 6-6 Task Expression for Chairman at "Conference Session" during Animation

Figure 6-6 illustrates an exemplary animation of the task expression shown in Figure 6-2 (here the full task tree is shown). The symbols attached to the task nodes represent the current state in accordance with Table 6-2 and Figure 6-4. The tasks *Enter Room, Welcome Presenter, Present Agenda, Announce Talk* and *Interrupt Talk* have been executed (represented by the *Completed* state). The tasks *Open Discussion, Close Session, Announce Open Discussion* and W*rap-up Session* are executable (denoted by the symbol for *Enabled* state). The abstract task *Manage Talks* is currently under execution and *Sit and Listen* has been skipped. *Leave Room* is not yet executable since it is in the state *Disabled*.

This far we have defined the execution semantics of individual collaborative task expressions. It is now continued with the definition of semantics of a collaborative task model. Thereby, the main principles are as follows:

1. For each role, based on the associated task expression, a network of communicating state machines (as shown previously) is created.

2. With respect to the selected Configuration, for each actor, an individual copy (instance) of the corresponding role state machine network is created.

3. The resulting state machine networks are composed and run concurrently at animation time. In essence, a collaborative task model is transformed into a set of concurrently running networks consisting of task state machines and operator state machines.

An exemplary animation of the Cooperation model in Figure 6-1 with the Configuration "Scenario 1" (see Figure 6-3) is depicted in Figure 6-7. The screenshot shows three columns, one for each actor. Each column is vertically divided in two parts. The upper part shows the currently enabled tasks for the actor (which can be activated on click) whereas the task expression animation for each role of the actor is shown in the lower part. A tree-like illustration is used in which the root nodes represent the role-based animations.

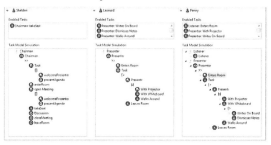

Figure 6-7 CTML Animation of "Conference Session" of "Scenario 1" (see Figure 6-3)

After having introduced the (informal) semantics of CTML specification the different facets of CTML specifications for modeling cooperation, devices, locations and the domain are examined in detail. The integration of those models into task modeling is achieved by means of preconditions and effects. More in detail, tasks are assigned preconditions making statements about a certain state to be fulfilled with respect to cooperation, devices, location and/or domain. On the other hand the execution of a task may result in a state change with respect to the devices, location and/or domain.

6.1.4 Cooperation / Team Modeling

Tasks of individuals in the context of multi user environments or systems are never performed isolated but need to be synchronized with actions of the other individuals involved. The dependencies of cooperational tasks performance can be quite complex and are influenced by different aspects such as relation of the individuals, context (work, leisure, etc.), organizational structure and others. With respect to task modeling not all such cases can be supported. However, as it had been shown previously the currently existing means to model cooperation on a high level of abstraction defining a precise behavior are very limited [Mori *et al.*, 2002; Penichet *et al.*, 2008; van der Veer & van Welie, 2000]. Moreover the cooperation of actor of a SmE can be defined on different levels of abstraction:

- **Team-based.** Tasks are often not orchestrated directly but by a higher level context. In a conference session an agenda usually defines the action items in temporal order. In CTML this model is called team model. It defines the orchestration of high level tasks and their definition by role based tasks. Exemplary one can define the team state *Introduction* which is based upon the task *Introduction* of the *Chairman*.

- **Role-based.** Specifying task dependencies on role based level integrates well with the CTML modeling approach as tasks are specified on a role based level generally. Basically one would specify that a *Presenter* needs to perform a certain task to let the *Chairman* perform another. As a role can be fulfilled by several actors simultaneously quantified statements are needed.

- **Actor-based.** Task dependencies are specified between two (or more) actors within a configuration. In this vein dependencies can be specified very accurate but need to be defined for each pair of actors in every configuration. Regarding the running example one would specify that *Leonard* needs to perform a certain task before *Sheldon* starts another. Due to the complexity of such specification mechanism this approach is dismissed and not followed in CTML.

In the following paragraphs the used approaches in CTML, namely team-based and role-based cooperation, are explained in detail.

As stated above, in CTML a dedicated team model synchronizes role based task specifications of actors.

In CTML team-based cooperation is modeled by a dedicated team task model. A team model is a certain type of task expression with the constraint that each atomic task is of the type *team* (denoted by a different symbol). In Figure 6-8 an example of a team model is depicted. It specifies that *Presentation 1*, *Presentation 2* and *Presentation 3* are given in arbitrary order and finally a *Discussion* is taking place. What constitutes to each team task is defined by means of triggers.

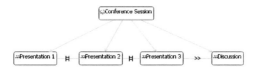

Figure 6-8 Team Model for "Conference Session"

A trigger defines the condition under which a certain team task is started respectively completed. The conditions are based on simulation states, quantified tasks states (see Table 6-2) or location of actors. The semantics of the two types of triggers are described in Table 6-3. The explanations in Table 6-3 show that team tasks are virtual tasks as they cannot be executed directly but their state is derived based upon states of role based tasks.

Trigger Type	Semantics
Start Trigger	Defines a condition under which a team task is started if it is enabled with respect to the semantics of the used temporal operators.
End Trigger	Defines a condition under which a running team task is completed. The next team task to be started is selected by examining the enabled task set and corresponding Start triggers.

Table 6-3 Semantics of Triggers

In Table 6-4 examples of Start and End Triggers are given. The first column specifies the team task the triggers are assigned to whereas the latter contains the triggers. The triggers of *Presentation 1* can be paraphrased as follows: *Presentation 1 is started if one Presenter has been started the task Start Presentation. Presentation 1 is finished if one Presenter has finished the talk.* In the same vein the semantics of the triggers of the task *Discussion* can be described but in contrast to the prior description the *allInstances* quantifier is used meaning the all actors fulfilling the role named in the trigger need to complete the task to pull the trigger.

The usage of quantifiers (oneInstance, allInstances) is a general approach in CTML whenever a statement is made about a set of tasks which can only occur if the role the task is belonging to is fulfilled by multiple actors. They quantifiers in CTML are comparable to the quantifiers of first-order logic ($\exists$, $\forall$).

Start Triggers	
Task	Trigger
Presentation 1	Presenter.oneInstance.StartPresentation
Discussion	Presenter.allInstances.FinishTalk
End Triggers	
Task	Trigger
Presentation 1	Presenter.oneInstance.FinishTalk
Discussion	Chairman.allInstances.CloseSession

Table 6-4 Exemplary Triggers for Team Model in Figure 6-8

So far the team model only observes the states of animation/simulation of CTML specifications. To be truly effective a mechanism is needed to influence the potential task execution. In CTML, precondition can be based on team tasks and their states (see Figure 6-4) as team tasks run through the same task life cycle by automated triggered transitions. In this vein the task execution can be restricted until a certain team state is reached. This allows for modeling rich dependencies in handy manner. In summary, team states can be defined over the task states of actors and the task execution of actors can be constrained by the employment of team tasks for preconditions.

The modeling of cooperation by means of a dedicated team model is one option in CTML. More precisely, CTML allows also for specifying task dependencies on the level of role-based task expressions as already hinted earlier. Before actual defining the dependencies an interface needs to be defined. Figure 6-9 shows the visual representation of such an interface by means of a link. The link specifies that the task execution of the role *Presenter* can be constrained and affected by tasks of the role *Chairman* (denoted by <<*uses*>>). The complete interface comprises also the actual tasks to be used in the affected task expression (*Presenter* in this case). This information is specified by a dialog which has been omitted here. Bidirectional dependencies are possible as well.

In CTML the definition of interfaces between model entities in the cooperation model is a general approach. It allows for separation of concerns and helps to manage complexity while defining preconditions and effects. Furthermore dependencies are made explicit and as such are visible at first glance.

Figure 6-9 Role Dependency for "Conference Session"

After defining explicitly the interface between two roles the cooperation can be modeled by means of preconditions on a role based level. Task based preconditions can address all tasks defined in the interface. Again, since several actors may fulfill more than one role quantified statements are needed.

Figure 6-10 Task Tree for Presenter at "Conference Session"

In Figure 6-10 a task expression for the role *Presenter* is presented. It specifies the process of giving a talk at a conference session. First, the Presenter introduces herself followed by the configuration of the equipment. The talk is given by explaining each slide denoted by an iteration (*). In the end the Presenter responds to the raised questions. Finally the presenter leaves the environment. With respect to the task expressions of the role *Chairman* (depicted in Figure 6-2) and the role *Presenter* (depicted in Figure 6-10) the preconditions shown in Table 6-5 can be defined.

Role	Task	Precondition
Presenter	Start Presentation	Chairman.oneInstance.Announce Talk
Presenter	Respond to Question	Chairman.oneInstance.Open Disucssion
Chairman	Announce Open Discussion	Presenter.allInstances.End Presentation

Table 6-5 Preconditions for Tasks of Role Presenter at "Conference Session"

The first precondition defines that the *Presenter* is only allowed to start her presentation if she had been announced by a *Chairman*. The second states that responding to questions can only be performed if the *Chairman* has opened the discussion. The precondition of the

Chairman states that an open discussion can only be announced if all *Presenters* have fi-nished the presentation. Preconditions defined on this level of abstraction integrate well with the CTML approach of role based descriptions. Quantifiers are able to specify how many actors fulfilling the role are addressed (one or all).

Please note that team-based modeling is very convenient way of specifying cooperational aspects of a CTML specification. However, they are actually syntactic sugar as each precon-dition addressing a team state can be replaced by an appropriate rephrasing of the trigger. This finding is especially important for the rigorous semantics given in 6.4.

6.1.5 Device Modeling

In HCI devices have usually been considered as platform on which a UI is rendered and which is used to interact with the user. However in SmEs this viewpoint is not sufficient. Additionally, devices are used to define the actual capabilities of a SmE and therefore the functional state of a device enables, disables respectively, the execution of a task. Therefore in CTML not only the static properties characterizing the capabilities are considered but also the behavior by means of functions and states.

In order to allow a high level description device types are specified. Moreover it is defined whether a certain role needs a certain device in order to assist the actor fulfilling the role during the task performance. Again, this is specified by dependencies on the level of the Cooperation Model as depicted in Figure 6-11.

Figure 6-11 Device Dependency for "Conference Session"

In Section 6.1.2 the concept of Configurations has been discussed. Amongst others it has been stated that actors fulfill roles. If a device dependency to a device types exists the actor naturally needs a device which fulfills the requirement defined in the dependency (e.g., a device capable of operating as Notebook in the given example). Therefore a mapping is needed to specify which devices of an actor fulfilling a certain role operate as needed device specification. In the same vein as roles abstract from actors, device specifications (e.g., Notebook) abstract from a certain device of an actor (e.g., the device of *Leonard*).

Besides such personal device specifications bound to a role also stationary devices exists. They define the permanent available devices in the environment. Projectors in meeting rooms are prominent examples of that issue. The same type of dependencies can be defined to roles but no mapping for actors is needed as stationary devices are deployed at runtime directly (one for each stationary device defined).

The properties of a device specification are defined by two different means:

- **Structural Properties.** Predefined device components for each device can be as-signed. They represent the in- and output, network and other capabilities of a device specification. Also a generic component exist which can be used to define custom properties.

- **Behavioral Properties.** State machines can be used to define the potential device state and transition between the states (called functions in the remainder of the thesis).

Please note that the behavior of devices cannot expressed by a finite state machine (due to the finity of states). However finite state machines can still be a valid way of abstraction. Moreover CTML has not been designed in order to operate a SmE but as means to do analysis, requirement engineering and design with respect to interaction. According to this field of application finite state machines are fully sufficient.

In Figure 6-12 a simplified device specification of a notebook used for presentation purposes is given. The notation is taken from the UML [2010]. Rectangles denote states whereas transitions are represented by direct edges. Moreover the final state is denoted by black dot with a circle and the initial state by a black dot.

The model specifies that the device starts in the state *off* and transits to *on* by executing the function *switchOn* (more precisely upon the event *switchOn*). Then, either the function *switchOff* or *startPresentation* can be executed which either leads back to *off* or the state *presentationStarted*, etc.

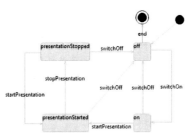

Figure 6-12 Simplified Behavioral Specification of Notebook for the "Conference Session"

In order to integrate device modeling into task modeling in CTML also preconditions and effects are used. In essence, preconditions assigned to a task with respect to device modeling express that the device needs to be in a certain state to execute the task. Contrary, an effect with respect to device modeling states the function to be executed when performing the task. In this vein the binding of task modeling and device modeling is achieved.

Role	Task	Precondition
Presenter	Start Presentation	self.device.presentationStarted
Presenter	Leave Room	self.device.off
Role	**Task**	**Effect**
Presenter	Set to Presentation Mode	self.device.startPresentation
Presenter	End Presentation	self.device.stopPresentation

Table 6-6 Preconditions and Effects for Role Presenter with respect to Device Modeling

In Table 6-6 example of preconditions and effects addressing the device model given above are presented. In essence, the device to be addressed needs to be specified. In the examples the standard device of the actor is addressed. They can also be addressed by name. Then, for preconditions the state needed to enable the task the precondition is assigned to follows. The first precondition can therefore be paraphrased as follows: the task *Start Presentation* can only be executed if the device of the actor is in the state *presentationStarted*. In order to leave the room the device needs to be in the state *off*. For effects, not states are defined but functions to be executed when performing a certain task. Thus, the first effect states that when executing the task *Set to Presentation Mode* the function *startPresenation* is executed (if possible). Hence, when ending the presentation the device stops the presentation.

Please note that deterministic finite state machines are demanded in order to perform formal analysis explained in Section 6.5 and Section 6.6.

6.1.6 Location Modeling

The integration of location modeling into task modeling for physical spaces is of enormous interest. When actors performing tasks in a physical environment like a SmE they move or change their places. Certain tasks may only be executable when standing at the right spot. This certainly needs to be considered while modeling tasks for SmE. For MB-UI development this is important to allocate the UI to an appropriate device whereas in implicit interaction location is used as source of context [Rodden *et al.*, 1998].

Different attempts have been made to model the spatial relation of objects and actors in physical environments. There are geometric models which define the spatial relation by coordinates of the objects. Applications can easily derive containment relation of objects and location. A disadvantage of those models is that properties like *is connected to* are not easy to derive.

Graph-based location models explicitly model this relation. A node specifies a location and edges represent connections between locations. Weights can be added to model distances between locations. Another type of models uses sets to specify locations and their decomposition into sub-locations. An atomic location is specified by a shape and position. Composed locations are defined by a set of existing locations. The containment relation of locations can be easily expressed using sub-set relations. Hierarchical models are also based on a set of locations which are ordered according to the containment relation. The most used types of model combine several modeling approaches to suit the special needs of the application [Becker & Dürr, 2005].

For CTML a local geometric model which uses a simple set of geometric figures (rectangle, ellipse, point) and their compositions. This enables the developer for specifying complex, nested locations without making location modeling a burden. In Figure 6-13 a screenshot of the location model (and its corresponding graphical editor) is shown. It uses a 2-d model of the SmartLab as background to ease location modeling. Moreover, several locations relevant for the scenario used before are defined. In essence, the door zone and outside zone are used to determine the entering, leaving respectively, presentation and whiteboard zone on the upper right hand side are used to define presentation areas. Several further zones are used to determining listening to presentations exist. Please note that the composed location *Chairs* aggregates all zones in which listening to a presentation is envisioned.

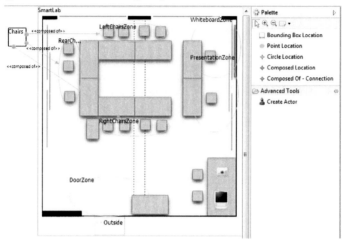

Figure 6-13 Location Model for "Conference Session"

Moreover, to model that a certain role uses the location model an appropriate dependency needs to be defined accordingly. In Figure 6-14 such a dependency is depicted. The rationale is analogous to the before mentioned dependencies. An interface can be used to define preconditions and effects based on the location model.

Figure 6-14 Location Dependency of Presenter to SmartLab

With respect to the task expression for the role *Presenter* denoted by Figure 6-10 the preconditions and effects given in Table 6-7 are defined. The first precondition explicitly demands the actor to be in the Presentation Zone to start the presentation. The same applies for the second preconditions which states that the actor needs to be in the Door Zone to execute the task *Leave Room*. Hence, the effect of leaving the environment has the results that the actor is now in the location Outside.

Role	Task	Precondition
Presenter	Start Presentation	self.isIn(Presentation Zone)
Presenter	Leave Room	self.isIn(Door Zone)
Role	**Task**	**Effect**
Presenter	Leave Room	self.is(Outside)

Table 6-7 Preconditions and Effects for Role Presenter with respect to Location Modeling

6.1.7 Domain Modeling

In several task modeling languages domain modeling has been integrated successfully. Tasks are always executed within a certain work environment and application domain. Considering the task model as isolated entity is often insufficient. During executing domain objects can be created, destroyed, manipulated or relations between objects are established. In other situations objects may need to be present or in a certain state in order to execute a task. In Section 3.4.3 an overview of existing task modeling languages and different extensions to CTT-like notations is given. Several extensions fall in the category of domain modeling. Three limitations according to the theory and practice of domain and task modeling have been identified:

- **Lack of Expressiveness.** Some approaches only support very limited capabilities of domain modeling. In certain cases only objects are defined (no abstraction of class and object). Common concepts like abstractions, associations and generalization are not considered. However domain modeling is a complex task which needs appropriate artifacts to truly reflect the domain adequately. In essence, more complex domain modeling concepts are needed to provide suitable means for domain modeling [Evans, 2003]. Approaches of this category are AMBOSS [Giese *et al.*, 2008] and VTMB [Biere *et al.*, 1999b].

- **Custom Notations for Domain Model.** In current software engineering practices domain modeling is performed via object oriented analysis and design. State of the art artifact for that are the UML class diagrams [Booch *et al.*, 2005; UML, 2010]. However in different approaches for task modeling objects are specified using other types of formalisms. Representatives of that kind are TaoSpec [Dittmar & Forbrig, 2003] and CTT [Paternò, 1999]. This is actually very unfortunate as a *lingua franca* is invaluable especially for practice.

- **Lack of Integration.** Most task modeling languages consider objects as at least noteworthy even though only a few integrate domain modeling in the task analysis and modeling process [Caffiau *et al.*, 2008]. Actually most languages consider domain objects as notes assigned to tasks. The integration with respect to executability of a task and the effect a task has on the environment has only been tackled by a few languages such as VTMB [Biere *et al.*, 1999b], TaoSpec [Dittmar & Forbrig, 2003], and K-MAD [Caffiau *et al.*, 2008].

In order to overcome the named limitations above UML class diagrams are used to specify domain models. The integration of task modeling and domain modeling is achieved by OCL (Object Constraint Language) constraints [UML, 2010; Warmer & Kleppe, 2003] which are used as preconditions and effects in CTML. Naturally only a subset of the OCL language is employed. OCL is a formal, declarative language based on predicate calculus to define additional constraints not expressible by other UML model (e.g., the class diagram). Models are enriched with OCL constraints to avoid ambiguity and misinterpretation [Fowler, 2004]. OCL constraints allow for navigating through the models and making statement about certain facts that need to hold and define assertion.

In order to illustrate the general rationale an example of a domain model with respect to the scenario is given in Figure 6-15. If the reader is not familiar with UML class diagrams [Booch *et al.*, 2005; UML, 2010] are suggested for further readings. In the illustration the relevant entities which have not been captured by the task, location, and device model are specified. More precisely devices can be modeled in the device model and domain model depending on the viewpoint and elements to be considered as important. Passive elements are modeled within the domain model, in contrast to active entities which are represented by the device model.

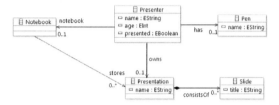

Figure 6-15 Domain Model for "Conference Session"

The domain model in Figure 6-15 represents the relevant entities for a presenter giving a talk in a conference session. In essence, it is specified that a presenter may have a pen and a notebook. Moreover a presentation can be stored on a notebook which in turn can be owned by the presenter. A presentation consists of slides having a title. Other properties are specified as well. For example, a flag has been defined in order to denote whether the presentation has been already given. Based on such a domain model precondition and effects can be defined representing the binding of task execution and the domain of interest.

In the same vein as for location and device modeling an interface to the role needs to be defined on the level of the Cooperation Model. The interface specifies the domain types needed for the role in order to execute the tasks successfully (see Figure 6-16). In essence, these types are used to define preconditions and effects with respect to the domain model.

Figure 6-16 Domain Dependency of Presenter to Domain Model

A domain precondition is basically a simplified OCL constraint with a Boolean value. An effect addressing the domain determines a value to be changed and set a new value. There are two ways of specifying preconditions and effects in CTML. Either by starting to navigate through the domain model from the actor fulfilling the current role (e.g., Presenter in this case) or by defining the context and making a general statement. The latter is used when a certain fact needs to be ensured for all instances of a certain type of the model. To illuminate both cases example are given in Table 6-8 and can be paraphrased as follows: The first precondition defines that the actor needs a notebook to execute the task *Start Presentation*. Next, it is stated that the notebook of the Presenter need to store the slides of the Presenter for that presentation. An effect defined in this particular case is that ending the presentation sets the flag of having presented.

Role	Task	Precondition
Presenter	Start Presentation	self.notebook<>null
Presenter	Start Presentation	self.notebook.stores->includes(self.owns)
Role	**Task**	**Effect**
Presenter	End Presentation	self.presented = true

Table 6-8 Preconditions and Effects for Role Presenter with respect to Domain Modeling

As explained before during animation a configuration is selected and used to "instantiated" the CTML specification. When using the domain model a representation of the object involved is needed. Object diagrams according to the guidelines of the UML are used [UML, 2010].

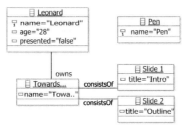

Figure 6-17 Example of an Object Diagram for Domain Model in Figure 6-15

In Figure 6-17 an example of potential objects is depicted. It represents a concrete situation of the domain (the state of the objects). The actor *Leonard* is defined by an object and he owns the presentation to be given. Moreover the presentation has a certain name and consists of two slides. With respect to Table 6-8 it can be stated that none of the given preconditions are fulfilled. However due to task execution the object model might change and the precondition may become satisfied. An example of an effect is given and results in changing the attribute *presented* of *Leonard* (if *Leonard* is the currently executing actor).

6.2 Executability

Having explained the modeling elements of CTML, their rationale and the reasons for design it is now continued with an important principle of CTML: *Validation by Animation* which is also referred as executability.

A full CTML specification consists of multitude of entities. When creating such an entity it is important to be able to inspect the model. Different ways for doing so exist. Graphical editors and viewers can help to foster the understanding of the artifact. Each editor (viewer) may highlight different characteristics of the entities. However, such a static view on the model is not always sufficient. If the behavior of the model is well-defined (the model is successfully validated) it should also be explorable by an interactive walkthrough. By allowing to explore each model isolated and in combination with other entities different viewpoints of the behavior are offered. Therefore, the following guidelines have been defined for CTML and its tool support:

1. **Animation.** Each entity exhibiting behavior should be interactively explorable in isolation and in combination with the whole CTML specification.

2. **Viewpoints.** Different tools for animation should be offered to highlight the behavior from different perspectives and on different levels of abstraction.

These rules have not only been applied for the task model but also for the device specifications which can also be animated isolated and in accordance with the complete CTML model.

6.3 Formal Syntax of CTML

After defining the syntax and intuitive semantics of CTML in section 6.1 it is now continued with a more rigorous definition of the syntax and semantics of CTML specifications. The state chart based approach to assign meaning to CTML is appropriated for an intuitive definition of the semantics. However, also other possibilities exist to do so. Especially in the area of process algebra prosperous approaches exist supporting verification algorithms out of the box.

Section 6.1 has already given an overview of the modeling concepts and their composition. The concrete syntax has been shown by means of screenshots of the graphical editors. In the following paragraphs only the abstract syntax is presented.

We start to define the syntax in a top-down approach. Basically we decompose a CTML model into its subcomponents until a convenient level of detail is reached.

Definition 6-1 ($CTML$): CTML is defined by the following tupel:

$$CTML = \langle Coop, \mathcal{C} \rangle$$

1. $Coop$ denotes the Cooperation Model (Section 6.1.1) and
2. $\mathcal{C}$ is the set of configurations (Section 6.1.2) used to hold runtime information for a concrete animation.

Definition 6-2 ($Coop$-Cooperation Model): The cooperation model is defined by the tupel:

$$Coop = \langle \mathcal{R}, \mathcal{T}, \tau, \mathcal{TE}, L, \mathcal{DS}, \mathcal{ST}, dev, \mathcal{DM} \rangle$$

$\mathcal{R}, \mathcal{T}$ are the set of roles, respectively task names. τ is a total function assigning each task name a certain task type:

$$\tau: \mathcal{T} \rightarrow \{application, interaction, system, user\}$$

$\mathcal{TE}$ denotes the set of task expressions with:

$$\mathcal{TE} = \{TE_r | r \in \mathcal{R}\} \ with \ TE_r \in \mathcal{TEXPR}_r$$

Please note that in the remainder of the thesis TE_r always denotes the task expression of the role r even though this is formally not correct as $\mathcal{TE}$ is a set. In detail, a function is needed to specify such mapping. For reasons of brevity this function is omitted as it is trivial.

$\mathcal{TEXPR}_r$ is the set of task expressions valid for the role r. To introduce $\mathcal{TEXPR}_r$ we need further definitions:

Definition 6-3 ($\mathcal{QT}_r$-Qualified Task Names for r): Let r be a role and $\mathcal{T}$ be a set of task names then $\mathcal{QT}_r$ is defined as:

$$QT_r \subseteq \{(r, t) | t \in \mathcal{T}\}$$

$\mathcal{QT}_r$ defines the set of qualified task names for the role r in accordance with the set of task names $\mathcal{T}$. Based upon this definition we define $\mathcal{TEXPR}_r$ inductively as follows:

Definition 6-4 ($\mathcal{TEXPR}_r$-Qualified Task Expressions for r): Let QT_r be the set of quali-fied task names of r. Let t_1 and t_2 be qualified task expressions ($t_1, t_2 \in \mathcal{TEXPR}_r$), $t \in QT_r$ and pre_{type_p} and eff_{type_e} be preconditions and effects with $type_p \in \{T, DOM, DEV, L\}$ and $type_e \in \{DOM, DEV, L\}$, then the following expres-sions are also qualified task expressions:

$$(t_1[]t_2), (t_1| = |t_2), (t_1 \parallel t_2), (t_1[> t_2), (t_1 | > t_2), (t_1 \gg t_2),$$

$$t, t_1{}^*, t_1{}^n, [t_1], \lfloor pre_{type_p} \rfloor t_1, t \lfloor eff_{type_e} \rfloor$$

Please note that no effect related to tasks exists. This is due to ensure semantic consistency throughout CTML as effects with respect to tasks would imply to manipulate tasks which are not executed by any actor of the system. Moreover, Definition 6-4 only allows the definition of effects for atoms (in contrast to preconditions). This restriction is necessary to allow a consistent semantics which is only feasible if atoms change the world state (e.g., what is the effect of a choice expression?).

Definition 6-5 (L-Location Model): L defines the location model (Section 6.1.6) of $Coop$. More precisely, L is defined by the tuple:

$$L = \langle \mathcal{L}, \eta \rangle$$

Let $\mathcal{L}$ be the set of location names, and η be an irreflexive, antisymmetric, transitive function assigning locations its super-ordinate locations (compose-of function):

$$\eta : \mathcal{L} \to \mathcal{L}$$

Definition 6-6 ($\mathcal{DS}$-Device Specifications): $\mathcal{DS}$ is a set of Device Specifications (D) whe-reas:

$$D = \langle name, \mathcal{S}, \mathcal{F}, s_0, \mathcal{Final}, \delta \rangle$$

With $name$ being a unique identifier, $\mathcal{S}, \mathcal{F}$ are non-empty sets of states and functions, respec-tively, $s_0 \in \mathcal{S}$ is the initial state, $\mathcal{Final} \subseteq \mathcal{S}$ defines the non-empty set of final states, $\delta : \mathcal{S} \times \mathcal{F} \to \mathcal{S}$ is the transition function mapping a pair of state and function with a proceed-ing state.

Definition 6-7 ($\mathcal{ST}$-Stationary Device Specifications): $\mathcal{ST}$ is the set of stationary devices which are denotes by:

$$\mathcal{ST} \subseteq \mathcal{DS}$$

As a device may be assigned to a role as equipment a relation is needed expressing this:

$$dev \subseteq \mathcal{R} \times \mathcal{DS} \backslash \mathcal{ST}$$

The formalization of UML class diagram is still a vita research area, in particular with respect to OCL constraints as the usage of the entire expressiveness of OCL leads to undecidability [Cabot et al., 2008] as first-order logic itself is undecidable in general and OCL is more expressive. In [Berardi et al., 2005] a formalization of UML class diagrams based on first order logic is proposed which does not only give advice how to formulize a certain class diagrams but also supports the definition of formulas ensuring certain validation (type consistency of associations, multiplicity of associations, inheritance properties such as disjointness, completeness, etc.). The general approach relies on introducing a predicate for each class, association, and attribute. Even though the approach has been defined for refactoring UML class diagram to prove congruence and equivalence between two specifications, it is also valid to formulize the domain model here. In order to do so, some syntactical elements are not considered here for reasons of understandability. The entire formulization can be found in [Berardi et al., 2005]. The definition of the domain model is very simple as the structural properties are not relevant during animation, execution respectively.

Definition 6-8 ($\mathcal{DM}$-Domain Model): The domain model is defined by the tuple:

$$\mathcal{DM} = \langle \mathcal{Cl}, \mathcal{Ass}, \mathcal{Att} \rangle$$

with $\mathcal{Cl}, \mathcal{Ass}, \mathcal{Att}$ being a set of predicates for classes, associations, and attributes, respectively.

In order to exemplify this rather simple definition it is shown how the domain model given in Figure 6-15 can be formulized using Definition 6-8. Here, only a part of the whole formalization is given. The complete model is given Appendix A.1.

For each class a unary predicate is defined which denotes that a certain object belongs to a class (here only for *presentation* and *slide*):

$$\mathcal{Cl} = \{Presentation(o), Slide(o)\}$$

For each association a binary predicate is defined denoting that two object in relation with each other (here only for *consistsOf*):

$$\mathcal{Ass} = \{consistsOf(o_1, o_2)\}$$

For each attribute a binary predicate is defined denoting the object and the corresponding value of that attribute (here only for *title*). Please note that types are omitted here:

$$\mathcal{Att} = \{name(o, value), title(o, value)\}$$

As stated before, in [Berardi et al., 2005] a set of formulas in first order logic are given which assures consistency and structural validity. A formula expressing that the attribute *title* can only be defined for objects of the type *Slide*:

$$\forall o: title(o, x) \implies Slide(o)$$

Having defined the major entities of the Cooperation Model, it is now continued with preconditions and effects of different types.

Definition 6-9 (pre_{TASK}-Task Precondition): A task precondition is defined by the tuple:

$$pre_T = \langle qt_r, quantifier \rangle$$

with $qt_r \in QT_r$ ($r \in \mathcal{R}$ of $Coop$) and $quantifier \in \{\forall, \exists, !\}$. Whereas the first defines the task to be addressed by the precondition the latter defines whether all actors fulfilling the role need to execute the task ($\forall$), only one actor need to perform the task ($\exists$) or only the currently executing actor (!).

Definition 6-10 (pre_{DOMAIN}-Domain Precondition): A domain precondition is defined by the tuple

$$pre_{DOM} = \langle o, name, value \rangle$$

with $o \in \pi_1(Objects)$(see Definition 6-19) being a object name, $name \in ass \cup att$ being an association or attribute name and $value$ being the value to be tested.

Definition 6-11 (pre_{DEVICE}-Device Precondition): A device precondition is defined by the tuple:

$$pre_{DEV} = \langle ds, state \rangle$$

with $ds \in DS$ and $state \in \mathcal{S}$ (of d). A device precondition defines that a certain device (denoted by ds) needs to be in a certain state in order to be fulfilled.

Definition 6-12 ($pre_{LOCATION}$-Location Precondition): A location precondition is defined by

$$pre_L = \langle l \rangle$$

with $l \in \mathcal{L}$ (of L of $Coop$). This definition states that the currently fulfilling actor needs to be at a certain location (l) to fulfill the precondition.

Definition 6-13 (eff_{DOMAIN}-Domain Effect):

$$eff_{DOM} = \langle o, name, value \rangle$$

with $o \in \pi_1(Objects)$(see Definition 6-19) being a object name, $name \in ass \cup att$ being an association or attribute name and $value$ being the value to be set.

Definition 6-14 (eff_{DEVICE}- Device Effect): A device effect is defined by the tuple:

$$eff_{DEV} = \langle ds, function \rangle$$

with $ds \in DS$ and $function \in \mathcal{F}$ (of d). A device effect defines that a function is executed on a certain device (denoted by ds).

Definition 6-15 ($eff_{LOCATION}$-Location Effect): A location effect is defined by

$$effect_L = \langle l \rangle$$

with $l \in \mathcal{L}$ (of L of $Coop$). This definition states that the currently fulfilling actor moves to the location (l) by executing the assigned task.

After having defined the tupel $Coop$ the abstract syntax of configurations $\mathcal{C}$ needs to be defined.

Definition 6-16 ($\mathcal{C}$ -Configurations): $\mathcal{C}$ is the set of configurations where each item has the following form:

$$Conf = \langle \mathcal{A}, Objects \rangle$$

A configuration is consisting of a set of actors and the objects.

Definition 6-17 (*Actor*): An actor is defined by the following tuple:

$$Actor = \langle name, location, \mathcal{I}ns, \mathcal{AR}, insToDevices, AE \rangle$$

with *name* being a unique identifier, *location* denoting the initial location of the actor *location* $\in \pi_1(L)$, and $\mathcal{I}ns$ being the set of device names belonging to the actor. π denotes the projection of a tuple ($\pi_i(\langle x_1, x_2, .., x_n \rangle) := x_i$). This notation is used in the remainder of the thesis.

$\mathcal{AR}$ defines the set of roles the actor is fulfilling:

$$\mathcal{AR} \subseteq \mathcal{R}$$

Moreover the total function *insToDevices* assigns each device specification assigned to the roles of the actor a corresponding device of the actor in order to fulfill the requirements of the device specification of the Cooperation Model.

$$\mathcal{DS}_a = \{ ds \mid (r, ds) \in dev \text{ and } r \in \mathcal{AR} \}$$

$$insToDevices: \mathcal{DS}_a \longrightarrow \mathcal{I}ns$$

The actor expression AE defines the temporal order of roles an actor is fulfilling:

$$AE \in \mathcal{AEXPR}$$

Definition 6-18 ($\mathcal{AEXPR}$ -Actor Expression of *a*): Let $\mathcal{AR}$ be the set of roles for the actor *a*. Let r_1 and r_2 be an actor expressions $(r_1, r_2 \in \mathcal{AEXPR})$, $r \in \mathcal{AR}$, then the following expressions are also actor expressions:

$$r, (r_1[]r_2), (r_1| = |r_2), (r_1 \parallel r_2), (r_1[> r_2), (r_1| > r_2), (r_1 \gg r_2), r_1{}^*, r_1{}^n, [r_1]$$

Definition 6-19 (*Objects*): Let $\mathcal{DM} = \langle \mathcal{Cl}, \mathcal{Ass}, \mathcal{Att} \rangle$ be a domain model, then the set of *objects* is defined by the tuple $\langle O, ass, att \rangle$ with O being a set of object names, ass being the set of existing associations according to the defined association predicates in $\mathcal{Ass}$, and att being the set of attributes for each object according to the defined predicates in $\mathcal{Att}$.

In order to exemplify the given definition above the Scenario shown in Figure 6-3 is formulized in the following paragraphs. Please note that not all specified information have visual counterparts in Figure 6-3. In such a case the reader is reminded and further information is given.

The Running Example – Configuration Scenario 1

A scenario is a tuple consisting of a set of actors and objects:

$$Scenario1 = \langle \mathcal{A}_{sc1}, Objects_{sc1} \rangle$$

The set of actors is defined as follows:

$$\mathcal{A}_{sc1} = \{ sh, le, pe \}$$

(Abbreviated for sh - Sheldon, le - Leonard, pe - Penny)

Each actor is a tuple as well. The first item denotes the name of the actor. The second one specifies the initial location of the actor which is specified with respect to the complete running example in Appendix A.1 (*out* is abbreviated for *outside*). There is no visual representation of the initial location in Figure 6-3. The location is specified in a dialog. Next, the set of device instances is defined which denotes the personal devices the actor is carrying with. Again no visual counterpart exists. This information is specified in a dialog as well. In the case of Sheldon (sh) the set is empty. Leonard (le) and Penny (pe) each carry a notebook. The next item defines the set of role the actors is fulfilling. Sheldon acts as Chairman (c), Leonard as Presenter (p) and Penny as Listener (l) and Presenter. Then, a mapping is specified which associates device specifications with device instance of the actors. This information is specified in a dialog as well. This mapping is needed to denote what kind of role the device instance is going to play in the scenario. Finally, the actor expression is given. In case of Sheldon and Leonard only the role name is used as actor expression. Therefore the behavior is only defined by the role task expressions defined in the Cooperation Model. In case of Penny a complex actor expression is specified. It specifies that Penny firsts acts as Presenter followed by being a Listener.

$$sh = (sh, out, \emptyset, \{c\}, \emptyset, c)$$

$$le = (le, out, \{le\_nb\}, \{p\}, \{(notebook, le\_nb)\}, p)$$

$$pe = (pe, rcz, \{pe\_nb\}, \{p, l\}, \{(notebook, pe\_nb)\}, p \gg l)$$

The object model of Scenario 1 is given in Figure 6-17 and can be formulized as follows:

$$Objects_{sc1} = (O, ass, att)$$

The set of object names is:

$$O = \{Leonard, Pen, Slide\ 1, Slide\ 2, Towards\ ...\}$$

The set of associations of the objects is:

$$ass = \left\{ \begin{matrix} owns(Leonard, Towards\ ...), consistsOf(Towards\ ..., Slide\ 1), \\ consistsOf(Towards\ ..., Slide\ 2) \end{matrix} \right\}$$

The set of attributes of the objects is:

$$att = \left\{ \begin{matrix} name(Leonard, Leonard), age(Leonard, 28), presented(Leonard, false), \\ name(Towards\ ..., Towards\ ...), name(Pen, Pen) \\ title(Slide\ 1, Intro), title\ (Slide\ 2, Outline) \end{matrix} \right\}$$

6.4 Semantics of CTML

After having defined the abstract syntax in an unambiguous manner it is now continued with a precise semantic definition of CTML.

CTML has been defined to model the potential behavior and interaction of users and system in SmEs. Moreover modeling is performed from user perspective and user tasks are the central driving force of progress in the model. However CTML is a model which may contain inconsistencies and therefore a rigorous semantic definition is beneficial.

For CTML an interleaving semantics is used as semantic foundation. This decision has been made for several reasons. First and foremost it is claimed that interleaving semantics is a suitable abstraction for task modeling. Naturally real world tasks are executed simultaneously but with respect to interaction interleaved execution is fully sufficient. Next, interleaving semantics is an intuitive semantic domain for CTML. The interleaving semantics of a task expression can already be comprehended at a glance for skilled users. This is particular of importance while designing the model to shorten feedback cycles. In the subsequent paragraphs it is shown that CTML can be straightforwardly transformed into in an appropriate artifact which in turn has already been mapped to interleaving semantics.

In comparison to the previously explained meaning of CTML based on state charts it can be said that interleaving semantics is a simplification of the state chart based approach of Section 6.1.3. Subsequently it is shown that the hierarchical decomposition of tasks is eliminated. Task models are therefore considered only as expression in which only leaf tasks are represented by their identifiers.

Precise semantics in CTML are assigned by a preprocessing step which normalizes CTML models. Then, based upon inference rules a LTS (see Definition 4-1) is derived. The LTS precisely defines the state space of the CTML specifications as well as the transitions by means of executing an action (an atomic task).

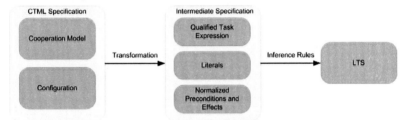

Figure 6-18 Semantic Definition of CTML

The basic idea is to derive a LTS based on a task expression (see Figure 6-18). In order to do so it is started with a Cooperation Model and a selected Configuration. Then, the model is transformed into a homogeneous qualified task expression and a representation of the initial world state by literals and functions assigning the qualified task (sub) expressions their normalized preconditions and effects. The first represents the task expression to be translated into a LTS whereas the second and third are used to give meaning to preconditions and effects. Afterward inference rules are used to derive a LTS from the qualified task expression which eventually defines the semantics precisely. More precisely the qualified task expression is stepwise translated into a LTS model.

6.4.1 Transformation

As depicted in Figure 6-18 the input for this phase is a CTML Specification with a selected Configuration. The result of the transformation is an intermediate specification consisting of a qualified task expression, a set of literals, and functions assigning task expression preconditions and effects (see Definition 6-26). In the following paragraphs the creation of each item is explained in detail.

More precisely, the transformed model represents the initial state of the LTS on which the inference rules are applied until the complete state space is explored. In this vein the resulting LTS is obtained.

Given a CTML ($CTML = \langle Coop, C \rangle$) with a select configuration ($C_i \in C$) the following definitions are needed in order to specify a transformation:

Definition 6-20 (QT_{CTML}-Qualified Task Names for CTML): Let $a_0, ..., a_n \in \mathcal{A}$ of C_i and let $roles(a_i) := \pi_5(a_i)$ (denoting the projection of the tuple, $\mathcal{AR}$ in this case), then we define the set of qualified task expression of a $CTML$ model as:

$$QT_{CTML} = \bigcup_{i=0}^{n} a_i \times QT_r \mid r \in roles(a_i)$$

QT_{CTML} consists of triples $\langle a, r, t \rangle$ with $a \in \mathcal{A}, r \in \mathcal{AR} (\subseteq \mathcal{R}), t \in \mathcal{T}$. It defines all atomic actions for a given CTML with respect to a selected Configuration C_i.

Definition 6-21 ($\mathcal{TEXPR}_{CTML}$-Qualified Task Expressions for CTML): Let QT_{CTML} be the set of qualified task names of a CTML model. Let t_1 and t_2 be qualified task expressions for a CTML specification ($t_1, t_2 \in \mathcal{TEXPR}_{CTML}$), $t \in QT_{CTML}$, pre_H, pre_S, eff_S be function symbols, then the following expressions are also qualified task expressions:

$$(t_1 [] t_2), (t_1 | = | t_2), (t_1 \parallel t_2), (t_1 [> t_2), (t_1 | > t_2), (t_1 \gg t_2),$$
$$t, t_1^*, t_1^n, [t_1], pre_H(t_1), pre_S(t_1), eff_S(t),$$

Please note that according to this definition preconditions may be assigned to complex qualified task expression whereas effects are only valid for atoms (qualified task names) as a state change of a system need to be bound to an action. By allowing complex task expressions it would not be possible to determine which action is responsible for a certain state change (e.g., the effect of $t_1 [] t_2$) is not clear).

In order to introduce the set of literals used in the prior given definition further definitions are needed. The definitions of terms, function symbols and predicates are adopted from First Order Logic [Russell & Norvig, 2003].

Definition 6-22 ($\mathcal{Term}$-Set of Terms): A term is inductively defined by:

(1) Any constant is a term (c).

(2) Any variable is a term (x, y, z).

(3) Function symbols are terms: $f(q_1, ..., q_n)$ denotes the function symbol f with $q_0, ..., q_n$ are terms themselves. n is the arity of the function symbol ($f(x), g(x, y)$).

Definition 6-23 ($\mathcal{P}$-Set of Predicates): Let $q_0, ..., q_n \in \mathcal{Term}$ be terms then all Predicates (e.g., P, F, T) defined over $\mathcal{Term}$ ($P(x), F(y, g(x, z), T(c)$) are belonging to $\mathcal{P}$.

Please note that this form of Predicates is often also referred as Atomic Sentences of First Order Logic [Russell & Norvig, 2003].

In order to define the transformation the set of terms and predicates for the domain of CTML need to be defined.

Definition 6-24 ($\mathcal{Term}_{CTML}$-Set of Terms for CTML): Terms for a CTML model are the following ($\mathcal{Term}_{CTML} \subset \mathcal{Term}$):

(1) All names of actors of the selected configuration are constants and as such are terms ($\mathcal{A}$ of C_i).

(2) All names of locations defined in the Location model of $Coop$ are constants and as such are terms ($\mathcal{L}$ of the L of $Coop$).

(3) All names of objects defined in the $Objects$ of the selected Configuration are constants and as such are terms ($Objects$ of $\mathcal{C}_i$).

(4) All names of devices specifications defined in the set of device specifications of $Coop$ are constants and as such are terms (D of $\mathcal{DS}$ of $Coop$).

(5) All device states of each device specification of the set of device specifications ($\mathcal{DS}$ of $Coop$) of $Coop$ are constants and as such are terms (denoted by the set $\mathcal{S}$ of D).

(6) All functions of each device specification of the set of device specifications ($\mathcal{DS}$ of $Coop$) of $Coop$ are constants and as such are terms (denoted by the set $\mathcal{F}$ of D).

(7) All names of devices of each actor of the selected configuration are constants and as such are terms (denoted by the set $\mathcal{Ins}$ of each actor).

Having defined the terms for a CTML model it is now continued with the definition of predicates specifying relations of terms:

Definition 6-25 ($\mathcal{Lit}_{CTML}$ -Set of Literals): Let $a, l, o, value, d, ds, s \in \mathcal{Term}_{CTML}$ be terms then the following predicates over $\mathcal{Term}_{CTML}$ are Literals ($\mathcal{Lit}_{CTML} \subset \mathcal{P}$):

(1) $location(a, l)$ associates a certain actor (name) with a certain location (name). The interpretation is that an actor is at a certain location.

(2) $attribute(name, o, value)$ associates a certain object (name) o with a certain attribute name with its value. The interpretation is that the attribute with the name $name$ of object o is of the value $value$. Please note that value can be of any kind. Thus also association relating two objects can be specified by means of the attribute predicate.

(3) $deviceState(d, ds, s)$ associates a certain device (name) with a certain device specification (name) and a certain device state (name). The interpretation is that a device is in a certain state by fulfilling a certain device specification.

(4) $trans(ds, s, f, s_f)$ associates a certain device specification (name) with a current state (name), a function (name) and the resulting state (name) after executing f.

Intuitively the terms define the entities in a CTML model. The predicates represent the knowledge about those entities necessary to interpret preconditions and effects. During the transformation process the abstract preconditions and effects introduced (in Definition 6-9 - Definition 6-15) are translated into statements querying or manipulating the defined knowledge ($\mathcal{Lit}_{CTML}$).

After having defined all necessary prerequisites it is now continued with the definition of the intermediate specification and its creation based on a CTML model and a selected configuration.

Definition 6-26 (IS_{CTML}-Intermediate Specification): The result of the transformation in Figure 6-18 is an intermediate specification which can be defined as the tuple

$$IS_{CTML} = \langle TE_{CTML}, S_0, pre_H, pre_S, eff \rangle$$

with $TE_{CTML} \in \mathcal{TEXPR}_{CTML}$ denoting the qualified task expression for a CTML specification with respect to a selected configuration (C_i). $S_0 (\in \mathcal{Lit}_{CTML})$ denotes the set of literals expressing the initial state of all actors and devices which are necessary information to evaluate preconditions and apply effects.

The unary function $pre_H : \mathcal{TEXPR}_{CTML} \rightarrow \langle q, \mathcal{T} \rangle$ (with $q = \{\forall, \exists\}, \mathcal{T} \in \mathcal{P}(\mathcal{QT}_{CTML})$) maps qualified task expressions to a tupel consisting of a quantifier and a sub set of qualified task names which serve as precondition. Informally the quantifier denotes which tasks (either all or one) of the qualified task names need to be executed in order to enable the precondition. pre_S is a unary function mapping qualified task expressions to a set of preconditions $(pre_S : \mathcal{TEXPR}_{CTML} \rightarrow \mathcal{P}(\mathcal{Lit}_{CTML}))$. $\mathcal{P}(x)$ denotes the power set of x.

In contrast eff is a unary function mapping qualified task names to tupels specifying the effects of the task. An effect is defined by the tupel $\langle Y, \mathcal{P}_e, \mathcal{E}^+, \mathcal{E}^- \rangle$. Y specifies the set of variables, $\mathcal{P}_e$ denotes the set of predicates with variables which needs to hold to apply the effect. $\mathcal{E}^+, \mathcal{E}^-$ define the set of positive, negative respectively effects to implement the effect.

In order to implement preconditions and effects the situation calculus is used. For each action manipulation or needing the world state in order to be executable entries in these functions are created. The functions define how the execution of an action affects the world state. Within an effect, the positive effects are facts which are true after execution (e.g., the actor is in front of the audience) whereas negative effects state the facts which are false after execution (e.g., the actor is not behind the audience). In the situation calculus the current world state is not defined explicitly but by the initial world state and the execution history manipulating the world state and thus defining the current world state implicitly [Russell & Norvig, 2003]. In CTML the preconditions and effects are rather simple with respect to the theory of the situation calculus. Thus functions are fully sufficient. Moreover negative effects are synthesized from the positive effects which is clarified in the subsequent paragraphs.

In order to create an initial state representing the knowledge about the entities in a CTML a sub set of $\mathcal{Lit}_{CTML}$ is created by applying the following rules:

(1) For each actor of the selected configuration the initial location is specified by the $location$ predicate $(\mathcal{A} = \pi_1(C_i))$.

$$\mathcal{L}_0 = \bigcup_{i=0}^{n} location(\pi_1(a_i), \pi_2(a_i)) \,|\, a_i \in \mathcal{A}$$

(2) For each object belonging to the selected Configuration the attributes are specified by the attribute predicate $(Objects = \pi_2(C_i), att = \pi_2(Objects))$. Please note that the elements in the set att are binary predicates with the predicate name denoting the name of the attribute. In the formalization of the world state a general attribute predicate is introduced taking as parameter the name of the attribute. Moreover associations also formulized by this approach.

$$\mathcal{O}_0 = \bigcup_{i=0}^{n} attribute(n, o, value) \,|\, att_i \in att, att_i = n(o, value)$$

$$\cup \bigcup_{i=0}^{n} attribute(n, o_1, o_2) \,|ass_i \in ass, ass_i = n(o_1, o_2)$$

(3) For each device belonging to an actor the device specifications the device is fulfilling and their initial state is captured.

$$\mathcal{D}_0 = \bigcup_{i=0}^{n} deviceState\big(d, \pi_1(ds), \pi_4(ds)\big) \,|\forall(ds, d) \in insToDevices = \pi_5(a_i), a_i \in \mathcal{A}$$

(4) For each stationary device specification a device is created and specified in the *deviceState* predicate in accordance with its initial state ($\mathcal{ST} = \pi_6(Coop)$).

$$\mathcal{ST}_0 = \bigcup_{i=0}^{n} deviceState\big(\pi_1(s_i), \pi_1(s_i), \pi_4(s_i)\big) \,|s_i \in \mathcal{ST}$$

(5) For each device specification the transitions function δ is expressed using the *trans* predicate.

$$T = \bigcup_{i=0}^{n} trans\big(\pi_1(ds_i), s, f, s_f\big)|\forall(s, f, s_f) \in \delta_i, \delta_i = \pi_4(ds_i)$$

The initial world state is therefore specified by the following formula:

$$\mathcal{S}_0 = \mathcal{L}_0 \cup \mathcal{O}_0 \cup \mathcal{D}_0 \cup \mathcal{ST}_0 \cup T$$

In (1) the initial locations of each actor are collected and specified as *location* predicate with the actor name (using the projection of tuples). (2) formulizes attributes and association of the objects of the domain using the *attribute* predicate. Next, (3), the personal devices of each actor are specified as literals with the device specification they are fulfilling and the initial state with respect to the device specification as state chart. In (4) the initial state of each stationary device is specified as literal. In the last formula the transition function of each device specification is expressed via the *trans* predicate. Whereas the rules (1) - (4) represent facts which may change over time the last rule specifies structural knowledge about the present device specifications. These facts are not adapted due to task execution but used in order to interpret effects.

In order to exemplify the given definition Scenario 1 in Figure 6-3 is consulted. The scenario has already been formulized in Section 6.3. Please note that the actors Sheldon and Penny are omitted here. The complete example can be found in Appendix A.1.

The Running Example – The Initial State of Scenario 1

The complete initial state is consisting of the following sets:

$$\mathcal{L}_0 = \{location(le, out)\}$$

For each actor (in the example only for Leonard) the *location* predicate is used to specify the initial location of the actor. The interpretation of the predicate is that *Leonard* is *Outside*.

$$O_0 = \left\{ \begin{array}{c} attribute(name, le, Leonard), attribute(age, le, 28), \\ attribute(presented, le, false), attribute(title, Slide2, Outline), \\ attribute(owns, le, Towards \dots), attribute(consistsOf, Towards \dots, Slide1), \\ attrbiute(consistsOf, Towards \dots, Slide2) \end{array} \right\}$$

For each attribute and association an *attribute* predicate is created which specifies the name of the attribute, association respectively, the object it is belonging to and the value. For example the predicate $attribute(name, le, Leonard)$ expresses that Leonard (le) has the name Leonard, etc.

$$\mathcal{D}_0 = \{deviceState(le\_nb, notebook, off)\}$$

For each device instance the assigned device specification with its initial state is specified by the *deviceState* predicate. In the example only Leonard has a device instance with the name le_nb which fulfills the device specification *notebook* whose initial state is off.

$$\mathcal{ST}_0 = \{deviceState(projector, projector, off)\}$$

In the same vein as for the device instance the standalone devices are formulized. The only difference is that the device instance is filled up with the device specification name. This is not necessary but avoids the definition of a binary *deviceState* predicate.

$$T = \left\{ \begin{array}{c} trans(projector, off, sOn, on), trans(projector, on, sOff, off), \\ \dots, trans(projector, pMOff, sPreM, pMOn), trans(notebook, off, sOn, on), \\ trans(notebook, on, sOff, off), \dots, trans(notebook, pSto, sOff, off) \end{array} \right\}$$

For each device specification the state transition relation is specified by the *trans* predicate. This is necessary to encode the device specification in the state to apply effects. For example the predicate $trans(projector, off, sOn, on)$ specifies that for the device specification $projector$ by executing the function sOn in the state off leads to on.

Having defined the initial state of CTML model with respect to a certain configuration it is now continued with the description of how to transform a CTML model with a certain Configuration into a homogenous task expression.

Let $a_0, \dots, a_n \in \mathcal{A}$ of C_i $(\pi_1(C_i))$, r_1, r_2 be actor expressions of a_i $(r_1, r_2 \in \mathcal{AEXPR}$ of $a_i)$, r be a role $(r \in \mathcal{AR}$ of $a_i)$, t_1, t_2, te be task expression of r $(t1, t2 \in TEXPR_r)$, t be a qualified task name of the role r $(t \in TE_r)$, then the qualified task expression of a CTML model $CTML$ is created as follows:

The transformation algorithm itself is top down algorithm starting with composing the qualified task expression of all actors of the selected configuration C_i using the concurrent operator (rule (1)):

(1)
$$TE_{CTML}(CTML, C_i) = \begin{cases} \Delta_a(a_1) & |\mathcal{A}| = 1 \\ \| \left(\Delta_a(a_1), \| \left(\Delta_a(a_2), \dots, \Delta_a(a_n) \right) \right) & , else \end{cases}$$

Table 6-9 Transformation of Actors

An actor is transformed by transforming the role expression of a (rule (2)) with $(roles(a) := \pi_6(a))$. Moreover the algorithm transforms complex actor expressions by transforming each sub expression (rule (3),(4),(5), and (6)). When a role is encountered the task expression TE_r is transformed by rule (7).

(2)	$\Delta_a(a) = \Delta_a(a, roles(a))$
(3)	$\Delta_a(a, \blacksquare(r1, r2)) = \blacksquare\big(\Delta_a(a, r_1), \Delta_a(a, r_2)\big), \blacksquare \in \{[], | = |, ||, [>, | >, \gg\}$
(4)	$\Delta_a(a, r_1^*) = \Delta_a(a, r_1)^*$
(5)	$\Delta_a(a, r_1^n) = \Delta_a(a, r_1)^n$
(6)	$\Delta_a(a, [r_1]) = [\Delta_a(a, r_1)]$
(7)	$\Delta_a(a, r) = \Delta_{te}(a, TE_r)$

Table 6-10 Transformation of an Actor

A task expression is transformed in the same vein as an actor expression by descending in the hierarchy of complex task expressions until an atom is reached (rules (8), (9), (10), and (11)). In addition preconditions and effects are part of task expressions and need to be transformed following the same approach (rule (13) and (14)).

(8)	$\Delta_{te}(a, \blacksquare(t_1, t_2)) = \blacksquare\big(\Delta_{te}(a, t_1), \Delta_{te}(a, t_2)\big), \blacksquare \in \{[], | = |, ||, [>, | >, \gg\}$
(9)	$\Delta_{te}(a, t_1^*) = \Delta_{te}(a, t_1)^*$
(10)	$\Delta_{te}(a, t_1^n) = \Delta_{te}(a, t_1)^n$
(11)	$\Delta_{te}(a, [t_1]) = [\Delta_{te}(a, t_1)]$
(12)	$\Delta_{te}\big(a, \lfloor pre_{type}\rfloor t_1\big) = \Delta_{pre}\big(\lfloor pre_{type}\rfloor, a, t_1\big)$
(13)	$\Delta_{te}\big(a, t_1 \lfloor eff_{type}\rfloor\big) = \Delta_{eff}\big(\lfloor eff_{type}\rfloor, a, t_1\big)$
(14)	$\Delta_{te}(a, t) = \Delta_{qt}(a, t)$

Table 6-11 Transformation of a Qualified Task Expression

As preconditions and effects in the role based task specifications contain abstract preconditions they need to be adapted in order to address the fulfilling actor. Therefore a transformation of those preconditions and effects need to be performed accordingly. In order to do so the type of precondition respectively effects is used. For each type a specific translation is given in Table 6-12 and Table 6-13.

The translation of task precondition depends on the used quantifier. In the intermediate specification the preconditions in the task expression are homogenous. Three different quantifiers exist: for all ($\forall$), exist ($\exists$) and exactly one (!). The first two are translated by adopting the quantifier and collecting the qualified task names to be addressed (rule (15)). The addressed tasks are all qualified task names of actors who are performing the role specified in the precondition. For the latter no counterpart in the intermediate specification exists. The meaning of the quantifier is that exactly the executing actor is addressed by the precondition. Therefore the quantifier can be rewritten by the all quantifier with the appropriate task name (rule (16)).

The subsequent preconditions (rule (17), (18), and (19)) do not address the tasks but the domain, devices and location of actors. In order to implement these formally first order logic introduced earlier is used. In essence, the current true facts during task execution are specified by means of literals according to Definition 6-25.

Domain preconditions specify that certain domain objects need to be present in order to execute a task. The specification of a domain precondition already contain all entities to create a suitable representation based on the predicate $attribute$ (rule (17)). More precisely, the preconditions are transformed by adding a suitable entry in the pre_S function which assigns task expression to evaluable preconditions.

Device preconditions define that a certain device needs to be in defined state in order to execute the addressed tasks. A CTML specification contains only abstract device preconditions which need to be translated accordingly. More in detail, during modeling device specifications are referenced. When translating the model into an intermediate specification those device specifications need to be bound to devices of actors (rule (18)). If the device is a stationary device then is used directly as name. In the other case the devices of the current actor are consulted in order to determine the device of the actor implementing the device specification of interest. The result of the translation is a statement which can be evaluated with respect to the set of literals for the CTML specification ($\mathcal{L}_{CTML}$).

In the same vein as device preconditions location preconditions are translated (rule (19)). More precisely, an abstract precondition is translated into a predicate evaluable with respect to the set of literals. As preconditions may not only be assigned to atomic task the nested task expression of the precondition needs to be transformed (denoted by $\Delta_{te}(a, te)$).

Please note that x_φ denotes the name of the element x. More precisely the following formula assigns to each element a name:

$$x_\varphi = \begin{cases} \pi_1(x) & , if \ x \in \mathcal{A} \\ \pi_1(x) & , if \ x \in \mathcal{DS} \\ x & else \end{cases}$$

As the sets $\mathcal{A}$ (denoting the actors of the selected Configuration) and $\mathcal{DS}$ (denoting the device specifications of $Coop$) consisting of tuples the projection to their names is used. Otherwise it is assumed that x is a name.

The overriding operator ($\oplus$) is used to update functions (such as pre_H, pre_S, eff) which creates a function based on two functions by the union of pairs but with the restricting of overriding the already mapped values of the first function with the values from the second one. The operator is adopted from Z [Woodcock & Davies, 1996].

$$\begin{aligned}
(15) \qquad &\Delta_{pre}(\lfloor pre_T \rfloor, a, te) = pre_H\big(\Delta_{te}(a, te)\big) \\
&pre_T = (qt_r, q), qt_r = (r, t) \ and \ q \in \{\forall, \exists\} \\
&pre_H := pre_H \oplus \big\{\big(\Delta_{te}(a, te), (q, \{(a_0, r, t), \dots, (a_n, r, t)\})\big)\big\},
\end{aligned}$$

$$a_0, \dots, a_n \in \{a \in \mathcal{A} \mid r \in \mathcal{AR} \text{ of } a\} \big(\mathcal{A} = \pi_1(Conf) \text{ and } \mathcal{AR} = \pi_5(a)\big),$$

(16)
$$\Delta_{pre}(\lfloor pre_T \rfloor, a, te) = pre_H\big(\Delta_{te}(a, te)\big)$$

$$pre_T = (qt_r, !) \text{ and } qt_r = (r, t),$$

$$pre_H := pre_H \oplus \{(\Delta_{te}(a, te), (\forall, \{(a, r, t)\}))\}$$

(17)
$$\Delta_{pre}(\lfloor pre_{DOM} \rfloor, a, te) = pre_S(\Delta_{te}(a, te)),$$

$$pre_{DOM} = (o, name, value)$$

$$pre_S := pre_S \oplus \{(\Delta_{te}(a, te), \{attribute(o_\varphi, name_\varphi, value_\varphi)\})\}$$

(18)
$$\Delta_{pre}(\lfloor pre_{DEV} \rfloor, a, te) = pre_S(\Delta_{te}(a, te)),$$

$$pre_{DEV} = (ds, state)$$

$$pre_S := pre_S \oplus \{((\Delta_{te}(a, te), \{deviceState(d_\varphi, ds_\varphi, state_\varphi)\})\}$$

$$d = \begin{cases} ds & , ds \in \mathcal{ST} \\ insToDevices(ds), insToDevices = \pi_4(a) & , otherwise \end{cases}$$

(19)
$$\Delta_{pre}(\lfloor pre_L \rfloor, a, te) = pre_S(\Delta_{te}(a, te)),$$

$$pre_L = (l)$$

$$pre_S := pre_S \oplus \{(\Delta_{te}(a, te), \{location(l_\varphi, a_\varphi)\})\}$$

Table 6-12 Transformation of Preconditions

In the same vein as the preconditions effects are translated accordingly. The general approach of substituting the abstract effects with function symbols which can be interpreted by inference rules with respect to the current world state is identical. However the function eff associates atoms (QT_{CTML}) with tuples specifying the effect of the action execution. An effect consists of the tuple $\langle Y, \mathcal{P}_e, \mathcal{E}^+, \mathcal{E}^- \rangle$. As the world state is of importance to apply an effect appropriately it is not an option to ground the terms already. For example the following state after executing a function on a device depends on the current state when applying an effect. Therefore variables are needed (Y). When applying the effect those variables are replaced by appropriate values depending on the world state. In order to do so statements are necessary characterizing the needed literals in the world state to apply an effect $(\mathcal{P}_e)$. When applying the effect the variables are grounded so that $\mathcal{P}_e$ is true in the current world state. This grounding is then applied to the positive and negative effects. Thus state dependent effects can be defined. If $\mathcal{P}_e$ does not contain any literals no restriction on the positive and negative effects is defined. All suitable literals are removed in case of negative effects or added in case of the positive effects to the world state.

An abstract domain effect is implemented by adding an entry to the function assigning a task expression to a transformed effect which is consulted during evaluation of the effect (rule (20)). According to the given explanations above the tuple of eff_t is constructed using only one variable x. The positive effects are specified by the attribute predicate which needs an object name, an attribute name and a value. The negative effects state that the old values need to be removed. If the tuple specified in the abstract domain effect represents an attribute (see Definition 6-19) then only the old value of the attribute needs to be removed. Associations are also specified by the attribute predicate and defined by only one literal. In essence, they are specified as ordinary attributes. However, as associations can also be navigatable from the other object involved both "sides" need to be considered. Thus, two literals are named in the negative effects $\mathcal{E}^-$ which represent both cases.

A device effect is transformed by a function symbol in the task expression (eff_S) and with appropriate entries in the function eff (rule (21)). The tuple of eff_t is constructed accordingly to the given explanation above. More precisely two variables are needed. x is representing the current state of the device whereas y is denoting the subsequent state which results from executing the device function f. In order to ground x and y, $\mathcal{P}_e$ states that the current device state need to exist in the world state ($deviceState(d_\varphi, ds_\varphi, x)$) and that the device is able to transit from this current state by the function f to the subsequent state ($trans(ds_\varphi, x, f_\varphi, y)$). The positive and negative effects are then defined accordingly. The positive effect is the new state of the device. The negative effect specifies that the old state of the device is not available anymore.

For location effects the approach is analogous but slightly simpler as no variable is needed to represent the subsequent location as this is not state dependent (rule (22)).

$$
\begin{aligned}
(20) \quad & \Delta_{eff}(\lfloor eff_{DOM}\rfloor, a, t) = eff_S(\Delta_{te}(a, t)), \\
& eff_{DOM} = (o, name, value) \\
& eff_t = \langle Y, \mathcal{P}_e, \mathcal{E}^+, \mathcal{E}^- \rangle \ with \ Y = \{x\}, \\
& \mathcal{P}_e = \{attribute(o_\varphi, name_\varphi, x)\} \\
& \mathcal{E}^+ = \{attribute(o_\varphi, name_\varphi, value)\} \\
& \mathcal{E}^- = \begin{cases} \{attribute(o_\varphi, name_\varphi, x)\} & , if \ name(o, value) \in att \\ \begin{pmatrix} attribute(o_\varphi, name_\varphi, x), \\ attribute(x, name_\varphi, o_\varphi) \end{pmatrix} & , if \ name(o, value) \in ass \end{cases} \\
& eff \coloneqq eff \oplus \{(\Delta_{te}(a, t), eff_t)\} \\
(21) \quad & \Delta_{eff}(\lfloor eff_{DEV}\rfloor, a, t) = eff_S(\Delta_{te}(a, t)), \\
& eff_{DEV} = (ds, f) \\
& eff_t = \langle Y, \mathcal{P}_e, \mathcal{E}^+, \mathcal{E}^- \rangle \ with \ Y = \{x, y\}, \\
& \mathcal{P}_e = \{deviceState(d_\varphi, ds_\varphi, x), trans(ds_\varphi, x, f_\varphi, y)\} \\
& \mathcal{E}^+ = \{deviceState(d_\varphi, ds_\varphi, y)\} \\
& \mathcal{E}^- = \{deviceState(d_\varphi, ds_\varphi, x)\} \\
& d = insToDevices(ds), insToDevices = \pi_4(a) \\
& eff \coloneqq eff \oplus \{(\Delta_{te}(a, t), eff_t)\}
\end{aligned}
$$

$$(22) \qquad \Delta_{eff}(\lfloor eff_L \rfloor, a, t) = eff_S(\Delta_{te}(a, t)),$$
$$eff_L = (l)$$
$$eff_t = \langle Y, \mathcal{P}_e, \mathcal{E}^+, \mathcal{E}^- \rangle \; with \; Y = \{x\},$$
$$\mathcal{P}_e = \{location(x, a_\varphi)\}$$
$$\mathcal{E}^+ = \{location(l_\varphi, a_\varphi)\}$$
$$\mathcal{E}^- = \{location(x, a_\varphi)\}$$
$$eff := eff \oplus \{(\Delta_{te}(a, t), eff_t)\}$$

Table 6-13 Transformation of Effects

The transformation result of qualified task name of an actor with a certain role is the triple of actor, role and task name. This is the most fine-grained entity in the intermediate specification. When an atom is reached ($t \in QT_r$) it is transformed by the function Δ_{qt} (rule (23)).

$$(23) \qquad \Delta_{qt}(a, (r, t)) = (a, r, t), with \; (r, t) \in QT_r, (a, r, t) \in QT_{CTML}$$

Table 6-14 Transformation of a Qualified Task Name

By applying the rules (1)-(23) a CTML model ($CTML = \langle Coop, \mathcal{C} \rangle$) with a selected configuration (C_i) is translated into a homogenous qualified task expression in which each atom has the form (a, r, t) with $a \in \pi_1(C_i)$, $r \in \pi_1(Coop)$, and $t \in \pi_2(Coop)$.

The Running Example – Transformation to Qualified Task Expression

In order to show the rationale of the previously described transformation algorithm an excerpt of the running example (which is completed described in Appendix A.1) according to the "Conference Session" is used. The task expression in Figure 6-19 has been selected. For each atomic task, *Welcome Presenter* and *Present Agenda*, a location precondition is defined to ensure that these tasks are only executable if the currently executing actor is in the *Presentation Zone* ($location(le, pz)$).

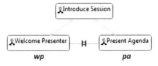

Figure 6-19 Partial Task Expression of the Role Chairman

The abstract syntax of the given task expression is as follows:

$$IS = | = |((pz)\rfloor(c, wp)\lfloor(pz)\rfloor(c, pa))$$

To be able to transform that task expression to an intermediate specification a scenario is needed, named *Scenario* 1', which precisely assigns actors to roles (amongst others). Taking a slightly adapted version of the Scenario 1 which defines that *Sheldon* acts as *Chairman* (with the task model for the chairman given above) the transformation can be started as defined by the given rules:

Rule(s)	$TE_{CTML_{Sc2}}(CTML_{ConferenceSession}, Scenario\ 1') =$
(1)	$\Delta_a\ (sh) =$
(2)	$\Delta_a\ (sh, c) =$
(7)	$\Delta_{te}\ (sh, IS) =$ $\Delta_{te}\left(sh, \lfloor = \lfloor(\lfloor(pz)\rfloor(c, wp), \lfloor(pz)\rfloor(c, pa))\right) =$
(8)	$\lfloor = \lfloor\left(\Delta_{te}\ (sh, \lfloor(pz)\rfloor(c, wp)), \Delta_{te}\ (sh,, \lfloor(pz)\rfloor(c, pa))\right) =$
(12), (19)	$pre_S := pre_S \oplus \{((sh, c, wp), \{location(pz, sh)\})\}$ $\lfloor = \lfloor\left(pre_S\left(\Delta_{te}\ (sh, (c, wp))\right), \Delta_{te}\ (sh, \lfloor(pz)\rfloor(c, pa))\right) =$
(12), (19)	$pre_S := pre_S \oplus \{((sh, c, pa), \{location(pz, sh)\})\}$ $\lfloor = \lfloor\left(pre_S\left(\Delta_{te}\ (sh, (c, wp))\right), pre_S\left(\Delta_{te}\ (sh, (c, pa))\right)\right) =$
(14),(23)	$\lfloor = \lfloor\left(pre_S((sh, c, wp)), pre_S\left(\Delta_{te}\ (sh, (c, pa))\right)\right)$
(14),(23)	$\lfloor = \lfloor\left(pre_S((sh, c, wp)), pre_S((sh, c, pa))\right)$

Accumulated the function assigning preconditions based on the state defined in $\mathcal{S}_0$ can be expressed by:

$$pre_S = \{((sh, c, wp), \{location(pz, sh)\}), ((sh, c, pa), \{location(pz, sh)\})\}$$

Having applied the previously rules and transformed the model into a homogeneous task expression with according functions specifying preconditions (pre_S as given above and $pre_H = \emptyset$) and effects ($eff = \emptyset$) the LTS can be created.

6.4.2 Inference Rules

Throughout this thesis LTSs (see Section 4.5 for the formal definition) are the semantic domain of choice. They define an interleaving semantics. In order to define a precise semantics for CTML the intermediate specification (see Figure 6-18) is translated to a LTS by a set of inference rules. The derivation is based inference rules which transform an expression into another when certain hypotheses are fulfilled. The basic structure of such an inference rule is as follows:

$$\frac{Hypothesis_1 \dots Hypothesis_n}{Conclusion}$$

The statement above the fraction defines the situation when the conclusion, the statement under the fraction, is derivable. Each rule defines how a certain expression is stepwise translated to a LTS. In more detail, an action (an atomic task) is only executable if and only if it is derivable from the inference rule. By the execution of an action the task expression is transformed by the applied inference rule. Additionally the action history and the word state needs to be adapted accordingly.

In order to understand the semantic domains of LTSs for CTML it has to be defined what constitute a state in the LTS. A state represents the current task expression which is to be further transformed (e.g., $c \gg d$), the action history (denoting the set of already executed actions) (e.g., $\mathcal{A} = \{a, b\}$) and the set of currently true literals (e.g., $\{location('Sheldon, 'Presentation Zone')\}$). The initial state of the LTS can be straightforwardly derived from the intermediate specification as the task expression is part of the tuple IS_{CTML}. The action history is empty in the initial state and the set of literal. In essence, a LTS state is defined by the tuple $\langle t, \mathcal{S}, \mathcal{A}\rangle$ with t being the task expression in the current state, $\mathcal{S}$ being the literals in the current state and $\mathcal{A}$ being the set of already executed tasks. The functions assigning preconditions and effects in the intermediate specifications are consulted but do not constitute the state because they not modified during creation of the LTS.

In terms of a LTS executing an action results in a transition from the current state into the subsequent state. Thus with each transition the task expression is translated until only an action is left which is also eventually translated to the empty task expression. Finally a special state is created denoting the termination.

In order to foster the understanding of this approach an example of a LTS is given here. The initial task expression is given by $a| = |(b \gg c \gg d)$.

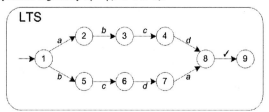

Figure 6-20 The Semantics of a Task Expression visualized as LTS

The LTS $LTS_{ex} = \langle\{1,2,3,4,6,7,8\}, \{a, b, c, d\}, \{(1, a, 2), (2, b, 3), (3, c, 4), (4, d, 8),(1, b, 5),$ $(5, c, 6), , (6, d, 7), (7, a, 8), (8, \checkmark, 9), 1\rangle$ can be visualized as the graph depicted in Figure 6-20. For reasons of clarity numeric labels instead of the actual task expressions are used (Table 6-15 explains the mapping). Please note that invisible actions and corresponding states are removed from the example in order to foster understanding.

Label	Expression	Label	Expression
1	$\langle a| = |(b \gg c \gg d), \emptyset, \emptyset\rangle$	6	$\langle d \gg a, \emptyset, \{b, c\}\rangle$
2	$\langle b \gg c \gg d, \emptyset, \{a\}\rangle$	7	$\langle a, \emptyset, \{b, c, d\}\rangle$
3	$\langle c \gg d, \emptyset, \{a, b\}\rangle$	8	$\langle SKIP, \emptyset, \{a, b, c, d\}\rangle$
4	$\langle d, \emptyset, \{a, b, c\}\rangle$	9	$\langle \Omega, \emptyset, \{a, b, c, d\}\rangle$
5	$\langle c \gg d \gg a, \emptyset, \{b\}\rangle$		

Table 6-15 Mapping of Labels to Expressions for the Example

A LTS is interpreted by its current state and the action enabled in its current state which are represented by outgoing transitions. In Figure 6-20 the initial state of the LTS is $a| = |(b \gg c \gg d)$. Thus the first action being executable are a and b. When b is activated the state of the LTS switches to $c \gg d \gg a$ in which c is enabled. The subsequent actions are performed in the same vein until the empty task expression $SKIP$ has been reached. Then the LTS propagates ✓ and successfully terminates in the state Ω (more precisely $\langle \Omega, \emptyset, \{a, b, c, d\} \rangle$). It is the special state which is added to the definition of a LTS for convenience in order to denote the termination. The other branch can be traced in the same manner.

In the following paragraphs for each operator and for preconditions and effects the inference rules are listed and explained. In order to illustrate the inference rules the intended semantics of the operators are explained in detail.

Again it is pointed out that not only the qualified task expression TE_{CTML} is stepwise translated but also the action history $\mathcal{A}$ (denoting the history of action executed) and the literals which are needed to give meaning to preconditions and effects (which are empty in the example above). Moreover the action history $\mathcal{A}$ is used to evaluate preconditions based on tasks.

Before introducing the inference rule some syntactical transformations are performed to reduce the number of inference rules. More precisely, the unary optional operator is replaced by the binary choice and the unary finite iteration operator is flattened by the binary enabling operator.

$$[t] = (t[]Skip)$$

An optional execution of a task can be rewritten by the choice of the task and the empty task expression. In order to simplify the rules the empty task expression is introduced. Following the convention of process algebra the empty task expression is named $Skip$.

The same applies for the finite iteration operator. The semantics of the unary finite iteration operator is the n-ary execution of t. It can be rewritten by $n - 1$ enabling expression. It is transformed by the following the recursive algorithms:

$$t^n = (t \gg t^{n-1}) \, with \, n > 1$$

$$t^1 = (t)$$

Having normalized optional and iterative task expressions, the inference rules for CTML are given and illustrated. Please note that the inference rules transform LTS states based on the initial state derivable from the intermediate specification. However, most rules focus on the pure task expression. Therefore the standard way of interpreting such a rule is only to consider the state as task expression. In this vein, obsolete projections on tuples are avoided. If the whole state including action history and state of literals is of interest it is explicitly stated.

The simplest task expression is the empty task expression. The only action $Skip$ can produce is ✓ after it terminates. The corresponding rule for this special term is as follows:

Successful Termination	(1)	$$\dfrac{\checkmark}{Skip \rightarrow \Omega}$$

The next rule specifies the execution of an action. There is no hypothesis as no condition is necessary in order to derive the LTS for this case. It defines that an action can be translated to an empty expression by defining a transition in the LTS between those states. Moreover it states that the execution of an action adds the action to the action history $\mathcal{A}$. In order to do so the complete LTS states need to be considered which is denoted by the tuples. More formally, the LTS state in which an element of QT_{CTML} (being an atom or action) represents the task expression can be transformed by executing t to the LTS state in which the task expression is the empty task expression ($Skip$) and the extended action history by t. The state of literals $\mathcal{S}$ is not changed.

As $Skip$ is produced each execution produces a $\checkmark$ before the final state is produced (see rule (1)). In certain situations this fact needs to be kept in mind when writing the rules (e.g., see the Enabling Operator).

Action Execution $t \in QT_{CTML}$	(2)	$$\dfrac{}{\langle (t), \mathcal{S}, \mathcal{A} \rangle \xrightarrow{t} \langle Skip, \mathcal{S}, \mathcal{A}_{+t} \rangle, \mathcal{A}_{+t} := \mathcal{A} \cup \{t\}}$$

The rule above also shows the structure of such rules. Under the fraction on the left hand side of the arrow an existing state of the LTS is given. The arrow defines which task is executed on the state. On the right hand side the resulting state of the LTS is given which if not present in the LTS is created. The same applies for the transition.

Now it is continued with complex task expressions. For the subsequent rules it is referred to t' as arbitrary qualified task expression of the specification ($t' \in TEXPR_{CTML}$)

The first one is the choice operator. In CTML the operator is interpreted as external choice. In process algebras it is distinguished between external and internal choice and also approaches in task modeling considered such a distinction [Roscoe, 1997; Sinnig $et\ al.$, 2007]. Thus the choice of actions is performed deterministically here. Let $(t_1 [] t_2)$ be a choice expression with $(t_1, t_2 \in TEXPR_{CTML})$ then by selecting an action of t_1 the second expression becomes unavailable (and vice versa). The rules define that the choice expression can be translated to another expression if one of the actions of the choice expression is translatable to t'. Please note that these rules also capture the case when t_1 or t_2 are atomic units as t' can be the empty task expression $Skip$. This applies for all subsequent operators as well. The handling of atomic actions is therefore completely solved by rule (4) and the $Skip$ expression. These two rules sufficiently define the choice operator.

As the choice operator does not affect the action history or the state of the literals the brief notation is used in this rule.

Choice $(t_1[]t_2)$	(3)	$\dfrac{t_1 \xrightarrow{a} t'}{(t_1[\ ]t_2) \xrightarrow{a} t'}$	$\dfrac{t_2 \xrightarrow{a} t'}{(t_1[\ ]t_2) \xrightarrow{a} t'}$

The order independent expressions is intended to define that two tasks can be performed in any order but once one the tasks is started the other has two wait until the first one terminates successfully. Therefore this operator can be defined by means of the enabling operator ($\gg$). Under the condition that one can transform t_1 to t' the order independent expression can be translated to the sequence of t' and t_2 as t_1 has already been started which restrict the execution to a simple sequence. The same rule is given for starting task t_2.

Order Independent $(t_1|=|t_2)$	(4)	$\dfrac{t_1 \xrightarrow{a} t'}{(t_1|=|t_2) \xrightarrow{a} (t' \gg t_2)}$	$\dfrac{t_2 \xrightarrow{a} t'}{(t_1|=|t_2) \xrightarrow{a} (t' \gg t_1)}$

With respect to an interleaving semantics concurrent means the interleaving of all actions of t_1 and t_2. Therefore no restriction is made by the inference rule given for the concurrent operator which reflects the intuition of the concurrent operator adequately. Rule (5) is not sufficient as each operand may produce a ✓ to notify its termination. This termination cannot be propagated as the expression is not terminated when one of its operands terminates but if both terminate successfully. Therefore synchronization between the termination of both operands is needed which is specified by rule (5), (6) and (7). To be more specific rule (6) specifies the need to catch the ✓ produced when the first operand terminates. Eventually the concurrent expression terminates successfully when both operands terminated (rule (7)). In this situation ✓ is propagated.

Concurrent $(t_1 \parallel t_2)$	(5)	$\dfrac{t_1 \xrightarrow{a} t'}{(t_1 \parallel t_2) \xrightarrow{a} (t' \parallel t_2)}$	$\dfrac{t_2 \xrightarrow{a} t'}{(t_1 \parallel t_2) \xrightarrow{a} (t_1 \parallel t')}$	$a \neq ✓$
	(6)	$\dfrac{t_1 \xrightarrow{✓} t'}{(t_1 \parallel t_2) \xrightarrow{\tau} (\Omega \parallel t_2)}$	$\dfrac{t_2 \xrightarrow{✓} t'}{(t_1 \parallel t_2) \xrightarrow{\tau} (t_1 \parallel \Omega)}$	
	(7)	$\dfrac{}{(\Omega \parallel \Omega) \xrightarrow{✓} \Omega}$		

The disabling (also referred as deactivation) operator defines that the second operand may disable the first operand at any time (rule (10)). Moreover when the first operand terminates successfully the ✓ is not propagated but the second operand needs to terminate first which is specified in rule (9). Rule (8) defines the normal case of executing actions of the first operand.

Disabling $(t_1| > t_2)$	(8)	$\dfrac{t_1 \xrightarrow{a} t'}{(t_1| > t_2) \xrightarrow{a} (t'| > t_2)}$	$a \neq \tau$

(9)		$$\dfrac{t_1 \overset{\checkmark}{\to} t'}{(t_1 \mid > t_2) \overset{\tau}{\to} (t_2)}$$
(10)		$$\dfrac{t_2 \overset{a}{\to} t'}{(t_1 \mid > t_2) \overset{a}{\to} (t')}$$

The intuitive meaning of the suspend resume operator is the iterative execution of the second operand (rule (12)) until the first operand is executed successfully (rule (11)). In any state of the first operand the second operand may be started (suspension). After termination the first operand may be continued. Please note that the second operand is defined as optional as a $\checkmark$ may be produced in rule (11) leading to termination.

Suspend Resume $(t_1[> t_2)$	(11)	$$\dfrac{t_1 \overset{a}{\to} t'}{(t_1[> t_2) \overset{a}{\to} (t'[> t_2)}$$
	(12)	$$\dfrac{t_2 \overset{a}{\to} t'}{(t_1[> t_2) \overset{a}{\to} \left(t' \gg (t_1[> t_2)\right)}$$

The enabling operator defines a sequential execution of both operands. The stepwise execution of the first operand is specified in rule (13). However if the first operand terminates rule (14) needs to be applied as the $\checkmark$ must not be propagated since the second operand needs to executed first. More in detail, when the first operand terminates the expression is transformed to the execution of the second operand.

Enabling $(t_1 \gg t_2)$	(13)	$$\dfrac{t_1 \overset{a}{\to} t'}{(t_1 \gg t_2) \overset{a}{\to} (t' \gg t_2)}$$	$a \neq \checkmark$
	(14)	$$\dfrac{t_1 \overset{\checkmark}{\to} t'}{(t_1 \gg t_2) \overset{\tau}{\to} (t_2)}$$	

After having defined the semantics of all binary operators it is now continued with the explanation of the unary operators. As the optional execution of a task denoted by $[t]$ has been eliminated beforehand (substitution by the binary choice operator) no rule for this operator exist.

The iteration operator specifies the repetitive execution of a certain task expression t. Once an iteration is started (rule (15)) it needs to be completed until a new iteration can be triggered. After having finished an iteration (denoted by $\checkmark$) either the repetitive execution may be stopped (*Skip*) or a new iteration cycle can be triggered (t^*) which is specified in rule (16).

Iteration (t^*)	(15)	$$\dfrac{t \overset{a}{\to} t'}{(t^*) \overset{a}{\to} (t' \gg t^*)}$$	$a \neq \checkmark$

(16)	$$\frac{t \xrightarrow{\checkmark} t'}{(t^*) \xrightarrow{\tau} (Skip\ [\quad]t^*)}$$

In the case of a task based precondition certain actions need to be executed in order to enable the precondition. As the history of actions is captured in the sequence A the evaluation of a task based precondition is straightforward. As seen in rule (2) when executing an action the sequence A is extended in order to define the current state (according to the situation calculus) and to evaluate task based preconditions. Moreover during the transformation process described in the last section the function pre_H is stepwise created. Please note that $pre_H(t)$ ($\in \mathcal{TEXPR}_{CTML}$) under the fraction is a term whereas $pre_H(t)$ above the fraction is a function assigning a qualified task expression its task based precondition. The evaluation of such a precondition is given in rule (17) and (18). Under the assumption that t can be transformed to t' by the action a the composed task expression $pre_H(t)$ can be transformed to t' given that the assigned precondition (being the tupel $\langle q, \mathcal{T} \rangle$) is fulfilled (with q being a quantifier and $\mathcal{T}$ being a set of qualified task names). The interpretation of the preconditions depends on the used quantifier q of the precondition. If an all quantifier is used all qualified task names need to be included in the action history $\mathcal{A}$ (rule (17)). In contrast if an exist quantifier has been used only one action of $\mathcal{T}$ needs to be contained in the sequence of actions already executed (rule (18)).

Precondition $pre_H(t)$	(17)	$$\frac{\langle t, \mathcal{S}, \mathcal{A} \rangle \xrightarrow{a} \langle t', \mathcal{S}', \mathcal{A}' \rangle, pre_H(t) = \langle \forall, \mathcal{T} \rangle, \forall \alpha \in \mathcal{T} : \alpha \in \mathcal{A}}{\langle pre_H(t), \mathcal{S}, \mathcal{A} \rangle \xrightarrow{a} \langle t', \mathcal{S}', \mathcal{A}' \rangle}$$
	(18)	$$\frac{\langle t, \mathcal{S}, \mathcal{A} \rangle \xrightarrow{a} \langle t', \mathcal{S}', \mathcal{A}' \rangle, pre_H(t) = \langle \exists, \mathcal{T} \rangle, \exists \alpha \in \mathcal{T} : \alpha \in \mathcal{A}}{\langle pre_H(t), \mathcal{S}, \mathcal{A} \rangle \xrightarrow{a} \langle t', \mathcal{S}', \mathcal{A}' \rangle}$$

In the same vein as a task based precondition state based preconditions are evaluated. More precisely the current situation denoted by $\mathcal{S}$ is consulted in order to check that the assigned state precondition $(pre_S(t))$ is fulfilled. A state based precondition is fulfilled iff the predicates assigned to the task expression are contained in the current world state $\mathcal{S}$.

Precondition II $pre_S(t)$	(19)	$$\frac{\langle t, \mathcal{S}, \mathcal{A} \rangle \xrightarrow{a} \langle t', \mathcal{S}', \mathcal{A}' \rangle, pre_S(t) \subseteq \mathcal{S}}{\langle pre_S(t), \mathcal{S}, \mathcal{A} \rangle \xrightarrow{a} \langle t', \mathcal{S}', \mathcal{A}' \rangle}$$

In contrast to preconditions effects denote the state change of the system due to the execution of an action. More precisely not only the positive effects but also the negative effects of an action need to be considered to define the world state consistently because the positive effects only state the facts which are true after executing which is not sufficient as some facts may be false after execution which needs to specify as well.

As effects are only assigned to qualified task names ($Q\mathcal{T}_{CTML}$) effects are applied in conjunction with action execution. As already state during the transformation of effects in the previous section effects are consisting of the following tuple $\langle Y, \mathcal{P}_e, \mathcal{E}^+, \mathcal{E}^- \rangle$. The reason for such a complex formalization is due to the state dependence of effects. When executing a function on a device as effect the new state of the device depends on the current state. Therefore effects need to take into account the current world state. To be able to do so variables are needed. Y denotes the set of variables for an effect. $\mathcal{P}_e$ specifies the needed situation containing variables which are substituted accordingly so that $\mathcal{P}_e$ is true in the current situation ($\mathcal{P}_e \subseteq S$). This substitution is then applied to the positive and negative effects which contain variables of Y. Thus all variables are eliminated.

Rule (20) states if t can be transformed to t' by the action a and a substitution of variables exists which eliminates all variables in $\mathcal{P}_e$ so that the grounded predicates in $\mathcal{P}_e$ are contained in the current situation S which means that $\mathcal{P}_e$ is true in that situation, then the effect can be applied. It is applied by transforming the task expression into t' and creating the new situation after executing a (denoted by S'). By applying the substitution for the positive and negative effects grounded predicates are created. The new situation is then derived by subtracting all negative effects from the current situation and adding all positive effects to it.

Effect $eff(t)$	(20) $\dfrac{\langle t, S, \mathcal{A}\rangle \xrightarrow{a} \langle t', S', \mathcal{A}'\rangle, eff(t) = (Y, \mathcal{P}_e, \mathcal{E}^+, \mathcal{E}^-), \exists \Theta_Y | \mathcal{P}_e \subseteq S}{\langle eff(t), S, \mathcal{A}\rangle \xrightarrow{a} \langle t', S', \mathcal{A}'\rangle, S' := S \backslash \mathcal{E}^-_{\Theta_Y} \cup \mathcal{E}^+_{\Theta_Y}}$

Having defined the inference rule the LTS representing the semantics of a CTML specification can be derived.

The Running Example – LTS Creation

Taking the running example of the "Conference Session" the example of the intermediate specification is now transformed into a LTS. According to the explanation given above a preprocessing step is necessary to eliminate optional tasks and finite iterations. As neither of them exists in the example no adaptation is necessary. In Table 6-16 and Table 6-17 the resulting LTS is specified. The visual presentation of the LTS is given in Figure 6-21. In Table 6-17 the applied inference rules in order to derive the subsequent state and the produced action are named.

Label	State
1	$\langle| = |\left(pres\big((sh,c,wp)\big), pres\big((sh,c,pa)\big)\right), location(le,pz), \emptyset\rangle$
2	$\langle\gg \left(Skip, pres\big((sh,c,pa)\big)\right), location(le,pz), \{(sh,c,wp)\}\rangle$
3	$\langle pres\big((sh,c,pa)\big), location(le,pz), \{(sh,c,wp)\}\rangle$
4	$\langle\gg \left(pres\big((sh,c,wp)\big), Skip\right), location(le,pz), \{(sh,c,pa)\}\rangle$
5	$\langle pres\big((sh,c,wp)\big), location(le,pz), \{(sh,c,pa)\}\rangle$
6	$\langle SKIP, location(le,pz), \{(sh,c,wp),(sh,c,pa)\}\rangle$
7	$\langle \Omega, location(le,pz), \{(sh,c,wp),(sh,c,pa)\}\rangle$

Table 6-16 Labels and States of Example LTS

The initial state of the LTS is given by the task expression in the intermediate specification, the set of true literals also defined in the intermediate specification and the empty set of already executed actions. This tuple entirely defines the initial state of the LTS. Not the inference rules are applied. Depending on the structure of the expression which is an order independent expression in the case of the initial state, the appropriate rule is applied. Hence, not only one rule is applied but in order to proof that the hypotheses above the fraction of the inference rule can be proven. To exemplify this approach the initial state of the LTS is used. As already stated the initial state is an order independence expression. Rule (4) can (and therefore is) applied if the hypothesis can be proven. The rule to be applied is:

$$\frac{t_1 \overset{a}{\to} t'}{(t_1|=|t_2) \overset{a}{\to} (t' \gg t_2)}$$

The rule can be paraphrased as follows: an order independence expression can be transformed into a enabling expression if the first operand can be transformed to t'. Therefore an appropriate inference rule for the first operand, namely $pre_S((sh, c, wp))$, is applied. As the expression is a state precondition rule (19) is consulted which checks whether the assigned precondition (the function pre_S defines the assigned precondition) is fulfilled in the current world state, here $location(le, pz)$. It is not only checked whether the precondition is fulfilled but also whether the inner expression of the precondition can be further derived $((sh, c, pa))$. As this an atom the action execution rule ((2)) can be applied which translated the atom to the empty task expression $SKIP$ and adds the executed action to the action history. The selection of the other operand of the order independence expression is analogous as this operator is symmetric (state 4).

Source State	Target State	Action	Inference Rules
1	2	(sh, c, wp)	(4),(19),(2)
2	3	τ	(14), (1)
1	4	(sh, c, pa)	(4),(19),(2)
4	5	τ	(14), (1)
3	6	(sh, c, pa)	(19),(2)
5	6	(sh, c, wp)	(19),(2)
6	7	✓	(1)

Table 6-17 Transition Matrix and Applied Inference Rule

Now the previously created enabling expression which represents partially state 2 is further derived. According to rule (14) an invisible action is created and the enabling expression resolved to the second operand if the action derivable from the first operand is ✓. As the first operand is $Skip$ which can be translated to Ω using rule (1) which in turn produces ✓ the hypothesis holds. Therefore rule (14) can be applied which produces τ and converts the enabling expression to the second operand which in turn is an atom and can be translated as described before. Finally the *Skip* expression is reached which can be further transformed into Ω. ✓ is used as action to denote the successful termination.

The other path through the LTS (by selecting the other task as first action to execute) is derived analogous.

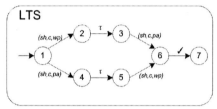

Figure 6-21 Visual Representation of the LTS

Semantics for Sub Specifications

During the creation of CTML specifications task expressions are created. The interactive exploration of those sub specifications is an important feature to be supported. The isolated interactive exploration of single task trees does not reveal their full semantics (as dependencies to other role based task models are not interpretable) but already show the meaning of the task structure and the results of the precondition and effects defined over the task expression and the domain model. Being able to animate intermediate specification helps to shorten feedback cycles and improve the artifact.

The approach of assigning semantics to a single task tree relies on synthesizing a simple CTML model based on the task tree. A configuration with a single actor which fulfills a synthesized role which in turn uses the task expression is created.

Let T be a single task expression of the following form $\langle \mathcal{T}_T, \tau_T, r, TE_T, \mathcal{DM}_T, \mathcal{O}_T \rangle$ with $\mathcal{T}_T$ being the set of task names of the task tree, τ_T assigning each task name a task type (in the same vein as in Definition 6-2), r being the role name, TE_T be the task expression according to Definition 6-4. $\mathcal{DM}_T$ being the domain model and $\mathcal{O}$ the corresponding objects, then a CTML model with $CTML = \langle Coop, \mathcal{C} \rangle$ and $Coop = \langle \mathcal{R}, \mathcal{T}, \tau, \mathcal{TE}, L, \mathcal{DS}, \mathcal{ST}, dev, \mathcal{DM} \rangle$ can be synthesized as follows. The cooperation model is defined by:

1. $\mathcal{R} = \{r\}$
2. $\mathcal{T} = \mathcal{T}_T$
3. $\tau = \tau_T$
4. $\mathcal{TE} = \{TE_T\}$
5. $L = \langle \{l\}, \emptyset \rangle$
6. $\mathcal{DS} = \mathcal{ST} = dev = \emptyset$
7. $\mathcal{DM} = \mathcal{DM}_T$

The set of configurations $\mathcal{C}$ is defined by the only one element:

1. $\mathcal{C} = \{C_T\}$

with $C_T = \langle \mathcal{A}, Objects \rangle$

1. $\mathcal{A} = \{a\}$ with $a = \langle actor, l, \emptyset, \{r\}, \emptyset, r \rangle$

2. $Objects = O_T$

In this vein the same formalism can be used to assign semantics for sub specifications of CTML model. Therefore all algorithms (such as refinement) are also usable for single task trees.

6.5 Refinement

During software development models are adapted and incremental refined. To answer the question whether a certain refined model is a valid adaptation of the base specification refinement checks are supportive. This applies particularly for models employed in an iterative, incremental process models. Therefore refinement is of interest for CTML models. In order to define an appropriate notion of refinement different refinement relations are examined and assessed with respect to the usage for CTML. As LTSs have been selected as ultimate semantic domain for CTML models refinement relation based on LTSs as examined in Chapter 4 can be used. However it is shown that those approaches are not sufficient in all cases. A more flexible approach is therefore proposed in the second part of this section.

6.5.1 Comparison Semantics for CTML

In Section 4.5 several notions of refinement have been examined. Here the different proposed comparison semantics are assessed with respect to CTML. Moreover it is shown that even though that some proposed semantics are suitable they do not fulfill all requirements in order to allow a flexible approach to introduce refinement for CTML specifications.

Trace semantics is the most coarse-grained semantics for LTSs. It gives meaning to a LTS with respect to what it is able to produce. However as there is no notion of successful termination it does not state what a LTS needs to do. Thus trace semantics gives only little information about the equivalence of two CTML specifications, respectively LTSs derivable from CTML models.

Definition 6-27 ($\mathcal{M}[\![m, c]\!]$ – Semantic Mapping): Let m be a CTML model and c the selected configuration of m, then $\mathcal{M}[\![m, c]\!]$ denotes the semantic mapping function with $\mathcal{M}: Coop \times Configuration \rightarrow LTS$ which assigns the CTML model and the selected configuration an LTS with respect to the given definitions in Section 6.4.

Definition 6-28 ($=_T$– Trace Equivalence): Let $CTML_A$ and $CTML_B$ be two CTML specifications, C_{A_i} and C_{B_i} the selected configurations of $CTML_A$ and $CTML_B$, respectively, then the CTML models are trace equivalent iff:

$$\langle CTML_A, C_{A_i} \rangle =_T \langle CTML_B, C_{B_i} \rangle \Leftrightarrow traces\big(\mathcal{M}[\![CTML_A, C_{A_i}]\!]\big) = traces\big(\mathcal{M}[\![CTML_B, C_{B_i}]\!]\big)$$

The set of traces of the LTS p is defined as follows:

$$traces(p) = \left\{ t \in \mathcal{A}ct^* \mid \exists q \in \mathcal{Q}: q_0 \xrightarrow{t} q \right\}$$

In the same vein trace inclusion and trace extension can be defined.

Completed trace semantics however introduces the notion of successful termination. This is of particular interest for CTML as task modeling relies on the hypothesis that task are executed in order to reach a goal which is not considered in trace semantics. Completed trace semantics is therefore a much more suitable semantic model for CTML. Moreover it is also an intuitive semantic model for CTML. This item should not be underestimated as the task modeler is able to comprehend the model while designing. Completed trace semantics offers this opportunity because it represents how people consider the execution of tasks (a task is complete when its goal has been reached e.g., cleaning a car is reached when the car is cleaned) and completed trace semantics is also assumed by most task modeling languages (but not formally defined) [Limbourg & Vanderdonckt, 2003; Paternò, 1999; van Welie *et al.*, 1998]. Due to the notion of successful termination also deadlock detection is possible in completed trace semantics.

Completed trace semantics consider to LTS equivalent if they have the same set of completed traces (successful terminated runs). Applied to CTML completed trace semantics defines the two CTML models are equal if they exhibit the same set of sequences of action reaching the goal.

Failure semantics not only states what a LTS needs to do but also examines a LTS with respect to what is not able to do. More precisely, failure semantics captures which actions are not executable after having executed a certain traces. As already stated earlier failure semantics includes completed trace semantics and as such is a finer comparison semantics. Due to the inclusion of completed trace semantics successful termination and deadlocks can be detected. However failures semantics is the semantics which investigate the structure of the model itself and not only the observations (executed actions). For modeling of human activity this is counterproductive as the internal structure of actions a human being cannot be investigated anyways.

The comparison semantics of LTSs form a lattice as already stated earlier. Having considered failure semantics as too fine for CTML no other comparison semantics (except for simulation semantics [van Glabbeek, 1990]) needs to be examined as all others are finer and therefore make less identifications over the set LTSs. Simulation semantics is independent of completed trace semantics and failure semantics but is not appropriate for CTML because it focuses additionally on the branching structure of the LTS which is not of interest for CTML (the branching structure represents the internal structure of the actions of a human being again).

Beside the comparison semantics to be used for CTML it needs to be examined what kind of refinement is allowed. Is a sub specification always an extension to its base specification or is a sub specification required to exhibit the exactly same behavior? This question cannot be answered by the examination of the modeling language but needs to be solved with respect to the usage of the modeling language within the development process. For CTML on the analysis level substantial model adaptation may be allowed but when moving from requirements to design this might be counterproductive. A cautious approach is needed in this case.

For CTML restricting the behavior in a sub specification is inappropriate as gradual refinement is one of the core concepts of hierarchical task modeling. During development atomic units are further refined constituting an extended behavior even though action refinement cannot be consistently defined with interleaving semantics. Equivalence behavior is desirable when only minor model adaptations are valid in the current phase of development (e.g., in the final phase of design). Extending the behavior of the base specification is definitely also a case to consider in order to define an appropriate refinement relation for CTML.

Under which circumstances the different types of refinement can be applied is answered in Chapter 7 which introduces a development approach by explicitly using the refinement relations proposed in the remainder of this chapter.

In the domain of LTS a completed trace refers to the successful run through the LTS. In task modeling an analogous term exists. A successful run through a task model is referred as scenario [Paternò, 1999; Wurdel *et al.*, 2008d]. As it has been shown previously completed trace semantics is an appropriate model of abstraction for CTML. In order to stick to the convention of task modeling the first comparison semantics for CTML is referred as scenario semantics:

Definition 6-29 ($=_S$– Scenario Equivalence): Let $CTML_A$ and $CTML_B$ be two CTML specifications, C_{A_i} and C_{B_i} the selected configurations of $CTML_A$ and $CTML_B$, respectively. Let further $\mathcal{M}[\![m, c]\!]$ be the semantic mapping assigning a CTML specification (m) and a selected configuration (c) its corresponding LTS as explained in Section 6.4, then the CTML models are scenario equivalent iff:

$$\langle CTML_A, C_{A_i}\rangle =_S \langle CTML_B, C_{B_i}\rangle \Leftrightarrow sce\big(\mathcal{M}[\![CTML_A, C_{A_i}]\!]\big) = sce\big(\mathcal{M}[\![CTML_B, C_{B_i}]\!]\big)$$

The set of scenarios of the LTS p is defined as follows:

$$sce(p) = \left\{t \in \mathcal{A}ct^* | \, \exists q \in \mathcal{Q}: q_0 \xrightarrow{s} q, s = \langle t^\wedge\checkmark\rangle\right\}$$

Accordingly scenario inclusion can be defined:

Definition 6-30 ($\subseteq_S$– Scenario Inclusion): Let $CTML_A$ and $CTML_B$ be two CTML specifications and C_{A_i} and C_{B_i} the selected configurations of $CTML_A$ and $CTML_B$, respectively, then $CTML_B$ refines $CTML_A$ by scenario inclusion iff:

$$\langle CTML_A, C_{A_i}\rangle \subseteq_S \langle CTML_B, C_{B_i}\rangle \Leftrightarrow sce\big(\mathcal{M}[\![CTML_A, C_{A_i}]\!]\big) \subseteq sce\big(\mathcal{M}[\![CTML_B, C_{B_i}]\!]\big)$$

This definition states a refinement which is based on extension. A sub specification needs to exhibit at least the behavior of its base specification. If additionally scenarios are defined scenario inclusion still holds. Scenario extension can be easily defined accordingly but is not of interest for CTML.

Those two given definitions are the basic notions of refinement in this thesis. In order to show the rationale of the definitions their applications are shown in the subsequent examples.

The Running Example – Scenario Equivalence and Inclusion

In Figure 6-22 an adapted version of the running example of the "Conference Session" is given. In this example managing talks is considered as atomic for reasons of brevity.

Figure 6-22 Base Specification for Role Chairman

The scenarios of the base specification are the following (please note that qualified task expression ($actor, role, task\ name$) are not used here, as actor and role are identical in all actions):

$$scenario(base) = \begin{cases} \langle er, wp, pa, mt, aod, wus, lr, \checkmark \rangle, \langle er, wp, pa, mt, wus, aod, lr, \checkmark \rangle, \\ \langle er, pa, wp, mt, aod, wus, lr, \checkmark \rangle, \langle er, pa, wp, mt, wus, aod, lr, \checkmark \rangle, \\ \langle er, wp, pa, aod, wus, lr, \checkmark \rangle, \langle er, pa, wp, wus, aod, lr, \checkmark \rangle \end{cases}$$

An adaptation of the model given above is depicted in Figure 6-23. In the refinement the order independent operators are substituted by the enabling operator and the task *Leave Room* is optional.

Figure 6-23 Refinement of Base Specification for Role Chairman

The scenarios of the refinement are the following:

$$scenario(ref1) = \{\langle er, wp, pa, mt, aod, wus, lr, \checkmark \rangle, \langle er, wp, pa, aod, wus, lr, \checkmark \rangle\}$$

Because of $scenario(base) \neq scenario(ref1)$ the models are not scenario equivalent. Moreover, $scenario(base) \not\subseteq scenario(ref1)$ no scenario inclusion exists between those models. The example exemplifies how scenario inclusion impacts the refinement process as it preserves the scenarios of the base specification. Such an approach ensures that defined requirements, design respectively, are not violated in later development steps.

Another adaptation is visualized in Figure 6-24. Here the order independent operator on the left hand side is replaced by the concurrent operator which allows the interleaved execution of all tasks. Moreover a new task *Make List of Participants* is introduced which is marked with the unary optional operator.

Figure 6-24 Another Refinement of Base Specification for Role Chairman

The scenarios of the second refinement are the following:

$$scenario(ref2) = \left\{ \begin{array}{l} \langle er, wp, pa, mt, aod, wus, lr, \checkmark \rangle, \langle er, wp, pa, mt, wus, aod, lr, \checkmark \rangle, \\ \langle er, pa, wp, mt, aod, wus, lr, \checkmark \rangle, \langle er, pa, wp, mt, wus, aod, lr, \checkmark \rangle, \\ \langle er, pa, wp, mt, aod, wus, mlp, lr, \checkmark \rangle, \langle er, pa, wp, mt, wus, aod, mlp, lr, \checkmark \rangle \\ \langle er, pa, wp, mt, aod, mlp, wus, lr, \checkmark \rangle, \langle er, pa, wp, mt, wus, mlp, aod, lr, \checkmark \rangle \\ \langle er, pa, wp, mt, mlp, aod, wus, lr, \checkmark \rangle, \langle er, pa, wp, mt, mlp, wus, aod, lr, \checkmark \rangle \\ \langle er, wp, pa, aod, wus, lr, \checkmark \rangle, \langle er, pa, wp, wus, aod, lr, \checkmark \rangle \end{array} \right\}$$

Because of $scenario(base) \neq scenario(ref2)$ the models are not scenario equivalent. However, as $scenario(base) \supseteq scenario(ref1)$ scenario inclusion exists between those models. The refined model preserves all existing scenarios before and adds some additional ones. This reflects the approach of adding iteratively requirements, designs respectively, to the models.

The examples already show that scenario equivalence and inclusion are efficient utilities in order to assure the valid implementation of base specifications. During model adaptation refinement checks can be applied repetitively in order to check whether the same (sub) set of scenarios are defined. However such a rigid approach exhibits also some drawbacks:

(1) **Model Adaptation.** Adapting models is part of engineering and as such is intended. Therefore especially in early phases models underlie substantial changes during development. Prototypes are created, adapted and dismissed. A more flexible approach is needed to support such a process. Moreover with gradual advance of modeling intermediate results are created which exhibit partially valuable results whereas other parts might still be constantly changing. Those more mature parts need to be treated with different quality criteria as the others.

(2) **Action Refinement.** As already explained in Section 4.5 action refinement cannot be consistently defined over interleaving semantics. Therefore another approach for gradual refinement of task models needs to be considered since action refinement or gradual refining atomic tasks is a common case in task modeling.

(3) **Detailed Design.** The general adaptation cycle consisting of adaptation and refinement check is expedient throughout all development stages. However when fine tuning the model in detailed design tasks might be introduced which are not conceptually important but necessary for technical reasons (e.g., in MB-UI development). In such a case it might be reasonable to exclude those tasks from the refinement checks. Therefore a more flexible approach is desired.

(4) **Structural Refinement.** The approaches so far, including scenario semantics, only observe the behavior of the system, model respectively. In many cases this is completely sufficient. Nevertheless also structural properties constitute the validity of a model and therefore also its refinement. What kind of properties are considered as important in order to refine a model validly with respect to its structure depend on the usage of model within the development process.

For these reasons a more flexible approach is introduced in the subsequent sections. The first approach examines the structure of CTML in order to define structural refinement. The second approach define a new semantic equivalence which makes use of so called meta operators to define which tasks are considered during the refinement checks. Therefore the

135

syntax and semantics of CTML is extended and new semantic equivalences are introduced. This will conclude the set of refinement relations for CTML. Subsequently it is shown when each method of refinement is appropriate in the development life cycle of CTML.

6.5.2 Structural Refinement

The structure of a whole CTML specification is quite complex. Various modeling elements can be examined in order to assure structural equivalence (or structural inclusion). Structural equivalence can be easily defined by equivalence of two CTML models. However such a notion of equivalence is not appropriate since it implies identity (or more general the existence of a bijection). Therefore a less rigid equivalence is used here.

Definition 6-31 ($\doteq$ – **Structural Equivalence**): Let $CTML_A$ and $CTML_B$ be two well-formed CTML specifications and there exists a bijective function φ assigning each element of $Coop_B$ an element of $Coop_A$, then the CTML models are structural equivalent iff the following conditions hold:

1. **Role Set.** The set of roles are identical.

$$\pi_1(Coop_A) = \pi_1(Coop_B) \wedge \forall r \in \pi_1(Coop_B): \varphi(r) = r$$

2. **Mapping Consistency.** Only elements of $Coop_A$ and $Coop_B$ are associated if they are of the same *type*. It assures that roles are only associated with roles, etc.

$$\forall i \in \{1, \dots, 9\}: \forall x \in \pi_i(Coop_B): \varphi(x) \in \pi_i(Coop_A)$$

3. **Task Structures.** The defined task expressions need to be identical in both models.

$$\forall r \in \pi_1(Coop_B), \forall te \in \pi_4(Coop_B): \varphi(te_r) = te_r$$

This definition states that there is a bijective mapping of the set of roles, set of task names, task type assignment, task expressions assigned to roles, locations, set of device specifications, set of stationary device specifications, device assignments to roles and domain models are equal of each cooperation model. Moreover, the task definitions are to be identical.

Please note that such a definition does not exact behavioral equivalence in any semantics examined before as the configurations are excluded from the definition. Therefore, two structural equivalent CTML specifications do not need to be trace or scenario equivalent even though this is possible.

Definition 6-32 ($\sqsubseteq$ – **Structural Inclusion**): Let $CTML_A$ and $CTML_B$ be two well-formed CTML specifications and there exists a surjective function φ assigning elements of $Coop_B$ to $Coop_A$, then $CTML_B$ structurally includes $CTML_A$ iff the following conditions hold:

1. **Role Set Inclusion.** The set of roles are extended by the refining model.

$$\pi_1(Coop_A) \subseteq \pi_1(Coop_B) \wedge \forall r \in \pi_1(Coop_A): \varphi(r) = r$$

2. **Mapping Consistency.** Only elements of $Coop_A$ and $Coop_B$ are associated if they are of the same *type*. It assures that roles are only associated with roles, etc. Explicitly excluded are task names as certain task names may not exist in the refining model.

$$\forall i \in \{1,3,4,5,6,7,8,9\}: \forall x \in \pi_i(Coop_B): \varphi(x) \in \pi_i(Coop_A)$$

3. **Task Structures.** The defined task expressions in the refining model $Coop_B$ are only allowed to refine former atomic actions into complex task expressions. Let te_r be the task expression for role r of the base model and $\varphi(te_r) = te_{r_{ref}}$ be the refining task expression for r, then $te_{r_{ref}}$ structural refines te_r validly if a function $\theta: Q\mathcal{T}_r \rightarrow \mathcal{TEXPR}_r$ exist which assigns atomic qualified task names their refinement. So that by replacing all atomic actions te with its assigned complex expression. This needs to apply for all role task expressions of the $CTML_A$.

Structural equivalence is very helpful in order to synchronize two CTML models according to their structural properties. For model refinement it is inoperative as it does not give for means adaptations. Contrary, structural inclusion is a very suitable device for refinement as it allows comparing two models even though one extends the other. More precisely, the definition of structural inclusion demands that the refining model extends the set of roles (identity is also understood as extension). Moreover the mapping function is only allowed to associate model elements of the same kind. The most interesting part of the definition is part three: *Task Structures*. Intuitively, the definition demands that only atomic actions in the base model are allowed to be refined in the refining model. Such a definition of refinement goes along with task modeling practices since intermediate specifications leaves certain tasks atomic which are to be refined in later modeling steps. Such a practice is supported by structural inclusion above.

The Running Example – Structural Inclusion

In order to show the rationale of structural inclusion an example according to the "Conference Session" is used. Structural inclusion (or structural refinement) is only exemplified for the third criteria. Therefore, the task expression given in Figure 6-22 is used as base specification. The refining model is depicted in Figure 6-25.The task *Manage Talks* has been structurally refined. No further adaptations are performed.

Figure 6-25 Structurally Refined Task Expression for Role Chairman

In order to highlight the rationale of the definition the function θ is specified (the role has been omitted here):

$$\theta(mt) = at \gg (st[> it) \gg od$$

6.5.3 Introducing Flexibility through Meta Operators

Section 6.5.1 has shown that strict comparison semantics adopted from interleaving semantics by means of LTSs are not appropriate in all cases. Scenario semantics seems to be a suitable semantic abstraction but lacks flexibility by means of prioritization of certain tasks and action refinement. Therefore this section introduces a set of unary operators which are assigned to tasks to denote their importance during refinement checks. Based on this syntactical change of CTML new comparison semantics can be defined which are still based on traces and scenarios. Preliminary results on this topic have been presented in [Wurdel *et al.*, 2008d].

Unlike temporal operators, meta operators do not determine the execution order of tasks, but define which tasks must be retained or may be omitted in the refining task model. As depicted in Table 6-18, we distinguish between four different meta operators: shallow binding, deep binding, exempted shallow binding, and exempted deep binding. All four operators denote tasks which need to be preserved in all subsequent refining task models. While shallow binding only applies to its direct operand task, deep binding applies to the entire subtask tree.

Operator	Symbol	Interpretation
Shallow Binding	⊙	Denotes a mandatory task which needs to be preserved in subsequent refining models. Subtasks may be omitted or modified and the task type may be changed.
Deep Binding	⊗	Denotes a mandatory task which, including all its subtasks and their types, needs to be preserved in subsequent refining models.
Exempted Shallow Binding	⊖⊙	Denotes a newly introduced mandatory task, which is not present in the base task model, but which should be preserved in all subsequent refining task models even though the subtasks can be modified.
Exempted Deep Binding	⊖⊗	Denotes a newly introduced mandatory task, which is not present in the base task model, but which (including all its subtasks) should be preserved in all subsequent refining task models.

Table 6-18 Meta Operators for CTML in Support for Behavioral Refinement

In Table 6-18 the existing meta operators for CTML are given. The first two are used to state a certain task (and all its subtasks in case of the deep binding operator) is mandatory in the subsequent development step (and all following). More precisely, the shallow binding operators define that a task is to be preserved but its hierarchical decomposition and the subordinated tasks can be freely adapted. This operator is especially helpful when redesigned work processes but considering the process itself as highly important. In contrast to the shallow binding operator, the deep binding operator does not allow any adaptation of the whole sub tree on which it is assigned. These operators provide the basic means for defining flexible behavioral refinement on CTML specifications. However in some cases more complex means are needed. The exempted binding operators help to solve such cases. They have been defined to enable the software designer to introduce new tasks which are not considered in the current refinement check (naturally in the refining model) but are considered in the subsequent refinement step (when the model becomes the base model). The distinction between shallow and deep has been made for the same reasons as the first two operators.

To be able to introduce the meta operators to CTML the syntax of CTML needs to be extended. Based on the Definition 6-4 which specifies how a task expression is syntactical valid a slightly adaptation is introduced:

Definition 6-33 ($\mathcal{TEXPR}_r^{meta}$-Qualified Task Expressions for r with Meta Operator): Let $\mathcal{TEXPR}_r$ be the set of qualified task expressions of r and $t \in \mathcal{TEXPR}_r$, then the following expressions are qualified task expressions with meta operator:

$$t^\odot, t^\otimes, t^{\ominus\odot}, t^{\ominus\otimes}$$

CTML with meta operators can then be straightforwardly defined by using Definition 6-33 as domain to form task expressions.

In order to perform the refinement check on two CTML specifications (base model and refining model) certain steps need to be executed in order to base the semantics on the previously introduced ones:

1. **Renaming of Tasks.** During adaptation certain tasks of the refining model might be renamed. This issue is supported by the refinement checker. A mapping of tasks of base and refining model can be established if necessary.

2. **Validation of Consistency of Nested Meta Operators.** Meta operators are not allowed to bet be nested without constraints. Therefore a syntactical validation of consistent nesting of meta operators is needed. Well-formedness criteria are defined later.

3. **Reduction of CTML Models.** The introduced meta operators of Table 6-18 already give a hint that a preprocessing step is needed in order to check refinement formally. Certain sub trees are chopped in the base and refining task model. This step is actually implementing the semantics of the meta operators. After that an ordinary, not annotated, CTML specifications is created representing the so called reduced CTML specifications.

4. **Refinement Check on Reduced CTML Models.** The refinement algorithms are the same as presented in Section 6.5.1 but use the reduced CTML specifications as input.

The steps are executed in order to provide the mandatory scenarios, respectively traces of the base and refining CTML models.

The first step can be defined by a simple mapping function assigning each qualified task name of the refining model a new name (potentially the identical name):

Definition 6-34 ($rename$ -Renaming Function): Let $Q\mathcal{T}_r$ be the set of task names of a CTML model, then, rename is a total function assigning another qualified task name:

$$rename: Q\mathcal{T}_r \rightarrow Q\mathcal{T}_r'$$

Definition 6-33 defines task expression with meta operators recursively. Therefore nesting of operators is syntactically correct. However, due to the semantics of the operators only a minor subset of nestings is also semantically useful (e.g., $(a \gg (b[\quad]c)^\otimes)^\odot$ is semantically not useful).

The check of validity of nested meta operators is performed with respect to the criteria given in Table 6-19. The reasons for permitting or forbidding the nesting are also given.

Assigned Operator to Task	Assigned Operator on Nested Task	Validity	Explanation
(exempted) Shallow	(exempted) Shallow	×	The shallow binding operator states that subtask can be freely adapted. This meaning is violated by such a nesting. Therefore it is not allowed.
(exempted) Shallow	(exempted) Deep	×	For the same reason as before such a nesting is also forbidden.
(exempted) Deep	(exempted) Shallow	×	The deep binding operator states that no adaptation is allowed in the subordinated task tree. This constraint is violated by a nested task which subtasks can be rearranged. Such a nesting is not permitted.
(exempted) Deep	(exempted) Deep	✓	As deep binding does not allow any adaptation this meta operator can be freely nested.

Table 6-19 Validity of Meta Operator Nesting

The reduction step is much more complex and distinguishes between base model and refining model. The reduction process itself is structured in four sub steps:

1. **Base Model: Shallow Binding Reduction.** According to the given interpretation of the meta operators in Table 6-18 the first step during the reduction of the base model is to remove all subordinated tasks marked with the (exempted) shallow binding operator as those sub trees can be freely defined in the refining model.

2. **Refining Model: Complex Task Reduction.** Complex tasks of the refining model which occur in the base model as leaf tasks are reduced in order to make base and refining task model comparable. This allows to compare the specification with respect to action refinement which is a common issue in interleaving semantics [van Glabbeek & Goltz, 2000]. This reduction is performed independent of any meta operators.

3. **Refining Model: Reduction of Exempted Tasks.** Tasks that are newly introduced in the model are not to be compared with the current base specification. Therefore subtasks of tasks marked with one of the exempted operators which have been introduced into the refining model in the current refinement step are chopped off.

4. **Based Model: Reduction of Ordinary Tasks.** If a task is not marked with any meta-operator and this applies recursively for all subtasks then these tasks can be removed from the CTML model. All meta operators can be dismissed to check refinement. The reduced based task model is created.

5. **Refining Task Model: Reduction of Ordinary Tasks.** In the same vein as in step 4 the not marked tasks of the refining model are also removed if recursively no subtasks are marked with a meta operator. All meta operators can be dismissed to check

refinement. The reduced refining task model is created. Moreover refinement of tasks marked with the shallow binding operator are reduced.

The complete process comprising renaming, validation and reduction can be considered as normalization of a CTML specification to its reduced form in ordinary syntax of CTML. Therefore the process is considered as function $norm(CTML^{meta})$ assigning each CTML model with meta operators a reduced one without meta operators. As base and refining model are normalized differently an index is attached to the function to denote the difference $(norm_{base}, norm_{ref})$

Having reduced the base and refining model the reduced version of each model is derived. This model provides the means to derive the mandatory scenario, traces respectively, in order to test for refinement of different kinds.

Definition 6-35 ($=_{MS}$− **Mandatory Scenario Equivalence**)**:** Let $CTML_A^{meta}$ and $CTML_B^{meta}$ be two CTML specifications with meta operators, C_{A_i} and C_{B_i} the selected configurations of $CTML_A^{meta}$ $CTML_A$ and $CTML_B^{meta}$, respectively, then $CTML_A^{meta}$ and $CTML_B^{meta}$ are mandatory scenario equivalent iff:

$$\langle CTML_A^{meta}, C_{A_i}\rangle =_{MS} \langle CTML_B^{meta}, C_{B_i}\rangle \Leftrightarrow \langle norm_{base}(CTML_A^{meta}), C_{A_i}\rangle =_{S} \langle norm_{ref}(CTML_B^{meta}), C_{B_i}\rangle$$

Accordingly scenario inclusion can be defined:

Definition 6-36 ($\subseteq_{MS}$− **Mandatory Scenario Inclusion**)**:** Let $CTML_A^{meta}$ and $CTML_B^{meta}$ be two CTML specifications with meta operators, C_{A_i} and C_{B_i} the selected configurations of $CTML_A^{meta}$ $CTML_A$ and $CTML_B^{meta}$, respectively, then $CTML_B^{meta}$ refines $CTML_A^{meta}$ by mandatory scenario inclusion iff:

$$\langle CTML_A^{meta}, C_{A_i}\rangle \subseteq_{MS} \langle CTML_B^{meta}, C_{B_i}\rangle \Leftrightarrow \langle norm_{base}(CTML_A^{meta}), C_{A_i}\rangle \subseteq_{S} \langle norm_{ref}(CTML_B^{meta}), C_{B_i}\rangle$$

Well-formedness Criteria for CTML with Meta Operators

In the following enumeration criteria of validity of the CTML specifications with meta operators are named. Naturally all criteria have to hold in order to validate a CTML specification successfully.

1. **Nesting of Meta Operators.** Table 6-19 already defines which kind of nesting of operators in one model is allowed. These rules are very important need to be observed.

2. **Conversion of Meta Operators.** During the diverse iteration cycles of refinement meta operators are naturally adapted. A shallow operator may become a deep operator. Therefore rules need to be provided defining also the valid adaptation of meta operators. The following rules apply:

    2.1. **Shallow to Deep.** The shallow binding operator can only be transformed into a deep binding operator. The rule is obvious with respect to their definition.

    2.2. **Exempted Shallow to Exempted Deep.** The same applies for the exempted operators. Only more a more rigid operators is allowed to use instead of an exempted shallow operator.

The Running Example – Refinement with Meta Operators

In Figure 6-26 an adapted version of the running example of the "Conference Session" is given. It is very similar to the one used to exemplify scenario equivalence and inclusion. Only *Introduce Session* is marked with the shallow binding operator and *Close Session* is marked with the deep binding operator.

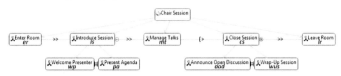

Figure 6-26 Base Specification with Meta Operators for Role Chairman

The model can be expressed by the following expression:

$$chairman_{base} = er \gg (wp| = |pa)^{\odot} \gg mt[> (aod| = |wus)^{\otimes} \gg lr$$

After having performed the first reduction step (1. Base Model: Shallow Binding Reduction) the model is reduced to this model:

$$chairman_{base_{red1}} = er \gg is \gg mt[> (aod| = |wus)^{\otimes} \gg lr$$

Now the final reduction step for the base model is performed which is only performed to reduce time and calculation steps while doing the refinement check (4. Based Model: Reduction of Ordinary Tasks).

$$chairman_{base_{red2}} = is^{\odot} \gg (aod| = |wus)^{\otimes}$$

The refining model is given in Figure 6-27. *Introduce Session* has been redefined and *Manage Talks* is not considered as atomic anymore. Moreover the *Leave Room* has been dismissed.

Figure 6-27 Refinement of Base Specification with Meta Operators for Role Chairman

The corresponding task expression is:

$$chairman_{ref} = er \gg (cpp| = |git)^{\odot} \gg (met^*[> tft)[> (aod| = |wus)^{\otimes}$$

Further refined tasks from the base specification are reduced according to step 2 (Refining Model: Complex Task Reduction):

$$chairman_{ref_{red1}} = er \gg (cpp| = |git)^{\odot} \gg mt[> (aod| = |wus)^{\otimes}$$

Next task marked with one of the exempted operators are reduced from the refining model (3. Refining Model: Reduction of Exempted Tasks). In this example no exempted operators are used. Therefore this step can be skipped.

$$chairman_{ref_{red2}} = chairman_{ref_{red1}}$$

The final step of normalization of the refining model comprises the reduction of ordinary tasks not marked with any of the meta operators (5. Refining Task Model: Reduction of Ordinary Tasks.):

$$chairman_{ref_{red2}} = is^{\odot} \gg (aod| = |wus)^{\otimes}$$

In both models the meta operators are removed. Now, the refinement check can be performed according to the previously defined scenario equivalence and scenario inclusion:

$$sceanrios(chairman_{base_{red2}}) = sceanrios(chairman_{ref_{red2}}) =$$

$$scenarios(is \gg (aod| = |wus)) = \{\langle is, aod, wus, \checkmark \rangle, \langle is, wus, aod, \checkmark \rangle\}$$

Therefore, $chairman_{base} =_{MS} chairman_{ref}$ holds.

6.5.4 Conclusion

In the last sections different notions of refinement for CTML have been defined and assessed, namely trace equivalence, scenario equivalence and inclusion, structural equivalence and inclusion and mandatory scenario equivalence and inclusion. Each of the introduced comparison semantics has its assets and drawbacks. Whereas behavioral comparison semantics are more suitable to analyze the runtime behavior of the model, structural properties can be better inspected via structural refinement. Scenario equivalence is the finest-grained semantic model for CTML proposed here (more fined-grained models can be defined such as bisimulation equivalence but are not suitable for CTML). Scenario equivalence is however rather inappropriate for model adaptation as it allows no additional scenarios. In contrast, scenario inclusion demands the scenarios of the base specification but also allows additional scenarios. Such a definition is much more suitable for adaptation processes in the software engineering lifecycle. The same argumentation can be applied for trace equivalence and inclusion. The drawback of trace semantics in general is the missing notion of successful termination. Structural equivalence and inclusion is, as stated before, a suitable validation device in order to asses that two models are structurally similar. Both comparison semantics do not demand any behavioral similarity. The most flexible notions of semantics are mandatory scenario equivalence and inclusion because the importance of a certain task within the refinement process is interactively assigned by so called meta operators. During the refinement check the base and refining models are analyzed with respect to the used meta operators in order to calculate the mandatory scenarios of each model. Mandatory scenario equivalence demands that both models need to define the same set of mandatory scenarios whereas mandatory scenario inclusion demands that the refining model needs to be comprise all mandatory scenario of the base model.

The defined refinement relations have not been defined to assess the quality of a certain model, but to compare a base specification with its refinement. The comparison criteria definitely change during the development process which makes it unfeasible to define only one comparison semantics. Therefore, the various comparison semantics defined in the last sections serve as toolbox and have to be smoothly integrated into the interaction development process. Such integration is proposed in Chapter 7.

6.6 Deadlock Analysis

Deadlock analysis has been tackled in a various fields of application. Having selected a semantic model with a notion of successful termination deadlocks can be detected. Informally with respect to LTSs a deadlock can occur if a LTS state exists which is not final and has no outgoing transitions.

Definition 6-37 (Deadlock on LTS): According to the Definition 4-1 a LTS is defined by the tuple $\langle Q, \mathcal{A}ct, \rightarrow, q_0 \rangle$, then a deadlock can occur in a LTS iff:

$$\exists q \in Q, t \in \mathcal{A}ct^*: q_0 \xrightarrow{t} q \wedge \forall a \in \mathcal{A}ct, \forall x \in Q: (q, a, x) \notin \rightarrow$$

Please note that $\mathcal{A}ct^*$ does not contain the symbol for successful termination ($\checkmark$). The definition states a certain state q have to be reachable via the action relation (without using $\checkmark$) and that this certain state has no outgoing transition defined by the action relation.

Accordingly deadlock freedom on LTS can be defined.

Definition 6-38 (Deadlock Freedom on LTS): According to the Definition 4-1 a LTS is defined by the tuple $\langle Q, \mathcal{A}ct, \rightarrow, q_0 \rangle$, then a LTS is deadlock free iff:

$$\nexists q \in Q, t \in \mathcal{A}ct^*: q_0 \xrightarrow{t} q \wedge \forall a \in \mathcal{A}ct, \forall x \in Q: (q, a, x) \notin \rightarrow$$

Using the semantic mapping defined before these definitions can be easily applied to CTML specifications.

The Running Example – Deadlock Analysis

By only using the temporal operators deadlock cannot be modeled. However, with the usage of arbitrary preconditions assigned to tasks deadlocks can be easily introduced into a model. In the example in Figure 6-28 a slightly adapted version of the task model for the role *Chairman* is used. In the given example another task specifying how to login into the conference management system is defined. Such a system is used to provide additional information regarding the current talk and the progress about the whole session. In detail, the task defines that first the login screen is presented and the user needs to provide her credentials. Finally the system either accepts or refuses the credentials. During managing a talk the chairman can mark a certain talk as given once it is finished. However this is only possible if the login has been successful which is expressed by the corresponding precondition.

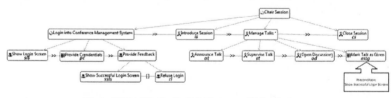

Figure 6-28 Specification for Role Chairman with Deadlock

According to Definition 6-37 a deadlock exists if not further action can be executed and $\checkmark$ has not been propagated yet. Such trace is $\langle sls, pc, rl, is, at, st, od \rangle$. After having executed *Open Discussion* the next potential executable task would be *Mark Talk as Given*. However this is prohibited by the precondition which requires *Show Successful Login Screen* to be executed earlier.

6.7 Tool Support for the CTML

One of the requirements for an adequate task modeling language stated in Section 5.1.2 is the supply of tool support for that language. To effectively make use of a language suitable tools need to be provided in order to foster creation, sharing, editing, visualization and usage in general of the language. For CTML four main areas of function can be identified: Creation and Editing, Visualization and Validation, Verification, and Interfaces. All areas are covered by the tool support for CTML and explained in the subsequent paragraphs. First, a basic introduction about the architecture of the tool support is given. Next, each area named above is examined thoroughly accompanied by screenshots exemplifying the usage of the tools. Finally some concluding remarks about the tool suite are given.

6.7.1 Architecture of the CTML Tool Suite

Software engineering usually comprises several languages edited and used in different IDEs. However this is a rather insufficient situation. The process model should be supported by one IDE covering all stages in which computer assisted manipulation of artifacts is taking place. Therefore the different components of CTML are all integrated into one environment. Moreover as other modeling languages are also relevant for CTML the de facto standard for coding and modeling has been selected as foundation for the CTML components, namely the Eclipse Platform as it furthermore supports a solid and flexible plug-in concept and diverse supportive libraries for development which are shown in Figure 6-29 on the first four layers. The EMF framework has been used for modeling the entities of CTML which also covers serialization to share models. Moreover a rudimental editor comes with EMF. On top of EMF the GEF and GMF framework have been used to create visual editors and validation tools. On top of that, custom code has been implemented separated in different modules. Hence, third level libraries have been used by certain modules which is denoted by black lines.

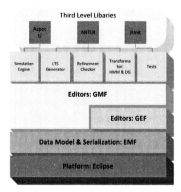

Figure 6-29 Layered Architecture of the CTML Tool Suite and its Modules

6.7.2 Creation and Editing

The creation of CTML models can be become quite complex as multiple entities on different levels of abstractions are involved. For each model in CTML (cooperation model, device model, location model, domain model, and task model) an appropriate visual editor has been implemented. Due to the fact that EMF always comes with a rudimental editor which is suitable for hierarchical models as it is tree-based multiple editors for a model exist. Figure 6-30 shows the high level editor for CTML models. It allows the designer to drag-and-drop the high level entities on the canvas in order to create the corresponding model entities. The palette is used to select the desired type of modeling element. Moreover, after having defined the CTML model tools exist to start or stop the current animation.

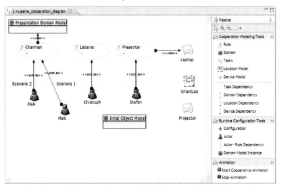

Figure 6-30 Visual Editor for Cooperation Model

After the high level entities are specified the model needs to be gradually refined. The meaning of the modeled elements can be defined by other visual editors (e.g., a role is specified by a task expression). A model created with the task model editor is given in Figure 6-2. In the same vein as in the Cooperation Model tasks can be easily created by simply dragging them onto the canvas. Relations, such as hierarchical decomposition and temporal operator, can be defined by connecting the tasks as desired. Syntactical validation is also supported. To use CTML effectively also preconditions and effects need to be defined. Figure 6-31 shows the dialog which supports the convenient creation of preconditions and effects for tasks. It can be accessed by opening the properties of tasks. The tabs are used to distinguish between the definition of preconditions and effects (a). The select box helps to distinguish between the different types of preconditions, effects respectively (e.g., location precondition, device precondition) in order to support their creation (b). A text field can be used to enter the preconditions, effects respectively by hand (c). Moreover for each type assistance in terms of selection support is provided (d) which helps to avoid syntactical errors.

Figure 6-31 Tool Support for Designing Preconditions and Effects

Visual editors for all types of models exist. Location modeling is supported by a bird view on the SmartLab to provide visual means to design the relevant location for the CTML specification. Device modeling is performed by a visual state chart editor. The domain model is defined by a UML class diagram. An appropriate editor is provided by the EMF framework delivered with the Eclipse distribution.

Specifying each entity separately can be quite cumbersome. Therefore the wizard pattern has been applied to create CTML specifications conveniently from scratch. A top-down approach is followed which starts with role creation (left hand side of Figure 6-32) and assigning appropriate task models (top of right hand side of Figure 6-32). Moreover devices and corresponding device specifications can be designed, created respectively. Eventually a configurations can created to test the model immediately. In this vein the creation process of CTML models is guided.

Figure 6-32 Two Wizard Pages of the CTML Creation Wizard

6.7.3 Visualization and Validation

Due to the complexity of a fully dressed CTML specification various visualizations and validation tools are offered. First and foremost the CTML editor shows the Cooperation Model with its Configurations (see Figure 6-30). It can be adequately adapted to emphasize the entities of interest (e.g., hiding of links and/or nodes of certain types, rearrangement, etc.). Moreover for each model several views may exist to highlight the model from different viewpoints. The same applies for all other graphical editors (e.g., location model, device model, etc.). Moreover for each model a tree-based editor generated by the EMF framework is integrated into the tool environment.

For validation purposes CTML specifications can be animated on different levels of abstractions and using different visualizations. A CTML model can be created following a top-down or bottom-up approach. In either way the different animation tools can be used which are explained here following a bottom-up approach.

Having created a task expression for a role using the graphical editor shown in Figure 6-2 it can be animated. During an animation the model is transformed into an executable specification according to the semantics defined in Section 6.4. In animation mode tasks are highlighted according to their current state by visual signs as shown in Figure 6-6. Tasks can be executed by double click or selection in a special widget. Further information such as execution history is displayed using other widgets. In the context of a Cooperation Model this animation enables the isolated validation of task expressions for roles. Naturally not all preconditions can be evaluated on this level of abstraction (e.g., a task precondition of another role).

Another entity which can be animated is the device model. Devices are specified by means of finite state machines (see Figure 6-12) whose behavior is defined by the words they produce. More precisely, within a certain state a set of action (being element of the alphabet) are accepted. In order to validate such a device specification an animation has also been implemented. In essence, the current state the finite state machine is in is visualized and the outgoing actions (transitions) can be selected. In this vein, the state space can be interactively explored.

Please note that the domain and location model do not have a behavior in a sense but give structure to the CTML model and are used to constrain the task execution. Therefore no behavioral animation of the models themselves can be defined. However for all editors syntactical and semantic checks are offered to check the rationale of the current edited artifact.

Have defined the low level entities of the CTML model the Cooperation Model can be designed (see Figure 6-30). This model actually consolidates the previously defined models, such as the device model. Due to the various specifications involved the fully-dressed CTML model can become quite complex and needs means for validation as well. In the same vein as for a single task expression an animation of a certain configuration can be started. For each actor a task animation is created and visualized (such an animation is given in Figure 6-7). Moreover when instantiating the animation the models to be considered during animation can be selected (so called Simulation Modes, see Section 6.1.2). This allows for testing the CTML model from different viewpoints and emphasizes a certain model (e.g., the impact of the location model on the CTML model). As the state of the current environment (the accumulation of device states, location of actors, etc.) is of importance during animation to evaluate preconditions and apply effects another widget display this information to the software designer.

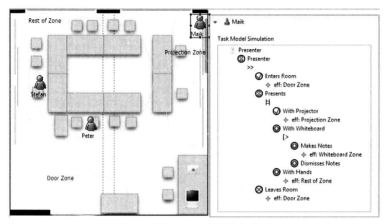

Figure 6-33 2D-View on CTML Animation

In order to make the animation more realistic another visualization of the animation of a CTML model has been implemented which is depicted in Figure 6-33. It uses the specified location model as basis to display the actors and their current position with respect to the (initial) locations. The actors can be selected to execute one of its tasks shown on the right hand side of Figure 6-33. This type of animation is especially helpful if location information is considered as particular important for the CTML model as changes in the location of actors can directly be investigated (which is the case in our experimental infrastructure, see Section 5.1.1).

6.7.4 Verification

Animation of CTML models is suitable to interactively explore the model and its state space. However due to the complexity certain features of the model may be kept concealed. Therefore more rigorous methods are needed to detect erroneous models. The CTML Verifier has been implemented to enable the software designer to perform refinement checks and deadlock analysis with respect to the definitions in Section 6.5 and 6.6.

The tool support for refinement checks can be accessed by the project explorer through the selection of two artifacts on which refinement is to be checked. These can either be fully-dressed CTML models or task trees (task expressions). Moreover several configurations of the same CTML specification can be checked for refinement as well. In Figure 6-34 the refinement check dialog for two task trees is depicted. Several properties can be adapted in order to make use of the different refinement types defined in Section 6.5. In order to ease the selection of properties predefined profiles exist which implement the guidelines of suitable refinement relation with respect to the development stages (a, see Section 7.3 for details). Besides that, it has to be specified which model is the base and refining model for this particular refinement check (b). Next, the concrete properties of this check are selected (c, e.g., which type of refinement: behavioral and/or structural, whether meta operators are taken into account, comparison semantics, and type of refinement (inclusion, equivalence, restriction)).

Finally, a name mapping can be defined in order to allow the user to rename tasks during adaptation. After entering these details or selecting a predefined profile which is part of the development methodology presented in Chapter 7 the refinement check is performed. The result is presented and if it is negative a counterexample is given.

Figure 6-34 Refinement Dialog for two CTML Models

6.7.5 Interfaces

As already discussed earlier task modeling is not the only activity during interaction design and implementation. In order to continue design and implementation within the same tool suite (semi) automatic transformations have been implemented whose results can be further adapted using the newly created or already existing editors integrated into the Eclipse IDE. More precisely, an interactive approach has been chosen to create dialog models based on CTML specifications (see Section 7.4.1) which is fully integrated and supported by the CTML Editor and Dialog Graph Editor. Basically after having created the task model a new dialog graph is created using the appropriate Eclipse Wizard. Then, the CTML specification is imported in the dialog graph and can be used as advised in Section 7.4.1 or in [Reichart *et al.*, 2004]. In order to use task models for implicit interaction an automatic transformation to HMMs has been implemented which serve as input for the intention recognition module of the SmartLab. In this approach CTML models are annotated with additional information to synthesize the HMM (see Section 7.4.2). During creation of the CTML model this kind of information can be added using the property view. Having finished task modeling a right click on the model is used to generate the HMM. An appropriate HMM Editor has also been implemented to further adjust the generated artifact. After that, it can also be exported into C Code which is used to operate the intention recognition system.

6.7.6 Conclusion

Tool support is a prerequisite to effectively make use of a modeling language like CTML. In the last sections the tool support for CTML has been presented from different viewpoints. In the beginning of the explanations the architecture of the tool suite has been examined. It is an Eclipse based tool which employs different libraries of the Eclipse community and other third parties. Beside the graphical editors which are based on the GMF and GEF framework different software modules have been implemented in order to implement CTML and its development approach.

Afterward the major functionalities provided by the editors and implemented modules are presented in detail. First, the creation and editing of CTML model and sub models have been explained, then different validation techniques are highlighted which are used to improve CTML models. Subsequently the interface of the refinement checker has been presented and its rationale is explained. It implements gradual refinement during the major phases of software engineering as proposed in Chapter 7. Finally the interfaces to subsequently used design artifacts have been shown. Concluding it can be stated the all phases in which CTML is relevant during interaction development are supported by the tool suite presented in the last sections.

Chapter 7
CTML Development Approach

In the last chapter CTML has been investigated in-depth. Now, the integration of CTML into a development process for interaction design is shown. It is based on an iterative, incremental model and offers several interfaces to other artifacts. CTML has been designed to specify the potential behavior and interaction in SmEs. Obviously the task model is not the only artifact involved during the software engineering lifecycle. Therefore task modeling needs to be applied in the appropriate phases and suitable artifacts need to be provided to derive a task model or being derivable from a task model.

It has already been shown that CTML has been developed for early phases of development and therefore the development approach primarily focuses on these stages. Three different phases are considered within the CTML development approach, namely analysis, requirements specifications and design. Common phases such as implementation, test, and maintenance are not covered by CTML as other artifacts are used in these phases. Two reasons can be stated why CTML primarily focuses on early stages of development:

- In SmEs requirements engineering is currently no standard discipline. Solutions are usually technical driven and thorough analysis and requirements elicitation is not performed.

- A lack of incorporation of user needs is observable. This issue actually relates to the first issue as user needs are gathered within the early stages of development.

Based on the insights of Section 3.2 an iterative, incremental process model for SmE is proposed to incorporate the principle of UCD and HCSE. The advantages of such an approach are the incorporation of the users' needs, short iteration and feedback cycles, and user involvement. In theory and practice it has been shown that iterative, incremental development approaches can be combined with UCD and HCSE [Göransson *et al.*, 2003] though the combination is not the case in general.

The named principles of UCD and HCSE cannot be implemented by the language itself but by guidelines how to use the language and the process model of the software system under construction. For example, user involvement cannot be provided by the language but by process model which demands user involvement to review each increment. Contrary, the tool support and the language may offer visualizations and prototypes which are understandable by the user to support user involvement. From our point of view task models in general, and CTML in particular, are able to support the principles of UCD and HCSE if employed in an appropriate process model. Task models enable rapid prototyping to fasten feedback cycles, are understandable by laypersons supporting user involvement and specify the system under construction from users' perspective.

Analysis   Interaction Specification   Detailed Interaction Design

Figure 7-1 Process Model for CTML for SmEs

The process model for early stages in SmEs is depicted in Figure 7-1. There are three different stages, namely Analysis, Interaction Specification, and Detailed Interaction Design, which roughly congruent to the classical software engineering phases analysis, requirements, and design but primarily focus on interaction development taking into account the special constraints of SmEs. Preliminary results have been published in [Wurdel *et al.*, 2008c]. During Analysis the interaction of the users are analyzed. When developing the SmE from scratch the pure human to human interaction is analyzed. However this is usually not the case. With the advent of cell phones, laptops and other mobile devices certain components constituting the SmE under construction are already present. Still, the purpose of the analysis phase is to analyze the human interaction in such an environment in order to have a valid image of a "normal" situation. Based upon that, the requirements with respect to interaction can be derived. The advantage of a dedicated analysis stage is that the existing work processes can be taken into account in the requirement specification (this issue has been investigated in Section 3.4.2). This allows for smooth transition between existing and new software system and accounts for user acceptance. The requirements are specified with respect to the whole SmE. It should be avoided to already specify which device is used to achieve a certain goal but a more abstract view is recommended. More precisely, the envisioned interaction flow of users and SmE is to be taken into account. Also other valuable facts can be specified in this stage: the domain types and locations relevant for executing tasks can be integrated to determine the dependencies of tasks and the environment. The result of the Interaction Specification phase should be an abstract interaction flow between user and system which can be enriched with domain and location information. In this vein an abstract interaction flow is specified which can be gradually refined in later stages. Interactions are reified with respect to modality and assignment to devices. This is performed in the Detailed Interaction Design stage. On this level of abstraction the device types potentially present in the SmE are specified with respect to their behavior (functions, states) and static properties (in- and output capabilities, network access, etc.). Moreover the binding of tasks to these devices is considered. "Which device types may support in which circumstances the execution of a task?" is a question to be answered here. The result of this stage is a fully dressed CTML specification being designed to serve as input for implicit or explicit interaction.

To be able to follow the interaction design process depicted in Figure 7-1 different means are offered to create the corresponding artifacts and increase their quality. The arrows in the figure already indicate the useful instruments for each stage. Naturally this mapping is rather a hint and can be adapted according to the needs in the process. The instruments used during the development lifecycle are explained in the following enumeration (except for refinement as it has been explained extensively before). Furthermore reasons are given for the suitability of the instruments for certain phases:

- **Discussion and Feedback.** Site visits to discuss the current used software system are very helpful during analysis but also feasible to discuss requirements and concrete design proposals [Hackos & Redish, 1998]. During analysis interviews and observations are used to get a picture about the current work situation. In subsequent stages instantiations (mock-ups, prototypes) of requirements or designs can be used to visualize the system under construction for the end user. Based on that feedback can be provided.

- **Animation.** Having a specification formalism with an operational semantics supports the idea of animating the model to show its behavior in a very concrete way. Either an interactive walkthrough or an automated run can show the currently specified behavior. Following a model-based approach the specification can be gradually refined, enriched and transformed to create more sophisticated prototypes. Therefore animation is used in all phases of development presented in this thesis. Also different ways of animating the very same model can be helpful to highlight certain viewpoints of the model.

- **Validation.** Animation is one way to validate a model. However syntactical and semantic validations are other means to improve the quality of a model. Checking consistency and cross references between models are representatives of this utility. During analysis too rigid validation constraints can even be counterproductive. The more mature the model becomes the more rigid validation can and should be applied.

- **Prototyping.** An animation can be considered as abstract prototype. However paper prototypes and high fidelity prototypes are other types which are very helpful to show the current design. Even though prototyping is often considered as technique to detect usability flaws ([Walker *et al.*, 2002]) it is actually an excellent utility to elicit requirements (by example) and evaluate potential design solutions.

- **Verification.** As soon as specifications become quite complex formal methods are needed to keep track of the properties of the model. Deadlock analysis and refinement checks are representatives of verification. During very early stages of development formal methods may be a burden to the designer as they restrict the creativity of the design. As soon as the specifications become more stable verification is invaluable.

These instruments are used to drive the design of the whole process. Some of them are not only used in intra stage design but also for inter stage design meaning that they are helpful to transit from one stage to the other. More in detail, it is claimed that refinement is an excellent vehicle to close the gap between the stages of development. The difference between intra and inter stage design is that the adaptations are much more fundamental when moving from one phase to another. This needs to be taken into account by the refinement relations used. This issue is addressed in Section 7.3.1.

7.1 Involved Artifacts

As stated before the task model is not the only artifact used in the development lifecycle of interaction. To provide a solid basis for the explanations of the phases in detail each artifact is illuminated briefly. To further elaborate on these topics references to literature is given.

7.1.1 Scenarios

Scenarios are narrative text descriptions of the usage of a system. They are concrete (e.g., using real names) and do not contain choices or decisions to make. Therefore, they actually describe one way through the usage of a system or specify how a system has been used in the retrospective. In Section 5.1.2 an example of a scenario in the domain of SmEs is given. Scenarios are a helpful technique for brainstorming. They are easily to understand and explain. End user can be involved and new scenarios can be developed based on existing ones until the main scenarios of the system are covered. For further information about scenarios [Carroll, 1995] is suggested. Please note that scenario in this sense are similar but yet not identical to scenarios of a task model. Scenarios here are artificial stories how the system might be used in the future to analyze and elicit requirement.

7.1.2 Use Cases

In contrast to scenarios and similar to task models use cases are generalized descriptions. As such they specify a set of runs through the system (potentially all possible runs). Use cases are the de facto standard in industry for specifying functional requirements and the basic interaction flow of events between user and system. They specify the flow stepwise by text descriptions what is happening in each step. According to the guidelines defined by Cockburn use cases should start with the most common way a goal is achieved ("main success scenario") and then add extensions to the ordinary case [2001]. Use case diagrams visualize the relation of several use cases (extension, generalization). In most software development processes use case modeling and specification are major steps while defining the requirements of the system under construction (e.g., RUP).

Figure 7-2 depicts an example of a use case with respect to the scenario of a presentation at a conference. First, the name of the use case can be seen ("Give Presentation") followed by the preamble. The primary actor is the subject who wants to achieve the goal and proactively interacts with the system. Secondary actors are supportive but do not take the initiative. Then the level of detail is specified which determines the granularity of the use case as they are modeled on different levels of abstraction. Here in the given example a precondition is defined denote the necessary state under which the use case can be started. After the preamble the main success scenario starts. It is a stepwise text-based description of the main path through the use case. The actions 1-6 represent the main success scenario. In action 6 a loop is described informally. Naturally the main success scenario does not cover all cases. Therefore extensions to it can be described. First, the condition under which the extension occurs and the entry point is specified (e.g., alternative path for action 5. is 5a. when time is expired).

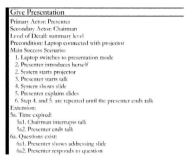

Give Presentation
Primary Actor: Presenter
Secondary Actor: Chairman
Level of Detail: summary level
Precondition: Laptop connected with projector
Main Success Scenario:
    1. Laptop switches to presentation mode
    2. Presenter introduces herself
    2. System starts projector
    3. Presenter starts talk
    4. System shows slide
    5. Presenter explains slides
    6. Step 4. and 5. are repeated until the presenter ends talk
Extension:
5a. Time expired:
    5a1. Chairman interrupts talk
    5a2. Presenter ends talk
6a. Questions exist:
    6a1. Presenter shows addressing slide
    6a2. Presenter responds to question

Figure 7-2 Use Case "Give Presentation" in Summary Level

Both artifacts explained before are requirement elicitation and specification tools. In the following paragraphs design artifacts for implicit and explicit interaction are explained as they are relevant in subsequent development steps based on CTML specifications.

7.1.3 Dialog Model

AUI specification languages exist in great numbers as shown in Section 3.3.2. Here, we focus on a particular representative as it is the most suitable artifact for GUI based system and integrates excellent with task modeling in general and CTML in particular. The dialog model introduced by Reichart *et al.* is an abstract visual representation of dialog structures based on task models [2004]. Formally it is a typed graph structure in which nodes represent different types of dialogs and transitions are represented by edges (see Figure 7-3). A dialog can only be instantiated once at a time but other can run concurrently (single dialog view) or multiple instances may exist (multiple dialog view). Moreover, another type of dialog blocks the whole application (model dialog view). Hence, different transitions exist. A sequential transition defines that the source dialog disappears while the target dialog is displayed. A concurrent transition creates a new dialog without close the source dialog when activated.

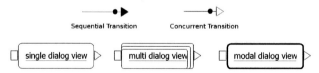

Figure 7-3 Modeling Elements in Dialog Model of Reichart

The integration of task modeling and AUIs, such as the dialog model, has been a research issue in HCI for years. A smooth transition from a high level model to AUI model is very difficult as work processes are mapped to abstract UI components [Limbourg *et al.*, 2001]. Semi-automated processes such the one of Reichart *et al.* exhibit higher quality with respect to usability than the generated solutions of Limbourg *et al.* Actually, in GUI-based systems a dialog is a grouping of tasks. Exactly this approach is implemented by the dialog model presented here. Tasks of a task model, such as a CTML specification, are assigned to dialog views. The execution of a task may or may not trigger a transition. The informal semantics are defined by the combination of the task model animation and the visibility of a task within the current visible dialogs during animation. If a task is not visible in any dialog it is not executable. Therefore dialog models add additional execution constraints to the task model.

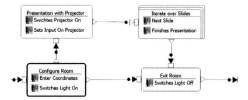

Figure 7-4 Example of Dialog Graph for "Give Presentation"

Figure 7-4 shows a dialog graph based on a CTML model for the role *Presenter*. *Configure Room* is the starting view. The user can either enter coordinates or can switch the light on. When giving a presentation the next view to be shown is *Presentation with Projector*. In this view the projector is configured. By setting the slides on the projector the next view becomes visible (without closing the prior one due to the concurrent transition). This view may be instantiated several times. When executing the task *Finishes Presentation* the final dialog appears which can be used to switch off the light.

The most expedient property of the dialog graph is its capability of being animatable. In the same vein as CTML, dialog graphs (enriched with CTML specifications) can be interactively explored. This integrates with the principles of agile development, UCD and HCSE. In Section 7.4.1 this approach is exemplified.

In order to continue the MB-UI chain an export to XUL can be triggered. Then, the abstract UI components can be replaced by more suitable ones based on the research conducted by Wolff [Wolff *et al.*, 2005]. By adapting the generated XUL models the links to the more abstract models (task model, dialog graph) can be retained allowing for reverse engineering of the UI.

7.1.4 Hidden Markov Model

For intention recognition probabilistic models are one way to model the structure of actions of persons. The advantage of such an approach is that uncertainty can be expressed which is important when handling sensor data (e.g., location tracking). HMMs are the most simple Bayesian Networks as the state of the system is represented by a single variable [Russell & Norvig, 2003]. Moreover the system model is first order Markovian: the current state depends only on the previous state and no other states. By further taking into account that typically the current state of the system cannot be observed directly, observations depending on (not observable) states are needed. So informally a HMM is a tuple consisting of a set of states, an initial probability of each state, a state transition relation with each transition having a certain probability to occur and a set of observations which are mapped to states with a certain probability to occur.

The HMM can be used to infer the current state of the system based on the observations and the assigned probabilities. Different algorithms exist to do so which are extensively explained in [Russell & Norvig, 2003]. However the algorithms on the HMM are not of interest here but the model is used as design artifact with respect to intention recognition. More in detail, the question of deducing the current state of the system from the observations can be straightforwardly applied to the human behavior within a SmE. Therefore in our research lab the intention recognition module is driven by HMMs. One issue faced by this kind of model is state explosion. As the system needs to be represented by a single state numerous states are needed to model the system adequately for sizable systems. This issue is addressed by CTML as well. In order to do so the model is introduced here formally.

Definition 7-1 (Hidden Markov Model): A Hidden Markov Model is defined by the tuple $\langle S, \pi, T, \tau, O, P \rangle$ with S being a set of numerable states, $\pi: S \to \mathbb{R}$ assigning each state an initial probability with $\sum_{s \in S} \pi(s) = 1$, $T \subseteq S \times S$ being the state transition relation and $\tau: T \to \mathbb{R}$ mapping transitions to probabilities with $\forall s \in S: \sum_{(s,s') \in T} \tau((s,s')) = 1$ representing state transition probabilities. O being a set of observations and $P: S \times O \to \mathbb{R}$ assigning states and observations a probability with $\forall s \in S: \sum_{o \in O} P(s, o) = 1$.

This rather abstract definition is exemplified by the following example which is depicted in Figure 7-5. Let $\langle S, \pi, T, \tau, O, P \rangle$ be the HMM with $S = \{One, Two\}$, $\pi(x) = 0.5$ for all $x \in S$. Let further $T = S \times S$, $\tau(One, One) = \tau(Two, Two) = 0.9$ and $\tau(One, Two) = \tau(Two, One) = 0.1$, using $O = \mathbb{R}$ with $P(One, i) = N_{(-1,2)}(i)$, $P(Two, i) = N_{(1,1)}(i)$. $N_{(\mu,\sigma)}$ denotes the normal distribution with mean μ and standard deviation σ. On the left hand side the state space of the HMM with its transition probabilities and initial probabilities is shown. On the right hand side the observation depending on the current state of the HMM are given.

Please note that the given example sticks to the formal definition of P even though the normal distribution is used as observation probability. The normal distribution is a function over the observations and therefore assigns each observation in the example an element of $\mathbb{R}$.

In a more concrete example according to the experimental infrastructure in the SmartLab the set of observations can be a set of locations defined by x-y coordinates (e.g., $O = \{(0,0), (100,150), (250,250)\}$) with $P(One, (0,0)) = P(One, (100,150)) = 0.3$ and $P(One, (250,250)) = 0.4$. An according definition needs to specified for $P(Two, o)$.

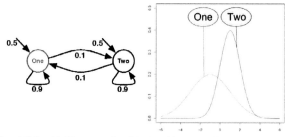

Figure 7-5 Graphical Representation of the Transition Model of the Example HMM

The introduced formal definition is used in Section 7.4.2 to formally defined how a CTML specification can be used to synthesize a HMM.

7.1.5 Conclusion

The artifacts examined in the previous sections have been partially designed for totally different purposes. However, all are relevant for the CTML development process. Whereas the first two models (scenarios and use cases) are used to support the design of a fully-dressed CTML model the latter two (dialog graph and HMM) are subsequent artifacts which can be derived based on a CTML specification.

Scenarios are very handy during very early stages of development as they help to interact with the end user and let one specify which tasks are performed by whom in the current setting. As it is stated in [Göransson *et al.*, 2003] use cases are the prevalent specification mechanism for requirements nowadays. Here use cases are considered as an intermediate specification helpful to specify the abstract interaction flow between SmE and user. Next, task models are used to specify the interaction more precisely with respect to modality, needed devices, location information and domain dependencies. However design is not finished here. Task models can be further transformed or derived. For explicit interaction the dialog graph formalism is considered as most suitable as it tackles the mapping problem stated in [Limbourg *et al.*, 2001] best. In a dialog graph the tasks relevant for the GUI are grouped and transitions between them are defined. A suitable further tool suite and development chain is provided to improve prototypes and eventually created the final UI. For implicit interaction probabilistic models are used. A first version of a HMM can be derived based on a CTML model. Further adaptations are usually necessary to design the detailed behavior not captured within the task model. The HMMs are employed to operate inference algorithms. The semantic relations of the artifacts are depicted in Figure 7-6.

7.2 Development Steps and Artifacts

During the development lifecycle which is shown in Figure 7-1 the involved artifacts are of different importance. As a rule of thumb, with respect to Figure 7-6 the artifacts on top are rather used in early stages and as more as fading to the bottom artifacts are more dominant in design. The mapping of artifacts to development phase and the used instruments to enhance the models is explained in Table 7-1. It actually combines Figure 7-1 and Figure 7-6.

Phase	Artifacts	Instruments
Analysis	Scenario, Use Case, Task Model	Discussion and Feedback, Animation, Validation, Refinement
Interaction Specification	Use Case, Task Model	Animation, Validation, Prototyping, Refinement, Verification
Detailed Interaction Design	Task Model, Dialog Graph, Hidden Markov Model, XUL	Animation, Validation, Prototyping, Refinement, Verification

Table 7-1 CTML Development Process, Artifacts, and Instrument

During analysis scenario, use cases and task models can be used depending on the system to be analyzed and the envisioned system. If interaction specification is to be emphasized in the current project task modeling is a suitable choice even for analysis purposes. However if the system is to be developed from scratch scenarios are useful to elicit the current work processes and specify them as use case or task model. The instruments to be used in this kind of phase to effectively make use of the models are first and foremost discussion and feedback with the end user, customer respectively, but also animating the first CTML specification can be very helpful to detect erroneous analysis models. Having specified some use cases and task models also syntactical and semantic validation may be helpful to rule out early defects.

In interaction specification scenarios are not useful as they are describing certain runs (one scenario – one run). More general description formalisms are needed. Use cases and task models are therefore more suitable. In general use cases are more abstract and independent of the type of modality and interaction devices and as such should be used before task modeling. Based on the specified use cases task models are designed. To assure consistency between both artifacts the approach of Sinnig can be used [2009]. Especially when already having designed task models during analysis they are suitable as a smooth transition from analysis to interaction specification is possible. Such a requirement specification is considered as contract between user, stakeholder respectively and software designer. This also applies for SmEs. To be able to create such a specification models are enhanced by the named instruments in Table 7-1. Animation and validation have the same purpose as in analysis. Prototyping is used to illuminate potential instantiations for the specified requirements and to collect feedback. More formal methods like refinement and verification of properties (such as deadlock freedom) can also be applied to assure quality and enhance models properly.

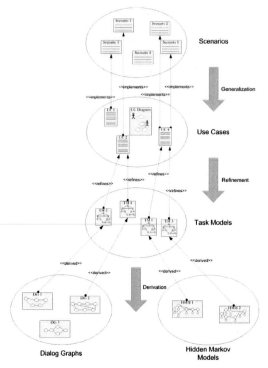

Figure 7-6 Semantic Relations of Involved Artifacts

In the detailed design phase only task models are still suitable. Use cases are not appropriate anymore as they only specify the interaction flow of user and the whole system. However in this stage the interaction is specified in a more concrete way. The device types constituting the environment are specified and their impact on the task world is designed. Therefore CTML specifications serve as foundation of this stage. However subsequent design artifacts are also used as design is not finished on the level of task modeling. Therefore for explicit interaction the dialog graph formalism and for implicit interaction the HMM are used. Naturally to continue design for explicit interaction via the MB-UI process the dialog model is transformed into AUI and final UI. UI description languages such as XUL are further used on this stage of the process.

In the last sections it has been examined which artifacts and instruments are used and applied to create valuable models for interaction design. However there are still some issues left. It is claimed that scenarios serve as input for use cases even though it has not been stated yet how to transit from a set of scenarios to a use case. The same applies for the task model. Moreover, it can be distinguished between intra stage transitions and inter stage transitions meaning that an artifact is either transformed in another in a certain development stage whereas the latter denotes the transformation of an artifact into another one between two stages of development. As task models are used on every stage of development their transition from one phase to another is of particular importance and is one of the major contributions of the thesis.

In order to provide guidance how artifacts are transformed to suit the needs of each phase properly the subsequent sections elaborate on these issues. More in detail, general advice is given how to work with scenarios, use case and task models and their transformations. Next, the transformations and their consistent adaptation during the CTML development lifecycle are examined thoroughly. Finally, the derivation of CTML models to design artifacts is explained.

7.3 Adapting CTML Specifications

Adaptation is a natural process in iterative incremental process models. The CTML development approach is no exception to this rule. In this section it is examined what constitutes valid refinement during the different steps of development in CTML.

Refinement can if applied appropriately be a very helpful device to ensure certain quality of the designed artifacts. It can furthermore support the transformation of artifacts and guide the phase transitions in a software engineering process. In essence, refinement can be a tool to avoid and detect failures. However a valid refinement check does neither state the correctness of the base nor of the refining model as it only indicates an adaptation which has been performed according to or contradict to the given refinement relation used. Whether a certain adaptation is useful or desired needs to be checked by the designer as it may contradict to the refinement relation proposed but has been performed at purpose. The interpretation of refinement within the whole development process is even more complicated. Refinement is a tool which is able to indicate erroneous adaptations and helps to ensure quality criteria but it cannot assure purposeful implementations.

7.3.1 Phase Transitions

Based upon the given explanations of the last section the adaptation mechanisms useful for the CTML development approach with respect to the involved artifacts are given in Table 7-2. In the first column the development stage or the transition phase of the two development stages are depicted. The second column specifies the artifact. The last column contains the instruments which are useful to enhance the particular artifact in this particular phase, phase transition respectively.

Phase / Transition	Artifact(s)	Instruments
Analysis	Scenario	Gradual Informal Refinement
	Scenario – Use Case	Informal Generalization
	Use Case	Structural Refinement
	Use Case – Task Model	Mapping of use case step to tasks

Phase / Transition	Artifact(s)	Instruments
From Analysis to Interaction Specification	Task Model	Refinement: Trace or Scenario Inclusion with Meta Operators, Structural Refinement
	Use Case	Restriction of User Choices [Sinnig, 2009]
	Use Case – Task Model	Restriction of User Choices [Sinnig, 2009]
Interaction Specification	Task Model	Refinement: Trace or Scenario Inclusion (with Meta Operators), Structural Refinement
	Use Case	Scenario Equivalence [Sinnig, 2009]
	Use Case – Task Model	Scenario Equivalence [Sinnig, 2009]
	Task Model	Refinement: Trace or Scenario Equivalence with Meta Operators, Structural Refinement
From Interaction Specification to Detailed Interaction Design	Task Model	Refinement: Scenario Equivalence with Meta Operators, Structural Refinement, Structural Refinement
Detailed Interaction Design	Task Model	Refinement: Scenario Equivalence (with Meta Operators), Structural Refinement

Table 7-2 Phase Transitions for each Artifact

As stated earlier all three artifacts are used during analysis of the current work processes and existing software systems. As scenarios are informal means to gather information and describe work processes in an end user friendly way only informal refinement can be performed. Existing scenarios are gradually refined by further detailing certain steps. When moving from scenarios to use case generalization is necessary as each scenario specifies a certain run whereas a use case specifies a set of runs (see Figure 7-6 for details). The generalization derives a set of use cases in which at least each scenario which is considered as relevant is represented by a run through a use case. This process cannot be supported by refinement checks as the scenario is informal. Once use cases are created they are refined as well. In [Sinnig, 2009] refinement relations between use cases and task models for different development phases are introduced. The approach is sound and partially used here. During analysis it is proposed to structurally enhance use cases meaning that previously atomic use case steps are further refined and detailed. When creating an analysis task model based on an analysis use case the relevant interactive parts of the use case are specified by means of tasks. The changes during analysis are rather fundamental and a flexible notion of refinement for such changes between use cases and task models does not exist. Therefore a mapping as described above is proposed. On the level of task modeling adaptations can be validated through the use of meta operators which have been explained earlier. They provide means to define what constitute a valid refinement in a flexible manner. On the analysis level major adaptations occur rather often. Due to this not too rigid refinement relations are needed. Therefore trace and scenario inclusion with meta operators are considered as valid during analysis. Moreover as models are designed gradual structural refinement is an excellent tool when adapting the model in a certain phase (intra stage transitions).

When moving from analysis to interaction specification only use cases and task models are considered as relevant as scenarios are too vague to describe the requirements with respect to interaction. Use cases are the standard device to specify functional requirements whereas task models are used to describe the UI requirements. However, usually the functional requirements are specified which are then examined with respect to the envisioned interaction. Therefore also use cases are relevant for this phase. Sinnig proposed to use a special notion of scenario refinement which only allows for restricting user choices. In this vein the basic set of scenarios are preserved but only potential interactions are restricted. Such an approach preserves the functional requirements defined in the use case but gives the freedom to adapt the interaction accordingly. Having created an analysis task model and using it to derive the UI requirements a flexible notion of refinement is mandatory as the analysis model represents the current work situation whereas the requirements model states the envisioned behavior with the software system under construction (see Section 3.4.2). Therefore refinement without meta operators is too rigid to allow a flexible adaptation process. With the support of meta operators it can easily be stated which tasks of the analysis task model (to which degree of detail) need to be preserved in the requirements model.

With the gradual refinement during interaction specification the models become more mature and stable. The more stable the model is the less adaptations are usually performed. Therefore the refinement relations can be more rigid as well. Structural refinement is especially for gradual refinement, meaning to detail a coarse-grained model, appropriate. For use cases the approach of Sinnig is taken up. Scenario equivalence is a rigid but valid refinement relation as once requirements are stated they need to be preserved in subsequent development to assure their valid implementation. The same applies for the transition of use cases to task models as requirements stated in the use case need to be transferred to the task model. On the level of task modeling the scenario equivalence with meta operators is considered as most suitable refinement relation. The scenarios based on the meta operator can be considered as contract of requirements which are needed to validly implement the system in the subsequent stages.

The defined requirements need to be transferred to the detailed design stage in which technology specific tasks are introduced. In order to do so scenario equivalence with meta operators are considered as important. During transformation design specific tasks are usually not marked with operator to avoid regarding them in the refinement checks.

Eventually, task model adaptations are performed in the detailed design stage. During that phase the most fine-grained CTML model is created. The model is gradually refined and therefore structural refinement can be used to guide this process. Moreover scenario equivalence based on meta operators is proposed as most suitable refinement relation. Obviously the refinement relation during design cannot be less rigid as in interaction specification to avoid corruption and weakening of the requirements. Therefore scenario equivalence with meta operator is used in this phase as well.

7.3.2 Guidance for Usage of Meta Operators

It has been shown that the meta operators allow a flexible way of prioritizing the tasks of a CTML specification. Naturally the defined operators have to be assigned with care with respect to the project stage (see Figure 7-1) and the selected refinement type (see Table 7-2). Therefore for each stage in which refinement with meta operators is applied advice is given how to make effectively use of the defined operators. The advice is based on the proposed refinement relations in Table 7-2.

Such general guidance is obviously not very detailed and cannot regard specific settings of the project and domain. During use particular guidance may evolve or can be defined which better suits the current needs. In this vein usage of patters can be created.

Analysis

The purpose of analysis is to understand users' behavior such that the requirements/design artifacts for the envisioned software can be defined as closely to "natural" human activity as possible. The analysis task model captures the current work situation and highlights elementary domain processes as well as exposes bottlenecks and weaknesses of the problem domain. It is important, that refinements of analysis models retain all crucial processes of the domain. As a rule of thumb, tasks that correspond to elementary business/interaction processes should be either marked with the shallow binding operator, or, if the process is crucial and fixed in its tasks, with the deep binding operator.

Starting with a coarse-grained analysis model leaf tasks are further refined until a fully-detailed version of the current work/interaction processes exists. During such chain of task models the shallow binding operators are very suitable. They allow for stating which tasks are necessary in subsequent development steps but allow for adapting their sub tasks. With respect to the transition to the interaction specification the shallow operators also allow for integrating the envisioned behavior smoothly. As a result the coarse-grained work processes on a high level of abstraction which are considered as necessary to be preserved in all subsequent steps should be marked with the shallow operators. Their definition can be adapted to the requirement and design in the according phases. The deep binding operators need to be used with caution. They define a fixed process within all subsequent adaptations. However if a new system is to be developed the work processes are usually restructured and reassigned to human/computer. Therefore this kind of operators can be a burden.

Finally, it is noted that an excessive usage of the meta operators is not advisable. When moving to the requirements stage, the changes to the model are usually substantial due to the introduction of the envisioned system. An overkill of meta operators (especially deep binding) unnecessarily restricts the specification of the requirements, which is often undesirable and counterproductive.

Interaction Specification

During interaction specification the UI requirements are manifested based on the analysis task model. Certain tasks are redefined and reallocated whereas others are dismissed or added. Generally, requirement task models specify the envisioned way tasks are performed using the system under development. The artifacts gathered during requirements specification are part of the contract between stakeholders about the future application. Therefore, it is recommended to mark crucial tasks with the deep binding operator to ensure that all refining models truly implement the requirements. However in certain situations a task is completely restructured due to design specific adaptations. If such a situation is anticipated the shallow binding operators should be used.

Detailed Interaction Design

During design, the various tasks of the requirements model need to be "instantiated" to a particular interaction technique. It is important to ensure that the design truly implements the requirements. Typically, when moving from requirements to design, mainly structural refinements are used, which further details a previously atomic task into a set of design specific subtasks. However as stated above, sometimes requirements are validly restructured (e.g., login task for a shop). Such an adaptation cannot be captured by structural refinement. Therefore, meta operators are used as well. During design the final task specification is created. For that reason basically all meta operators can be used here. Once a task tree is considered as final it can be marked with the deep binding operators. In this vein further adaptation is forbidden. If adaptations are envisioned for subsequent design steps only sub trees should be marked with the deep binding operators or the task itself should be marked with one of the shallow binding operators.

7.4 Creating the Design Artifacts

The artifacts and their relation used in CTML according to the process model are depicted in Figure 7-6. The figure shows that based upon task models both explicit and implicit interaction development are performed. In order to make the process feasible guidance is needed how to transit from a fully-dressed CTML specification to the artifact of choice for explicit interaction, namely dialog graphs, and implicit interaction, the HMM. In this section this issue is tackled. More precisely, a semi automatic approach for creating dialog graphs from CTML specifications is proposed as such an approach exhibits higher quality than fully automated algorithms even though they can be a good start. For implicit interaction an automated approach for the creation of HMMs is introduced. The main reason for that is the size of the HMMs for this field of application. HMMs become quite complex as the number of states easily reaches the thousand.

7.4.1 Explicit Interaction: From CTML Specifications to Dialog Graphs

The assignment of interactive tasks to dialog structures is a complex task and depends on various factors to create a usable system. The presented dialogs of the final UI need to be suitable for the device (e.g., suitable amount of tasks in one dialog on a small device) and user (e.g., avoid cognitive overload due to numerous devices). Due to the sensibility of the UI with respect to the task assignment an interactive approach is followed for CTML. Tasks are dragged & dropped onto dialogs in order to assign them. Moreover dialog transitions can be defined by means of task execution. Basically for each role a dialog graph can be defined individually which is instantiated during animation time, respectively runtime. If an actor fulfills several roles both dialog graphs are being displayed concurrently.

The Running Example

In accordance with the running example of the "Conference Session" a dedicated task model for explicit interaction is presented here.

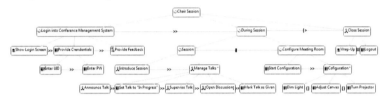

Figure 7-7 Task Model for Role Chairman for Explicit Interaction

In Figure 7-7 such a task tree for the role chairman is given. This model exhibits more tasks related to explicit interaction such as entering data or login/logout. On the left hand side of the task model authentication of the user for a conference management system is specified. During the talk of the presenter the chairman can set the talk in the system as in progress and eventually as been given. Moreover the chairman can configure the meeting room by dimming the light, adjusting the canvases and controlling the steerable projector.

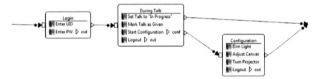

Figure 7-8 Dialog Graph for Role Chairman for Task Model in Figure 7-7

A possible dialog graph grouping the interactive tasks of the task model appropriately is given in Figure 7-8. The start dialog is called *Login* in which the credentials are entered. Having finished entering the password the dialog for the current talk is shown. While the talk is been given the progress can be set in the conference management system. First, the talk can be marked as in progress and eventually as finished. Moreover, a new dialog can be opened by executing *Start Configuration*. *Logout* finishes the use of the conference management system. In the *Configure Room* dialog the controllable components of the meeting room can be adjusted. Again, *Logout* leads to quitting the system.

Having created the dialog graph the entire model can be animated and validated based on the task model animation and the defined dialog model. Figure 7-9 depicts such an animation in progress. On the left hand side the abstract prototypes of the instantiations of the dialogs are shown (*During Talk* and *Configure Room* are active). Moreover, within each dialog the assigned tasks are represented as buttons. If a task is not executable the corresponding button is disabled. Enabled buttons can be pressed in order to trigger the execution of the task. Furthermore, on the right hand side the entire task model animation is shown. As the task model is a complete model of the behavior of the actor within the environment not all tasks are grouped in dialogs (e.g., *Introduce Session*). Therefore some tasks are executed without using the GUIs under construction. To tackle this issue those tasks need to be triggered independently which is possible on the right hand side.

Figure 7-9 Canonical Abstract Prototypes during Dialog Graph Animation

Such an abstract prototype is the first functional canonical prototypes following the model-based UI design paradigm. The designed navigation can be tested with respect to the temporal operators of the task model

The dialog graph can be exported as XUL file which is the AUI definition language in this process. The XUL files can be adapted and the buttons (serving as default placeholders for tasks) can be further refined and replaced by other AUI elements such as text fields, select boxes, etc. or complex AUI elements. In Figure 7-10 such a refined dialog based on the export of the dialog graph in XUL is shown. It is a rendered XUL file and represents the CUI, final UI respectively.

Figure 7-10 Refined Dialog "Configure Room"

7.4.2 Implicit Interaction: From CTML Specifications to Hidden Markov Models

The semantic domain of LTSs is actually very helpful to provide an interface to HMMs as the general structure of execution is quite similar. In the HMM nodes represent tasks under execution whereas edges represent transitions between those tasks under execution. The LTS specifies these information implicitly as each transition in the LTS represents a task under execution. Therefore, to derive the HMM transitions in the LTS are interpreted as nodes in the HMM. The same applies for the states in the HMM which are derived based on the transitions (actions) in the LTS.

According to Definition 7-1 more information need to be synthesized in order to create a valid HMM based on CTML specifications. More precisely, the derived LTS does not contain information about the initial probability of states, transition probability, observations and corresponding observation probabilities. In order to fill in those missing information two basic concepts are used. Either meta information are annotated to the task specification in order to synthesize the missing information or suitable default values are generated.

To be able to generate a HMM the following additional properties are necessary:

1. **Transition Probability.** The transition probability in the HMM is synthesized by assigning each atomic task of the CTML model a priority. The transition probability is then calculated by the relative priority of the task with respect to all enabled tasks.

$$prio: \bigcup_{r \in \mathcal{R}} Q\mathcal{T}_r \to \mathbb{N}$$

with $Q\mathcal{T}_r$ being the set of qualified task names for the role r.

2. **Set of Observations.** The set of observations is defined with respect to intention recognition. Such information is not specified within the process of task modeling. Usually observations are not constants but probability density functions mapping observations to probabilities (see the example in Section 7.1.4). The set of observations is denoted by $\mathcal{O}$.

3. **Observation Probability.** The same applies for the probability that a certain observation occurs. For each atomic task an observation is assigned. The probability of this observation is 1. Formally this is implemented by the function o.

$$o: \bigcup_{r \in \mathcal{R}} Q\mathcal{T}_r \to \mathcal{O}$$

Having defined all necessary preliminaries it is now continued with the derivation of the HMM based on a CTML specification and the necessary information above.

Let $\langle Coop, Conf \rangle$ be a CTML model, C_i the selected configuration with $C_i \in Conf$ and $\langle Q, \mathcal{A}ct, \to, q_0 \rangle$ (see Definition 4-1) be the assigned LTS according to Definition 6-27, then the corresponding HMM $\langle \mathcal{S}, \pi, \mathcal{T}, \tau, \mathcal{O}, \mathcal{P} \rangle$ is defined as follows:

- $\mathcal{S} = \{initial\} \cup \{(q_1, a) | (q_1, a, q_2) \in \to\}$
- $\pi(s) = \begin{cases} 1 & , if \ s = initial \\ 0 & , else \end{cases}$
- $\mathcal{T} = \begin{cases} \{(initial, (q_0, a)) | (q_0, a, q) \in \to\} \cup \\ \{((q_i, a), (q, b)) | (q_i, a, q) \in \to \land (q, b, q_j) \in \to \land b \neq \checkmark\} \end{cases}$
- $\tau(s_i, s_j) = \frac{prio((r,t)) \ with \ s_j = (q,(a,r,t))}{\sum_{(s_i,s) \in \mathcal{T}} prio((r,t)) \ with \ s = (q,(a,r,t))}$
- $\mathcal{O}$ is defined in the preliminaries
- $\mathcal{P}(s_i, o_j) = \begin{cases} 1 & , if \ o(s_i) = o_j \\ 0 & , else \end{cases}$

Please note that the set $\mathcal{A}ct$ contains elements of the set of qualified task names of a CTML model QT_{CTML} (see Definition 6-20) of the following form: (a, r, t) with a being an actor, r being a role and t being a task name.

As already stated before the LTS and HMM are structural similar. Actions in the LTS are states in the HMM. In order truly enroll the HMM properly not only the actions represent a state in the HMM but the tuple of source state and actions. This approach is taken in order to preserve the execution history implicitly defined in the LTS as it makes a difference in the HMM whether an action is executable at the beginning or having executed a certain set of actions. A special case is the initial state of the HMM which is added additionally. The initial probabilities are synthesized by assigning the initial state the probability 1 whereas for all other it is 0. The transitions of the HMM are derived based on the state space of the LTS. More precisely, for each state in the LTS a set of according HMM transition is created using the incoming and outgoing actions of the state.

Having defined the structure of the state space it is now continued with additional properties which are not part of the CTML model and LTS model itself. The transition probability is synthesized with the support of the *prio* function which assigns each qualified task name (QT_r) a priority. In order to calculate the transition probability the relative priority of the action (HMM state) of interest and to the sum of the priorities of all potential actions (HMM states) is consulted. The set of observations is defined according to the needs of the intention recognition (e.g., location information, RFID information) and is not part of the task modeling process. The observation can be imported accordingly. As each task is only assigned one observation the probability of the occurrence of this observation is 1, for all others it is 0.

The Running Example

In order to exemplify the creation of a HMM based on a CTML specification the running example is consulted. To keep the example as comprehensible as possible the derivation is only shown for a single task expression (more precisely for a single actor, *Sheldon*, fulfilling only one role, *Chairman*). However during the derivation process also other actors acting as *Presenter* are used (*Leonard, Penny*). The task expression used to exemplify the derivation process is shown in Figure 7-11. It is in line with example used in the whole and specifies how a chairman may chair a conference session with two talks to present. Such situation is typical in our SmartLab.

Figure 7-11 Task Tree for Implicit Interaction in SmartLab

The example is actually more concrete then the task models used in the other examples in the thesis as it precisely defines that two talks are to be given. In this vein, it becomes more easily to derive the currently executing task as each talk has different observations.

The corresponding LTS to the given task tree is depicted in Figure 7-12. Please note that invisible actions are already removed. Due to space constraints abbreviated action names are used (the names is abbreviated and the actor and role are omitted). The branching of states is a typically result of the usage of the orderindependence operator ($| = |$).

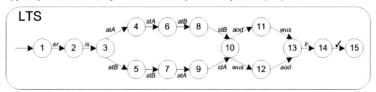

Figure 7-12 LTS for the Task Tree of the SmartLab

Formally the LTS can be represented by the tuple $\langle Q, \mathcal{A}ct, \rightarrow, q_0 \rangle$ with:

- $Q = \{1,2,3,4,5,6,7,8,9,10,11,12,13,14,15\}$

- $\mathcal{A}ct = \{er, is, atA, stA, atB, stB, aod, wus, lr\}$

- $\rightarrow = \left\{ \begin{array}{l} (1, er, 2), (2, is, 3), (3, atA, 4), (4, stA, 6), (6, atB, 8), (3, atB, 5), \\ (5, stB, 7), (7, atA, 9), (8, stB, 10), (9, stA, 10), (10, aod, 11), \\ (10, wus, 12), (11, wus, 13), (12, aod, 13), (13, lr, 14), (14, \checkmark, 15) \end{array} \right\}$

- $q_0 = 1$

In order to derive the corresponding HMM the additionally needed information need to be provided. A function assigning qualified task names a certain priority is given by:

$$prio(t) = \begin{cases} 40 & , t = atA \\ 10 & , t = atB \\ 60 & , t = aod \\ 40 & , t = wus \\ 1 & , else \end{cases}$$

Moreover an observation for each action to be executed needs to be defined in order to derive the currently executed action at runtime. Such a mapping represents the binding of the model to the world state. In this example locations of the SmartLab are used as observations. Given the location model in Figure 6-13 the following locations exist: *SmartLab, Outside, Presentation Zone, Whiteboard Zone, Door Zone, Right Chairs Zone, Rear Chairs Zone, Left Chairs Zone* and an accumulation of the different chair zones by *Chairs*. Moreover the observations are qualified with the actors in the environment in order to create an evaluable statement. Therefore, the observations of this example are:

$$O = \mathcal{A} \times \mathcal{L}$$

with $\mathcal{A}$ ($\{sh, le, pe\}$) being the set of actors in the environment and $\mathcal{L}$ being the set of locations ($\{out, pz, wz, dz, rcz, recz, lcz, c\}$).

The observations are mapped to atomic tasks with a certain probability. Here and in Definition 7-1 the simplest case is used. Only one observation is assigned for each action. Such an observation defines where each of the actors are in the environment. Therefore the probability of its occurrence is one. Please note that in this particular example the initial state does not have assigned an observation as it is the only possible starting state.

$$o(t) = \begin{cases} \{(sh,dz),(le,sl),(pe,sl)\} & ,t=er \\ \{(sh,wz),(le,sl),(pe,sl)\} & ,t=is \\ \{(sh,sl),(le,pz),(pe,sl)\} & ,t=atA \\ \{(sh,c),(le,sl),(pe,sl)\} & ,t=stA \\ \{(sh,sl),(le,sl),(pe,pz)\} & ,t=atB \\ \{(sh,c),(le,sl),(pe,sl)\} & ,t=stB \\ \{(sh,pz),(le,sl),(pe,sl)\} & ,t=aod \\ \{(sh,wz),(le,sl),(pe,sl)\} & ,t=wus \\ \{(sh,out),(le,sl),(pe,sl)\} & ,t=lr \end{cases}$$

Now, all information needed to create a HMM based on the LTS is given. The resulting model is depicted in Figure 7-13. Formally it is represented by $\langle S, \pi, \mathcal{T}, \tau, \mathcal{O}, \mathcal{P}\rangle$ with:

- $S = \{initial, er, is, atA, stA, atB, stB, atA_2, stA_2, atB_2, stB_2, wus, wus_2, aod, aod_2, lr\}$

- $\pi(s) = \begin{cases} 1 & ,if\ s = initial \\ 0 & ,else \end{cases}$

- $\mathcal{T} = \left\{ \begin{array}{l} (initial, er), (er, is), (is, atA), (atA, stA), (stA, atB), (atB, stB), \\ (is, atB_2), (atB_2, stB_2), (stB_2, atA_2), (atA_2, stA_2), (stB, wus), (stB, aod), \\ (stA_2, wus), (stA_2, aod), (wus, aod_2), (aod, wus_2), (aod_2, lr), (wus_2, lr) \end{array} \right\}$

- $\tau(s_i, s_j) = \begin{cases} 0.8 & ,s_i = is \wedge s_j = atA \\ 0.2 & ,s_i = is \wedge s_j = atB_2 \\ 0.4 & ,s_i = stB \wedge s_j = wus \\ 0.6 & ,s_i = stB \wedge s_j = aod \\ 0.4 & ,s_i = stA_2 \wedge s_j = wus \\ 0.6 & ,s_i = stA_2 \wedge s_j = aod \\ 1 & ,else \end{cases}$

- $\mathcal{O} = \mathcal{A} \times \mathcal{L}$ (as described above)

- $\mathcal{P}(s_i, o_j) = \begin{cases} 1 & ,o_j \in o(s_i) \\ 0 & ,else \end{cases}$

The states of the HMM represent the task under execution. The states have been renamed. Given the definitions above a state is represented by the tupel $\langle s,t\rangle$ with s being the source state in the LTS and t being the action. The source state has been eliminated and an index is introduced in order to avoid multiple occurrences of state names. In Figure 7-13 a visual representation of the HMM is given. Black circles represent states, directed edges defines state transitions. Numbers assigned to direct edges are transition probabilities. If a state has only one outgoing transition the transition probability is 1. In such case the number is not visualized in Figure 7-13. Red lines assign observations to states which in turn are visualized by red circles. For each state, except for the initial state, three observations are assigned: for each involved actor a sensor observation is needed to precisely describe the situation under a state is reached. In Figure 7-13 for each state only one observation is shown. The two other observations are not depicted as they only define that the other actors need to be present somewhere in the environment (e.g., for the state er the not shown observations are

$(le, sl), (pe, sl)$). The initial probability, the probability that a state is the initial state, is only visualized for the state *Initial* as this is the only state with value other then 0. It is given by the number in the underpart of the state.

In the last paragraphs it has been shown that annotated CTML specifications can be transformed into fully-dressed HMMs. The lower quality of the generated HMM pays off when the models become more complex (an HMM can easily reached the size of thousands of states). Moreover, the generated artifact can be further refined and perfectly based on the software designer needs. In this vein, task models are used on a high level of abstraction in order to specify the basic structure of the behavior with its temporal and causal dependencies which eventually results in a CTML specification which in turn is transformed into the HMM. The HMM is used to derive the current tasks under execution at runtime. Based on such intention recognition process the assistive technology can be smoothly introduced in order to truly assist the user.

The assessment whether a HMM is appropriate and of sufficient quality is a complex task. Of course, syntactical validation and consistency checks can be defined and implemented. However the rationale of the specified model is not revealed by such analysis. In [Burghardt *et al.*, 2009] an approach is presented which uses recorded or artificial sensor data in order to assess the quality of a defined HMM. This approach can also be used for the task model-based HMM.

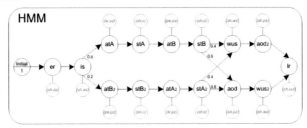

Figure 7-13 The derived HMM for Implicit Interaction in the SmartLab

7.5 Integration with further Software Engineering Disciplines

The CTML development approach and the language itself rely on common concepts and best practice methods from the area of HCI and software engineering. Naturally in both areas further application domains exist. In this section it is exemplified and substantiated which disciplines can be smoothly integrated with CTML and its development approach. More precisely, three disciplines have been assessed as most suitable for task modeling in general and CTML in particular.

Developing the interaction of a software system in a model-based way has the advantage of being able to use the models to perform usability tests in early phases. Usability evaluation cannot only be performed after having created the final UI, intention recognition respectively, but also during all stages of development as proposed in [Propp *et al.*, 2008]. Hence, task models are a very suitable artifact for usability evaluation as they focus on the user perspective and the accomplishment of goals of the user which is the one major interests of usability evaluation. Numerous techniques have been used to assess the usability of interaction for desktop systems. In his PhD Thesis Propp discusses different techniques to enable usability evaluation for SmEs based on task models. In essence, the major phases of software engineering are covered with appropriate usability evaluation techniques suitable for the artifacts in use. Techniques such as Wizard of Oz experiments, expert evaluation and cognitive walkthrough are offered and tool supported. The results of the thesis have also been published in [Burghardt *et al.*, 2009] and [Propp *et al.*, 2008].

Besides the interaction, the application core of the system under construction needs to be designed and implemented as well. In his PhD thesis Sinnig proposed an integrated development methodology for software system in general which employs task models as artifact for UI requirements and use case as artifact for functional requirements [2009]. In this vein the requirements of the software system are specified in a comprehensive manner and refinement checks and validity checks can be performed between task models and use cases. CTML can be integrated seamlessly into this prosperous methodology as the semantic domain of CTML is very similar to Sinnig's approach.

Reuse and knowledge sharing is a common challenge in software engineering. Pattern-based (pattern-oriented) design of software systems is one approach to tackle this issue. A pattern is an adaptable best practice solution to a recurrent problem on a certain level of abstraction [Gamma *et al.*, 1995]. In [Forbrig *et al.*, 2004] a two-folded approach for system development based on patterns is proposed. In a unified step the first models are created, amongst other the task model. Then, two separate approaches are followed to develop the application core and the UI which are both based on patterns. On the one hand design patterns of Gamma and the architectural patterns of Fowler ([2002]) are used to develop the application core. On the other hand the UI is created through the employment of HCI patterns. This and similar approaches relying on patterns exist for interaction design. The main advantage of such an approach is the reuse of solutions that have been successfully applied for similar problems and therefore exhibit a higher quality than custom tailored solutions. In the research field of HCI MB-UI development has already been enhanced by the application of pattern. In particular, several approaches introduced task pattern as reusable task structures [Breedvelt *et al.*, 1997; Sinnig, 2004]. In the domain of SmEs the usage of patterns seems to be fruitful as the incorporation of a particular domain may reveal different patterns of usage but also other patterns are conceivable (e.g., location patterns describing the layout of a particular SmE for a certain purpose). Therefore the integration with pattern-oriented UI design can be achieved and would enhance the development approach of CTML.

7.6 Further Application Areas

CTML and its development approach are not limited to the integration with other disciplines but are also applicable for other applications in the field. A model of the tasks being currently executed and are going to be executed in future is supportive for numerous applications in

SmEs. Provisioning of resources of any kind (e.g., establishing a network connection, transferring data, etc.) and preparation of long lasting functions (e.g., steering a projector, shutting the blinds, etc.) are prevalent general application areas of task models. However, also more human centered related application areas exist which are illuminated in the subsequent paragraphs.

The various enabled tasks in SmEs can also be a burden especially for novice users who are not used to assistive technologies. Therefore highlighting the system state and the anticipated tasks under execution of the user may help to explain certain decisions by the system. Such an approach allows for making a SmE less autonomous from users' perspective. Users may feel more comfortable if decisions are made explicit based on the assumption the system has about the user by means of a task model. Moreover the enabled tasks a user has and their potential outcome can be explained and the user can be guided through the use of the system.

Hence, as already stated the task model is actually an assumption about the users' intention and actions. Such an explicit model and its visualization can be used to correct the assumptions and adapt the model according to the feedback of the user. Such approaches are generally referred to as end-user development [Sutcliffe, 2005].

7.7 Summary and Conclusion

In this chapter the CTML development methodology has been introduced. It is based on an iterative, incremental development model and proposes different artifacts to be used. The central building block is the developed language of this thesis: CTML. Moreover it has been shown how a task model is created based on other artifacts such as scenarios or use cases. Hence, the derivation of task models to models used in the development process of the different interaction types, namely explicit and implicit interaction, has been exemplified. Naturally, the development methodology not only shows how to transform an artifact to a task model and vice versa, but also shows how to enhance a CTML properly depending on the stage of development. As this process of enhancing a CTML model is guided by refinement with and without meta operators the development methodology also guides the designer how to assign meta operators to tasks in a certain development stage. Beside guidance how to perform each development step also other application domains and interfaces to other software engineering disciplines have been provided.

Chapter 8
Conclusion & Outlook

8.1 Summary

In this thesis we proposed an integrated development methodology for the interaction development of SmEs based on the concept of *tasks*. The interaction in SmEs is significantly more complex compared to ordinary desktop systems due to the diverse in- and output devices, their individual capabilities and limitations and situatedness of task execution (e.g., unforeseen changes in the configuration of the SmE because of a mobile device entering or leaving the ensemble). This issue naturally also raises the complexity of interaction development. Task analysis and modeling have been successfully applied to interaction development over decades in order to provide a basis to start development from. One particular application, MB-UI development, tackles the question whether UIs can be created via a model-driven process in which task modeling is used as starting point. In this thesis it is investigated whether such a model-driven development process is feasible and prosperous for interaction in SmEs.

Explicit & Implicit Interaction

To address these issues a distinction of interaction is proposed and used to establish a robust and holistic interaction framework comprising **explicit** and **implicit interaction**. Whereas explicit interaction is the predominant method of interaction in WIMP systems, implicit interaction is a new interaction paradigm which makes use of user actions not primarily performed to interact with the system but being interpreted by the system (e.g., walking). Both interaction types have been mainly treated separately even though they occur interleaved. In order to develop convenient means of interaction both interaction types need to be developed in an integrated matter as they are relying on the same work processes and domain. Therefore, the integrated development methodology here is based on the common concept of tasks. Such a high level description mechanism is able to specify how goals are achieved by means of task execution which in turn can be used to develop explicit and implicit interaction.

The Collaborative Task Modeling Language

Task modeling has been considered as a normative and idealized model of task performance. However with the advent of model-driven development such idealized models are not sufficient anymore. The special characteristics of SmEs are the diverse sensors used to derive knowledge about the user and the devices constituting the SmE which are used as means for in- and output. Especially the first is important for implementing implicit interaction as ac-

177

tions of the user need to be recognized. The latter issue is important for explicit interaction as in- and output and as computing resource in general. Based upon these insights a set of requirements has been distilled which are necessary to adequately reflect tasks in SmEs. These requirements can be categorized into the following categories:

- **Modeling Approach.** On a high level of abstraction task modeling is suitable for representing the work processes involved in the domain of interest. This also applies for SmEs. Therefore a modeling language has been build around the concept of *task*. Moreover, as SmEs are inherently multi-user environments means for cooperation have been built into the language.

- **Context Modeling.** A set of models for characterizing the context during the task execution have been integrated into task modeling by preconditions and effects. A certain task is only executable if a certain contextual property holds (e.g., the actor is at a certain location). On the other hand task execution may lead to a change of the contextual properties (e.g., the actor is in front of the audience). Three types of models have been considered as most important: Location modeling, device modeling, and domain modeling. However, the architecture allows for integrating further models with minimal effort.

- **Means of Engineering.** In this category issues are subsumed which are needed to make effectively use of the language. A suitable development methodology and a tool suite supporting the development methodology are defined. Besides the designed language, the development methodology and corresponding tool support are also part of the thesis.

In order to address these requirements a new task modeling language, CTML, has been designed. In order to share CTML models and rule out any ambiguities a **formal syntax and semantics** have been defined. Whereas the syntax is based on applied set theory the ultimate semantic domain of choice are labeled transition systems (LTS). A CTML model is translated to a LTS by two-step process in which the model is first converted into a homogenous intermediate specification and eventually translated into a LTS by inference rules.

Refinement

As modeling is usually not performed in a single sweep but rather iteratively instruments for supporting such an approach are meaningful for CTML. Refinement answers the question whether a certain adaptation is still a valid refinement of its origin. Therefore different refinement algorithms have been examined and a sub set has been selected. Based upon the semantic domains of LTSs the refinement relations **trace** and **scenario inclusion** and **trace** and **scenario equivalence** have been formally defined for CTML models in order to compare two specifications with respect to their (allowed) behavior. In certain situations behavioral refinement is not always purposeful. In such cases structural properties can be used to check refinement. Type consistency and **structural refinement** of non atomic tasks are checked within such a refinement check.

While refining a task model a prioritization of tasks is desirable. Therefore a more flexible approach using so called **meta operators** has been defined. Tasks marked with one of the meta operators are treated in special manner during the refinement checks. More precisely they define whether a certain task (ant its sub tasks) are considered during the refinement check. In this vein a totally new approach to refinement has been defined and implemented. Case studies have shown that the flexibility pays of the raised effort of assigning the meta operators.

The CTML Development Approach

The extended expressiveness of CTML compared to other task modeling languages and the developed refinement algorithms are much more valuable if applied in a coherent development methodology. Therefore such a methodology has been created in order to develop interactive systems for SmEs comprising explicit and implicit interaction. The approach is based on model-driven development which uses the task model as first formal model (scenarios and use cases are used to elicit and specify requirements). Based on the developed task models the artifacts dedicated for each interaction type, namely the dialog model for explicit and the HMM for implicit interaction, can be derived. In case of the first, an interactive approach is proposed whereas the latter can be automatically derived based on further meta information.

The development approach comprises three stages which are mainly congruent with current software engineering practices of analysis, requirements specification and design stage. Naturally, the CTML development methodology is more focused on interaction and therefore takes into account UI requirements and functional requirements. The phases are:

- **Analysis**
- **Interaction Specification**
- **Detailed Interaction Design**

For each stage the relevant artifacts have been identified and guidance is offered how to apply them properly and advance development. Special attention has been paid to phase transitions when one artifact is transformed into another type of artifact (e.g., use case – task model, task model – dialog graph). For those phase transitions the development methodology gives concrete advice how to perform them best.

With respect to refinement the methodology specifies which refinement relation for CTML models is most suitable in which stages and whether meta operators should be considered during the refinement steps. The development approach also defines how meta operators should be assigned relative to the current development stage. This is of high importance as the meta operators are a new concept which may overtax the modeler. In order to ease this burden concrete guidance is offered.

Tool Suite

CTML, its methodology and the refinement algorithms are complemented with appropriate tool support. As task modeling is not the only activity throughout the whole development lifecycle the Eclipse IDE has been chosen as platform because it is one of the major standard software tools for development and coding and provides a solid and robust plug-in concept in order to develop editors and tools for other artifacts (such as the dialog model or HMM).

179

Integrated in the Eclipse IDE the CTML tool suite comprises the CTML Editor, Validator and Verifier. Whereas the CTML Editor enables the creation, manipulation, visualization and animation of CTML models, the Validator checks well-formnedness criteria. The CTML Verifier implements the refinement algorithms with and without meta operators. The components are aligned to serve the development methodology by supporting each step regarding task modeling and providing shortcuts for common use cases with respect to the development methodology (e.g., type of refinement for each stage).

8.2 Outlook

In this thesis task modeling for SmEs has been investigated thoroughly. However, some research questions still remain open, which are discussed next.

Even though CTML has been designed to be able to specify tasks in SmEs the usage scenario through the thesis was a particular SmE: a multi-user meeting setting. Further research need to be conducted to evidence the hypothesis that CTML is also feasible for other types of SmEs, such as home entertainment and elderly care. For the latter experimental modeling sessions have shown promising results.

The models which have been integrated with task modeling (such as the location model) are the most salient ones. Naturally, especially with regard to the usage scenarios involving of explicit and implicit interaction **further models** can be considered as well. Location information for example is only one source of sensor data. Physical properties such as temperature, day time, etc. can be considered as well and may have an impact on task execution. The same applies for other models as well. CTML and its tool suite are designed to allow for easy integration of new types of models with minimal effort.

The creation of CTML models can become quite complex. The developed tool support tries to hide complexity as much as possible. A wizard has been implemented to ease the creation of a CTML model from scratch. Nevertheless, reuse on a higher level of abstraction is desirable. **Patterns** are one way to achieve such kind of reuse. Most prominent in software engineering with the famous Gang of Four Design Patterns ([Gamma *et al.*, 1995]) patterns have also entered HCI [Tidwell, 2005; van Duyne *et al.*, 2006]. Even on the level of task modeling approaches exist which tackle the question whether task patterns can be used to enhance task modeling by offering generic solution to recurrent problems [Breedvelt *et al.*, 1997; Wurdel, 2006]. These ideas can be further extended and applied to SmEs in which certain tasks are recurrent in different configurations. Moreover the models integrated in CTML may also exhibit patterns which can be applied in future models.

The symbolic animation of CTML models is part of the tool suite and supports visualizations of the animated models on different levels of abstraction. A software interface, a text-based GUI, a tree-based animation and a 2-D bird view on the SmartLab have been implemented to allow the designer to animate the model from different viewpoints. Beyond that, a **3D visualization** could be the next step in order to create an even more concrete feeling about the CTML model under construction. This would allow to examine the model more thoroughly and to detect usability flaws regarding viewpoint occlusions and spatial issues.

One of the assets of model-driven development is the possibility of using the models at run-time and evaluating the system with respect to the developed models. This allows for evaluation on a higher level of abstraction (e.g., measuring the time performance of a certain task). Propp discussed the usage of task-based evaluation techniques in his PhD Thesis ([Propp *et al.*, 2008; Propp *et al.*, 2009]) and showed how different classical usability techniques such as Wizard of Oz experiments can be conducted based on the concepts of task modeling. The work of Propp and the thesis here propose an integrated approach to modeling and evaluation. CTML has been used by Propp to enable **usability methods**. Further integration of these methods with CTML is another interesting research question. Especially with respect to the models which have been integrated as these models specify the context which is of high importance for the reason of executing a certain task in a certain manner.

References

Aarts, E. and B. de Ruyter (2009). "New research perspectives on Ambient Intelligence." Journal of Ambient Intelligence and Smart Environments **1**(1): 5-14.

Aarts, E., R. Harwig and M. Schuurmans (2002). Ambient intelligence. The invisible future: the seamless integration of technology into everyday life, McGraw-Hill, Inc.: 235-250.

Abowd, G. D. (1999). "Classroom 2000: an experiment with the instrumentation of a living educational environment." IBM System Journal **38**(4): 508-530.

Annett, J. and K. D. Duncan (1967). "Task Analysis and Training Design." Journal of Occupational Psychology **41**: 211-221.

Baeten, J. C. M. and W. P. Weijland (1990). Process algebra. Cambridge, Cambridge University Press.

Basnyat, S., P. Palanque, B. Schupp and P. Wright (2007). "Formal socio-technical barrier modelling for safety-critical interactive systems design." Safety Science **45**(5): 545-565.

Bauer, M., L. Jendoubi and O. Siemoneit (2004). Smart factory - mobile computing in production environments, University of Stuttgart : Collaborative Research Center SFB 627 (Nexus: World Models for Mobile Context-Based Systems).

Beck, K. (2000). Extreme programming explained : embrace change. Boston, MA, USA, Addison-Wesley.

Becker, C. and F. Dürr (2005). "On location models for ubiquitous computing." Personal Ubiquitous Computing **9**(1): 20-31.

Bellotti, F., R. Berta, M. Margarone and A. D. Gloria (2008). "oDect: an RFID-based object detection API to support applications development on mobile devices." Softw. Pract. Exper. **38**(12): 1241-1259.

Berardi, D., D. Calvanese and G. D. Giacomo (2005). "Reasoning on UML class diagrams." Artif. Intell. **168**(1): 70-118.

Bergstra, J. A. (2001). Handbook of Process Algebra, Elsevier Science Inc.

Bergstra, J. A. and J. W. Klop (1990). An introduction to process algebra. Applications of Process Algebra. J. C. M. Baerten, Cambridge University press.

Biere, M., B. Bomsdorf and G. Szwillus (1999a). Specification and simulation of task models with VTMB. CHI '99 extended abstracts on Human factors in computing systems. Pittsburgh, Pennsylvania, ACM.

Biere, M., B. Bomsdorf and G. Szwillus (1999b). The Visual Task Model Builder. Proceedings of the third international conference on Computer-aided design of user interfaces. Louvain-la-Neuve, Belgium, Kluwer Academic Publishers.

Blumendorf, M. (2009). Multimodal Interaction in Smart Environments: A Model-based Runtime System for Ubiquitous User Interfaces. PhD in Elektrotechnik und Informatik. Berlin, Germany, Technische Universität Berlin.

Blumendorf, M., S. Feuerstack and S. Albayrak (2007). "Multimodal user interaction in smart environments: Delivering distributed user interfaces." Proc. AMI'07 Workshop on MDSE for AmI Applications.

Blumendorf, M., S. Feuerstack and S. Albayrak (2008). Multimodal user interfaces for smart environments: the multi-access service platform. Proceedings of the working conference on Advanced visual interfaces. Napoli, Italy, ACM.

Boehm, B. W. (1988). "A spiral model of software development and enhancement." Computer 21(5): 61-72.

Bolognesi, T. and E. Brinksma (1987). "Introduction to the ISO specification language LOTOS." Comput. Netw. ISDN Syst. 14(1): 25-59.

Bomsdorf, B. (2007). "The WebTaskModel Approach to Web Process Modelling." TaMoDia 2007 4849: 240-253.

Booch, G., I. Jacobson and J. Rumbaugh (2005). The Unified Modeling Language User Guide. Upper Saddle River, NJ, Addison-Wesley.

Booch, G., R. Maksimchuk, M. Engle, B. Young, J. Conallen and K. Houston (2007). Object-oriented analysis and design with applications, third edition, Addison-Wesley Professional.

Boy, G. A. and T. R. Gruber (1990). Intelligent Assistant Systems: Support for Integrated Human-Machine Systems, Knowledge Systems, AI Laboratory, Stanford University.

BPMN. (2010). "Business Process Modeling Notation, V2.0 beta." Retrieved March 13, 2010, from http://www.omg.org/cgi-bin/doc?dtc/09-08-14.

Breedvelt, I., F. Paternò and C. Severiins (1997). Reusable Structures in Task Models. Proceedings Design, Specification, Verification of Interactive Systems '97, Granada, Springer Verlag.

Brinksma, E., G. Scollo and C. Steenbergen (1995). Lotos specifications, their implementations and their tests. Conformance testing methodologies and architectures for OSI protocols, IEEE Computer Society Press: 468-479.

Brookes, S. D., C. A. R. Hoare and A. W. Roscoe (1984). "A Theory of Communicating Sequential Processes." J. ACM 31(3): 560-599.

Brooks, R. A. (1997). The Intelligent Room project. Proceedings of the 2nd International Conference on Cognitive Technology (CT '97), IEEE Computer Society.

Brumitt, B., B. Meyers, J. Krumm, A. Kern and S. Shafer (2000). EasyLiving: Technologies for Intelligent Environments. Handheld and Ubiquitous Computing: 97-119.

Burghardt, C. and T. Kirste (2008). Synthesizing probabilistic models for team-assistance in smart meetings rooms. Adjunct Proceedings of the 2008 ACM Conference on Computer Supported Cooperative Work, San Diego, CA, USA.

Burghardt, C., S. Propp, T. Kirste and P. Forbrig (2009). Rapid Prototyping and Evaluation of Intention Analysis for Smart Environments. Intelligent Interactive Assistance and Mobile Multimedia Computing, Springer Berlin Heidelberg. 53: 239-250.

Cabot, J., R. Claris and D. Riera (2008). Verification of UML/OCL Class Diagrams using Constraint Programming. Proceedings of the 2008 IEEE International Conference on Software Testing Verification and Validation Workshop, IEEE Computer Society.

Caffiau, S., P. Girard, D. L. Scapin, L. Guittet and L. Sanou (2008). Assessment of Object Use for Task Modeling. Engineering Interactive Systems 2008. Pisa, Italy.

Card, S., T. P. Moran and A. Newell (1983). The Psychology of Human Computer Interaction. Hillsdale, N.J., Erlbaum.

Cardelli, L. and A. Gordon (1998). Mobile ambients. Foundations of Software Science and Computation Structures, Springer Berlin / Heidelberg. 1378: 140-155.

Carroll, J. M. (1995). Scenario-based design : envisioning work and technology in systems development ; Workshop, on June 8, 1993. New York, NY u.a., Wiley.

Charniak, E. (1997). Statistical Parsing with a Context-free Grammar and Word Statistics. Proceedings of the Fourteenth National Conference on Artificial Intelligence.

Christopher, R. C., C. K. Hess, M. Román and R. H. Campbell (2001). Gaia: A Development Infrastructure for Active Spaces. Workshop on Application Models and Programming Tools for Ubiquitous Computing. 6: 65-67.

Cleaveland, R. and S. Smolka, A. (1996). "Strategic directions in concurrency research." ACM Comput. Surv. 28(4): 607-625.

Cleaveland, W. R., G. Lüttgen and V. Natarajan (2000). Priority in Process Algebras. Handbook of Process Algebra, Elsevier

Clerckx, T., C. Vandervelpen, K. Luyten and K. Coninx (2006). A task-driven user interface architecture for ambient intelligent environments. Proceedings of the 11th IUI. Sydney, Australia, ACM.

Cockburn, A. (2001). Writing effective use cases. Boston u.a., Addison-Wesley.

Coen, M., B. Phillips, N. Warshawsky, L. Weisman, S. Peters and P. Finin (1999). Meeting the computational needs of intelligent environments: The metaglue system. MANSE'99. Dublin, Ireland.

Constantine, L. L. and L. A. D. Lockwood (1999). Software for use : a practical guide to the models and methods of usage-centered design. Reading, Mass. u.a., Addison Wesley u.a.

Constantinos, P. (2000). UIML: A Device-Independent User Interface Markup Language. PhD in Computer Science, Virginia Polytechnic Institute and State University: 249.

Cook, D. and S. Das (2004). Smart Environments: Technology, Protocols and Applications (Wiley Series on Parallel and Distributed Computing), Wiley-Interscience.

Cook, D., M. Schmitter-Edgecombe, A. Crandall, C. Sanders and B. Thomas (2009). Collecting and disseminating smart home sensor data in the CASAS project. Proc. of CHI09 Workshop on Developing Shared Home Behavior Datasetsto Advance HCI and Ubiquitous Computing Research.

Cooper, A. (2004). The Inmates Are Running the Asylum: Why High Tech Products Drive Us Crazy and How to Restore the Sanity (2nd Edition), Pearson Higher Education.

Das, S. and D. Cook (2005). Designing Smart Environments: A Paradigm Based on Learning and Prediction. Pattern Recognition and Machine Intelligence: 80-90.

Demeure, A. and G. Calvary (2003). Plasticity of user interfaces: towards an evolution model based on conceptual graphs. 15th French-speaking conference on human-computer interaction. Caen, France, ACM.

Dey, A. K. and G. D. Abowd (2000). Towards a Better Understanding of Context and Context-Awareness. CHI 2000 Workshop on The What, Who, Where, When, Why and How of Context-Awareness.

Dijkstra, E. W. (1972). Notes on Structured programming. Structured programming. O.-J. Dahl, E. W. Dijkstra and C. A. R. Hoare. London u.a., Acad. Press: 1-82.

Dittmar, A. and P. Forbrig (1999). Methodological and tool support for a task-oriented development of interactive ssytems. Computer-Aided Design of User Interfaces. Louvain-la-Neuve, Belgium, Kluwer Academic Publishers.

Dittmar, A. and P. Forbrig (2003). Higher-Order Task Models. Interactive Systems. Design, Specification, and Verification: 219-230.

Dittmar, A., P. Forbrig, S. Heftberger and C. Stary (2004). "Tool Support for Task Modelling - A Constructive Exploration." Proc. EHCI-DSVIS'04.

Dix, A., J. Finlay, G. Abowd and R. Beale (1997). Human-computer interaction, Prentice-Hall, Inc.

Duarte, C. and L. Carri (2006). A conceptual framework for developing adaptive multimodal applications. Proceedings of the 11th IUI. Sydney, Australia, ACM.

Edwards, W. K. and R. E. Grinter (2001). At Home with Ubiquitous Computing: Seven Challenges. Proceedings of the 3rd international conference on Ubiquitous Computing. Atlanta, Georgia, USA, Springer-Verlag.

Evans, E. (2003). Domain-Driven Design: Tackling Complexity in the Heart of Software, Addison-Wesley Professional.

Ferre, X., N. Juristo and A. M. Moreno (2004). Improving Software Engineering Practice with HCI Aspects. Software Engineering Research and Applications: 349-363.

Feuerstack, S. (2009). A Method for the User-centered and Model-based Development of Interactive Applications endnote. PhD in Elektrotechnik und Informatik. Berlin, Germany, Technische Universität Berlin.

Feuerstack, S. and M. Blumendorf (2007). Prototyping of Multimodal Interactions for Smart Environments based on Task Models. Workshop Proceedings of AmI 2007. Darmstadt, Germany.

Feuerstack, S., M. Blumendorf, V. Schwartze and S. Albayrak (2008). Model-based layout generation. Working conference on Advanced visual interfaces. Napoli, Italy, ACM.

Fokkink, W. (2000). Introduction to process algebra : with 11 figures and 11 tables. Berlin u.a., Springer.

Forbrig, P., A. Dittmar, D. Reichart and D. Sinnig (2003). User-Centered Design and Abstract Prototypes. Proceedings of BIR 2003. SHAKER. Berlin: 132 - 145.

Forbrig, P., A. Dittmar, D. Reichart and D. Sinnig (2004). From Models to Interactive Systems Tool Support and XIML. IUI / CADUI. Funchal, Portugal, CEUR-WS.org.

Forbrig, P. and M. Wurdel (2010). Integrating Collaborative Task Modeling with Device Specifications. IADIS International Conference Interfaces and Human Computer Interaction. Freiburg, Germany, IEEE.

Fowler, M. (2002). Patterns of Enterprise Application Architecture, Addison-Wesley Longman Publishing Co., Inc.

Fowler, M. (2004). UML Distilled: A Brief Guide to the Standard Object Modeling Language Addison-Wesley Professional.

Franklin, D. and K. Hammond (2001). The intelligent classroom: providing competent assistance. Proceedings of the fifth international conference on Autonomous agents. Montreal, Quebec, Canada, ACM.

Gamma, E., R. Helm, R. Johnson and J. Vlissides (1995). Design Patterns : Elements of Reusable Object-Oriented Software. Reading, Mass., Addison-Wesley.

Garavel, H. and R.-P. Hautbois (1993). An Experiment with the Formal Description in LOTOS of the Airbus A340 Flight Warning Computer. First AMAST International Workshop on Real-Time Systems. Iowa City, Iowa, USA.

García, J., J. Vanderdonckt and C. Lemaigre (2008a). Identification Criteria in Task Modeling. Human-Computer Interaction Symposium: 7-20.

García, J. G., C. Lemaigre, J. M. G. Calleros and J. Vanderdonckt (2008b). "Model-Driven Approach to Design User Interfaces for Workflow Information Systems." Journal of Universal Computer Science 14(19): 3160--3173.

Garcia, J. G., J. Vanderdonckt and J. M. G. Calleros (2008). "FlowiXML:; a step towards designing workflow management systems." Journal of Web Engineering 4(2): 163-182.

Garg, V. K. (2002). Elements of distributed computing, John Wiley & Sons, Inc.

Garlan, D., D. Siewiorek, A. Smailagic and P. Steenkiste (2002). "Project Aura: Toward Distraction-Free Pervasive Computing." IEEE Pervasive Computing 1(2): 22-31.

Garrido, J. L. and M. Gea (2002). A Coloured Petri Net Formalisation for a UML-Based Notation Applied to Cooperative System Modelling. DSV-IS 2002, Springer-Verlag.

Giersich, M. (2009). Concept of a Robust & Training-free Probabilistic System for Online Intention Analysis in Teams. PhD in Faculty of Computer Science and Electrical Engineering. Rostock, Germany, University of Rostock.

Giersich, M., P. Forbrig, G. Fuchs, T. Kirste, D. Reichart and H. Schumann (2007). "Towards an Integrated Approach for Task Modeling and Human Behavior Recognition." Human-Computer Interaction 4550: 1109-1118.

Giese, M., T. Mistrzyk, A. Pfau, G. Szwillus and M. von Detten (2008). AMBOSS: A Task Modeling Approach for Safety-Critical Systems. Engineering Interactive Systems. Pisa, Italy: 98-109.

Göransson, B., M. Lif and J. Gulliksen (2003). Usability Design-Extending Rational Unified Process with a New Discipline. Interactive Systems. Design, Specification, and Verification: 303-310.

Gulliksen, J. and B. Goransson (2001). Reengineering the Systems Development Process for User Centred Design. Proceedings of IFIP INTERACT'01: Human-Computer Interaction.

Gulliksen, J., B. Göransson, I. Boivie, J. Persson, S. Blomkvist and Å. Cajander (2005). Key Principles for User-Centred Systems Design. Human-Centered Software Engineering - Integrating Usability in the Software Development Lifecycle, Springer-Verlag Netherlands. 8: 17-36.

Hackos, J. and J. Redish (1998). User and Task Analysis for Interface Design, Wiley.

Hallerstede, S., M. Leuschel and D. Plagge (2010). Refinement-Animation for Event-B - Towards a Method of Validation. Proceedings ABZ 2010, Springer-Verlag.

Heider, T. (2009). A Unifed Distributed System Architecture for Goal-based Interaction with Smart Environments. PhD in Faculty of Computer Science and Electrical Engineering. Rostock, Germany, University of Rostock.

Heider, T. and T. Kirste (2002). Supporting Goal-Based Interaction with Dynamic Intelligent Environments. 15th European Conference on Artificial Intelligence. Lyon, France.

Heider, T. and T. Kirste (2005). Multimodal appliance cooperation based on explicit goals: concepts & potentials. Proc.of the SOC-EUSAI 2005, Grenoble, France, ACM.

Hermann, F., R. Blach, D. Janssen, T. Klein, A. Schuller and D. Spath (2009). Challenges for User Centered Smart Environments. Human-Computer Interaction. Ambient, Ubiquitous and Intelligent Interaction: 407-415.

Herzog, U. (1990). Formal Description, Time and Performance Analysis. A Framework. Entwurf und Betrieb verteilter Systeme, Fachtagung des Sonderforschungsbereiche 124 und 182, Springer-Verlag.

Hevner, A. R., S. T. March and J. Park (2004). "Design Science in Information Systems Research." MIS Quarterly 28: 75-105.

Hoare, C. A. R. (1978). "Communicating sequential processes." Commun. ACM 21(8): 666-677.

Hong, J. I. and J. A. Landay (2004). An architecture for privacy-sensitive ubiquitous computing. Proceedings of the 2nd international conference on Mobile systems, applications, and services. Boston, MA, USA, ACM.

Huber, P., K. Jensen and R. Shapiro (1991). Hierarchies in coloured petri nets. Advances in Petri Nets 1990: 313-341.

ISO (1989). ISO 8807:1989 Information processing systems - Open Systems Interconnection - LOTOS - A formal description technique based on the temporal ordering of observational behaviour. Geneva, Switzerland.

ISO (1999). ISO 13407:1999 - Human-centred design processes for interactive systems. Geneva, Switzerland, ISO.

Jensen, K. (1987). Coloured Petri nets. Petri Nets: Central Models and Their Properties, Springer. 254: 248-299.

Jeong, C., Y. Kim and Y. Chung (1997). TIV: A Toolset for Interactive Verification of Basic LOTOS Specifications. International Conference on Advanced Computing.

Johanson, B., A. Fox and T. Winograd (2002). "The Interactive Workspaces Project: Experiences with Ubiquitous Computing Rooms." IEEE Pervasive Computing 1(2): 67-74.

Johnson, P. (1992). Human-computer interaction : psychology, task analysis and software engineering. London u.a., McGraw-Hill.

Ju, W., B. A. Lee and S. R. Klemmer (2008). Range: exploring implicit interaction through electronic whiteboard design. Proceedings of the 2008 ACM conference on Computer supported cooperative work. San Diego, CA, USA, ACM.

Ju, W. and L. Leifer (2008). "The Design of Implicit Interactions: Making Interactive Systems Less Obnoxious." Design Issues 24(3): 72-84.

Khendek, F., S. Bourduas and D. Vincent (2001). Stepwise Design with Message Sequence Charts. Proceedings of the IFIP TC6/WG6.1, Kluwer, B.V.

Kidd, C. D., R. Orr, G. D. Abowd, C. G. Atkeson, I. A. Essa, B. MacIntyre, E. D. Mynatt, T. Starner and W. Newstetter (1999). The Aware Home: A Living Laboratory for Ubiquitous Computing Research. Proceedings of the Second International Workshop on Cooperative Buildings, Integrating Information, Organization, and Architecture, Springer-Verlag.

Kiefer, P. and K. Stein (2008). A Framework for Mobile Intention Recognition in Spatially Structured Environments. 2nd Workshop on Behavior Monitoring and Interpretation

(BMI08), 31st German Conference on Artificial Intelligence Kaiserslautern, Germany.

Kientz, J. A., S. N. Patel, B. Jones, E. Price, E. D. Mynatt and G. D. Abowd (2008). The Georgia Tech aware home. CHI '08 extended abstracts on Human factors in computing systems. Florence, Italy, ACM.

Kirste, T. (2006). Smart Environments. True Visions. E. Aarts and J. L. Encarnacao. Heidelberg, Springer: 323-339.

Kirste, T., T. Herfet and M. Schnaider (2001). EMBASSI: multimodal assistance for universal access to infotainment and service infrastructures. Proceedings of the 2001 EC/NSF workshop on Universal accessibility of ubiquitous computing: providing for the elderly. Alcácer do Sal, Portugal, ACM.

Kirwan, B. and L. K. Ainsworth (1992). A Guide to Task Analysis: The Task Analysis Working Group, Taylor & Francis.

Klug, T. and J. Kangasharju (2005). Executable Task Models. TaMoDia 2005. Gdansk, Poland.

Koskinen, I., K. Kuusela, K. Battarbee, A. Soronen, F. Mäyrä, J. Mikkonen and M. Zakrzewski (2006). Morphome: a constructive field study of proactive information technology in the home. Proceedings of the 6th conference on Designing Interactive systems. University Park, PA, USA, ACM.

Kruchten, P. (2003). The Rational Unified Process: An Introduction, Addison-Wesley Longman Publishing Co., Inc.

Kumar, S. (2009). Challenges for Ubiquitous Computing. Fifth International Conference on Networking and Services, Valencia, Spain

Lamport, L. (1994). "The Temporal Logic of Actions." ACM Trans. Program. Lang. Syst. 16(3): 872-923.

Langheinrich, M., V. Coroama, J. Bohn and F. Mattern (2005). "Living in a Smart Environment - Implications for the Coming Ubiquitous Information Society." Telecommunications Review 15: 132-143.

Larman, C. (2004). Applying UML and Patterns: An Introduction to Object-Oriented Analysis and Design and Iterative Development (3rd Edition), Prentice Hall PTR.

Le Gal, C., J. Martin, A. Lux and J. L. Crowley (2001). "Smart Office: Design of an Intelligent Environment." IEEE Intelligent Systems 16: 60-66.

Lesser, V., M. Atighetchi, B. Benyo, B. Horling, A. Raja, R. Vincent, T. Wagner, P. Xuan and S. X. Q. Zhang (1999). The UMASS intelligent home project. Proceedings of the third annual conference on Autonomous Agents. Seattle, Washington, United States, ACM.

Limbourg, Q. and J. Vanderdonckt (2003). Comparing Task Models for User Interface Design. The Handbook of Task Analysis for Human-Computer Interaction. D. Diaper and N. Stanton, Lawrence Erlbaum Associates: 135-154.

Limbourg, Q., J. Vanderdonckt, B. Michotte, L. Bouillon and V. López-Jaquero (2005). USIXML: A Language Supporting Multi-path Development of User Interfaces. Engineering Human Computer Interaction and Interactive Systems: 200-220.

Limbourg, Q., J. Vanderdonckt and N. Souchon (2001). The Task-Dialog and Task-Presentation Mapping Problem: Some Preliminary Results. Interactive Systems Design, Specification, and Verification: 227-246.

Logrippo, L., A. Obaid, J. P. Briand and M. C. Fehri (1988). "An interpreter for LOTOS, a specification language for distributed systems." Softw. Pract. Exper. 18(4): 365-385.

Luyten, K. (2004). Dynamic User Interfaces Generation for Mobile and Embedded Systems with Model-Based user Interface Development. PhD in. Maastricht, Universiteit Maastricht.

Luyten, K., J. V. den Bergh, C. Vandervelpen and K. Coninx (2006). "Designing distributed user interfaces for ambient intelligent environments using models and simulations." Computers & Graphics 30(5): 702-713.

Luyten, K., T. Van Laerhoven, K. Coninx and F. Van Reeth (2003). "Runtime transformations for modal independent user interface migration." Interacting with Computers 15: 329-347.

MacColl, I. and D. Carrington (2000). "Translating UAN into CSP." ICFEM '00: Proceedings of the 3rd IEEE International Conference on Formal Engineering Methods: 121.

Magee, J. and J. Kramer (2000). Concurrency : state models & Java programs. Chichester u.a., Wiley.

Marr, C. (2007). Capturing Conflict and Confusion in CSP. Integrated Formal Methods: 413-438.

Mazurkiewicz, A. (1977). Introduction to Trace Theory. The book of traces. V. Diekert and G. Rozenberg. Singapore u.a., World Scientific.

MDA. (2010). "Model Driven Architecture."   Retrieved January 15, 2010, from http://www.omg.org/mda/.

Milner, R. (1980). A Calculus of Communicating Systems. Berlin, Heidelberg ;Springer,.

Molich, R. and J. Nielsen (1990). "Improving a human-computer dialogue." Commun. ACM 33(3): 338-348.

Molina, A. I., M. A. Redondo, M. Ortega and U. Hoppe (2008). "CIAM: A Methodology for the Development of Groupware User Interfaces." Journal of Universal Computer Science 14: 1435-1446.

Molina, P. J. (2004). A Review to Model-Based User Interface Development Technology. MBUI 2004. Funchal, Madeira, Portugal.

Montero, F. and V. López-Jaquero (2008). IdealXml: An Interaction Design Tool. Computer-Aided Design Of User Interfaces V: 245-252.

Mori, G., F. Paternò and C. Santoro (2002). "CTTE: Support for Developing and Analyzing Task Models for Interactive System Design." IEEE Trans. Softw. Eng. 28(8): 797-813.

Mozer, M. C. (1998). The neural network house: An environment that adapts to its inhabitants. American Association for Artificial Intelligence Spring Symposium on Intelligent Environments, Menlo Park, CA, USA, AAAI Press.

Mozer, M. C. (2004). Lessons from an Adaptive Home. Smart Environments. S. K. D. Diane J. Cook: 271-294.

Murata, T. (1989). "Petri nets: Properties, analysis and applications." Proceedings of the IEEE 77(4): 541-580.

Norman, D. A. (2000). The design of everyday things. London, MIT Press.

Oleson, C., M. Hagan and C. DeMoss (2009). Achieving IT Service Quality: The Opposite of Luck, Synergy Books.

Oliver, N. and F. Flores-Mangas (2006). MPTrain: a mobile, music and physiology-based personal trainer. Proceedings of the 8th conference on Human-computer interaction with mobile devices and services. Helsinki, Finland, ACM.

Ouyang, C., W. M. P. van der Aalst, M. Dumas and A. H. M. ter Hofstede (2006). "Translating BPMN to BPEL."

Oviatt, S. (1999). "Ten myths of multimodal interaction." Commun. ACM 42(11): 74-81.

Paolucci, M. and K. Sycara (2003). "Autonomous Semantic Web Services." IEEE Internet Computing 7(5): 34-41.

Paternò, F. (1999). Model-Based Design and Evaluation of Interactive Applications. London, UK, Springer-Verlag.

Paternò, F. and C. Santoro (2001). The ConcurTaskTrees Notation for Task Modelling. Technical Report at CNUCE-C.N.R.

Paternò, F., C. Santoro, J. Mantyjarvi, G. Mori and S. Sansone (2008). "Authoring pervasive multimodal user interfaces." Int. J. Web Eng. Technol. 4(2): 235-261.

Payne, S. J. and T. R. G. Green (1986). "Task-Action Grammars: A Model of the Mental Representation of Task Languages." Human-Computer Interaction 2(2): 93 - 133.

Peled, D. (1993). All from One, One for All: on Model Checking Using Representatives. Proceedings of the 5th International Conference on Computer Aided Verification, Springer-Verlag.

Penichet, V. M. R., M. D. Lozano, J. A. Gallud and R. Tesoriero (2008). Analysis models for user interface development in collaborative systems. CADUI 2008. Alabcete, Spain.

Penichet, V. M. R., M. D. Lozano, J. A. Gallud and R. Tesoriero (2009). "User interface analysis for groupware applications in the TOUCHE process model." Adv. Eng. Softw. 40(12): 1212-1222.

Penichet, V. M. R., M. D. Lozano, J. A. Gallud and R. Tesoriero (2010). "Requirement-based approach for groupware environments design." Journal of Systems and Software 83(8): 1478-1488.

Petri, C. A. (1962). Fundamentals of a theory of asynchronous information flow. IFIP Congress'62. Munich, Germany: 386-390.

Ponnekanti, S. R., L. A. Robles and A. Fox (2002). User Interfaces for Network Services: What, from Where, and How. Proceedings of the Fourth IEEE Workshop on Mobile Computing Systems and Applications, IEEE Computer Society.

Pontico, F., C. Farenc and M. Winckler (2007). Model-Based Support for Specifying eService eGovernment Applications. TaMoDia.

Pratt, V. (1986). "Modeling concurrency with partial orders." International Journal of Parallel Programming 15(1): 33-71.

Propp, S., G. Buchholz and P. Forbrig (2008). Task Model-Based Usability Evaluation for Smart Environments. Engineering Interactive Systems, Springer Berlin / Heidelberg. 5247: 29-40.

Propp, S., G. Buchholz and P. Forbrig (2009). "Integration of Usability Evaluation and Model-Based Software Development." Adv. Eng. Softw. 40(12): 1223-1230.

Ramchandani, C. (1974). Analysis of Asynchronous Concurrent Systems by Timed Petri Nets, Massachusetts Institute of Technology.

Reed, G. and A. Roscoe (1986). A timed model for communicating sequential processes. Automata, Languages and Programming: 314-323.

Reichart, D., A. Dittmar, P. Forbrig and M. Wurdel (2008). Tool Support for Representing Task Models, Dialog Models and User-Interface Specifications. DSV-IS.

Reichart, D., P. Forbrig and A. Dittmar (2004). Task models as basis for requirements engineering and software execution. TAMODIA, ACM: 51-58.

Reisse, C., C. Burghardt, F. Marquardt, T. Kirste and A. Uhrmacher (2008). Smart Environments Meet the Semantic Web. Proceedings of the 7th International Conference on Mobile and Ubiquitous Multimedia. Umea, Sweden, ACM Press: 88-91.

Rodden, T., K. Chervest, N. Davies and A. Dix (1998). Exploiting Context in HCI Design for Mobile Systems. in Workshop on Human Computer Interaction with Mobile Devices.

Ronzani, D. (2009). "The Battle of Concepts: Ubiquitous Computing, Pervasive Computing and Ambient Intelligence in Mass Media." UbiCC Journal 4(2).

Roscoe, B. (1997). The Theory and Practice of Concurrency, Prentice Hall PTR.

Royce, W. W. (1987). Managing the development of large software systems: concepts and techniques. ICSE '87: Proceedings of the 9th international conference on Software Engineering, Monterey, California, United States, IEEE Computer Society Press.

Russell, N., A. ter Hofstede, D. Edmond and W. van der Aalst (2005). Workflow Data Patterns: Identification, Representation and Tool Support. Conceptual Modeling – ER 2005.

Russell, S. and P. Norvig (2003). Artificial Intelligence: A Modern Approach (Second Edition), Prentice Hall.

Scapin, D. and C. Pierret-Goldbreich (1989). Towards a method for task description : MAD. Proceedings of Work with Display Units (WWU '89), North-Holland: Elsevier Science.

Schilit, B., N. Adams and R. Want (1994). Context-Aware Computing Applications. IEEE Workshop on Mobile Computing Systems and Applications, Santa Cruz, CA, US.

Schmidt, A. (2000). "Implicit Human Computer Interaction Through Context." Personal and Ubiquitous Computing 4(2/3).

Schmidt, A., M. Beigl and H. W. Gellersen (1998). There is more to Context than Location. Karlsruhe, University of Karlsruhe.

Schmidt, A., M. Kranz and P. Holleis (2005). "Interacting with the ubiquitous computer: towards embedding interaction." sOc-EUSAI '05: Proceedings of the 2005 joint conference on Smart objects and ambient intelligence: 147-152.

Schwaber, K. and M. Beedle (2001). Agile Software Development with Scrum, Prentice Hall PTR.

Seffah, A., J. Gulliksen and M. Desmarais (2005). Human-Centered Software Engineering - Integrating Usability in the Development Process (Human-Computer Interaction Series), Springer-Verlag New York, Inc.

Seffah, A. and H. Javahery (2004). Multiple User Interfaces : Cross-Platform Applications and Context-Aware Interfaces. Hoboken, NJ, J. Wiley.

Selic, B. (2003). "The Pragmatics of Model-Driven Development." IEEE Softw. 20(5): 19-25.

Sharples, S., V. Callaghan and G. Clarke (1999). "A multi-agent architecture for intelligent building sensing and control." Sensor Review 19: 135-140.

Sheridan, T. B. (2002). Humans and Automation: System Design and Research Issues, John Wiley \& Sons, Inc.

Shirehjini, A. N. (2007). A Multidimensional Classification Model for the Interaction in Reactive Media Rooms. Human-Computer Interaction. HCI Intelligent Multimodal Interaction Environments, Springer Berlin / Heidelberg. **4552**: 431-439.

Sinnig, D. (2004). The Complicity of Patterns and Model-Based Engineering.

Sinnig, D. (2009). Use Case and Task Models: Formal Unification and Integrated Development Methodology. PhD in Computer Science and Software Engineering. Montréal, Canada, Concordia University.

Sinnig, D., M. Wurdel, P. Forbrig, P. Chalin and F. Khendek (2007). Practical Extensions for Task Models. TaMoDia 2007, Springer. **4849**: 42-55.

Sommerville, I. (2006). Software Engineering. Boston, MA, USA, Addison-Wesley Longman Publishing Co., Inc.

Sottet, J.-S., G. Calvary and J.-M. Favre (2008). Models at Run-time for Sustaining User Interface Plasticity. Models@Runtime workshop at Models 2008: 1-10.

Sottet, J.-S., G. Calvary, J.-M. Favre, J. Coutaz, A. Demeure and L. Balme (2006). Towards Model Driven Engineering of Plastic User Interfaces. Satellite Events at the MoDELS 2005 Conference: 191-200.

Sutcliffe, A. (2005). "Evaluating the costs and benefits of end-user development." SIGSOFT Softw. Eng. Notes **30**(4): 1-4.

Tidwell, J. (2005). Designing Interfaces, O'Reilly Media, Inc.

Trætteberg, H. (2008). "Integrating Dialog Modeling and Domain Modeling - the Case of Diamodl and the Eclipse Modeling Framework." JUCS **14**(Human-Computer Interaction).

Uchitel, S., J. Kramer and J. Magee (2004). "Incremental elaboration of scenario-based specifications and behavior models using implied scenarios." ACM Trans. Softw. Eng. Methodol. **13**(1): 37-85.

Ullmer, B. and H. Ishii (2000). "Emerging frameworks for tangible user interfaces." IBM Syst. J. **39**(3-4): 915-931.

UML. (2010). "Unified Modeling Language." Retrieved August 10, 2010, from http://www.uml.org/.

UsiXML. (2010). "USer Interface eXtensible Markup Language." Retrieved March 10, 2010, from http://www.usiXML.org/.

van den Bergh, J. and K. Coninx (2007). "From Task to Dialog Model in the UML." TAMODIA **4849**: 98-111.

van der Veer, G., B. Lenting and B. Bergevoet (1996). "GTA: Groupware Task Analysis - Modeling Complexity." Acta Psychologica **91**: 297-332.

van der Veer, G. and M. van Welie (2000). Task based groupware design: putting theory into practice. Proceedings of the 3rd conference on Designing interactive systems: processes, practices, methods, and techniques. New York City, New York, United States, ACM.

van Duyne, D. K., J. A. Landay and J. I. Hong (2006). The Design of Sites: Patterns for Creating Winning Web Sites (2nd Edition), Prentice Hall PTR.

van Glabbeek, R. (1990). The linear time - branching time spectrum. CONCUR '90 Theories of Concurrency: Unification and Extension: 278-297.

van Glabbeek, R. and U. Goltz (2000). "Refinement of actions and equivalence notions for concurrent systems." Acta Informatica **37**(4-5): 229-327.

van Welie, M., G. van der Veer and A. Eliëns (1998). An Ontology for Task World Models. DSV-IS 98. Abingdon, United Kingdom, Springer.

Vanderdonckt, J. (2008). Model-Driven Engineering of User Interfaces: Promises, Successes, Failures, and Challenges. Romanian National Conference of Human-Computer Interaction -- RoCHI 2008, Bucarest, Romania.

Vanderdonckt, J., Q. Limbourg, B. Michotte, L. Bouillon, D. Trevisan and M. Florins (2004). USIXML : a User Interface Description Language for Specifying Multimodal User Interfaces. W3C Workshop on Multimodal Interaction WMI'2004

Vanderdonckt, J., H. Mendonca and J. P. Molina Massó (2008). Distributed User Interfaces in Ambient Environment. Constructing Ambient Intelligence, Springer Berlin Heidelberg. **11**: 121-130.

Walker, M., L. Takayama and J. A. Landay (2002). "High-Fidelity or Low-Fidelity, Paper or Computer? Choosing Attributes When Testing Web Prototypes." Human Factors and Ergonomics Society Annual Meeting Proceedings **46**: 661-665.

Warmer, J. and A. Kleppe (2003). The Object Constraint Language: Getting Your Models Ready for MDA, Addison-Wesley Longman Publishing Co., Inc.

Weiser, M. (1991). The Computer for the 21st Century. Scientific American. **265:** 94-104.

Weiser, M. (1993). "Hot topics-ubiquitous computing." Computer **26**(10): 71-72.

Welie, M. v., G. v. d. Veer and A. Eliëns (1998). An Ontology for Task World Models. International Eurographics Workshop on Design Specification and Verification of Interactive Systems, Abingdon, UK.

White, S. A. (2004). "An Introduction to BPMN." BPTrends: 1-11.

Wilson, S., P. Johnson, C. Kelly, J. Cunningham and P. Markopoulos (1993). Beyond Hacking: a Model Based Approach to User Interface Design. Human Computer Interaction, University Press: 217-231.

Winskel, G. (1980). Events in Computation. PhD Thesis in Department of Computer Science. Edinburgh, University of Edinburgh.

Wirth, N. (1971). "Program development by stepwise refinement." Commun. ACM **14**(4): 221-227.

Wolff, A., P. Forbrig, A. Dittmar and D. Reichart (2005). Linking GUI elements to tasks: supporting an evolutionary design process. Proceedings of the 4th international workshop on Task models and diagrams. Gdansk, Poland, ACM.

Woodcock, J. and J. Davies (1996). Using Z: specification, refinement, and proof, Prentice-Hall, Inc.

Wooldridge, M. J. (2002). An introduction to multiagent systems. Chichester, Wiley.

Wurdel, M. (2006). Tool Support of Patterns for Task Models. University of Rostock.

Wurdel, M. (2009). Towards an Holistic Understanding of Tasks, Objects and Location in Collaborative Environments. HCII. San Diego, USA.

Wurdel, M., C. Burghardt and P. Forbrig (2007). "Supporting Ambient Environments by Extended Task Models." Proc. AMI'07 Workshop on MDSE for AmI Applications.

Wurdel, M., C. Burghardt and P. Forbrig (2009). Making task modeling suitable for smart environments. International Conference on Ultra Modern Telecommunications & Workshops, 2009. ICUMT '09.

Wurdel, M. and P. Forbrig (2009). Use Cases and Task Models as Driving Forces to Identify Requirements in Smart Environments. IMC.

Wurdel, M., S. Propp and P. Forbrig (2008a). HCI-Task Models and Smart Environments. Human-Computer Interaction Symposium: 21-32.

Wurdel, M., D. Sinnig and P. Forbrig (2008b). "CTML: Domain and Task Modeling for Collaborative Environments." JUCS **14**(Human-Computer Interaction).

Wurdel, M., D. Sinnig and P. Forbrig (2008c). Task-Based Development Methodology for Collaborative Environments. Engineering Interactive Systems 2008. Pisa, Italy, Springer. **5247**: 118-125.

Wurdel, M., D. Sinnig and P. Forbrig (2008d). Task Model Refinement with Meta Operators. DSV-IS 2007. Kingston, Canada.

Wurdel, M., D. Sinnig and P. Forbrig (2008e). Towards a Formal Task-based Specification Framework for Collaborative Environments. CADUI. Albacete, Spain.

You, J., D. Lieckfeldt, F. Reichenbach and D. Timmermann (2009). Context-aware geographic routing for sensor networks with routing holes. Proceedings of the WCNC, Budapest, Hungary, IEEE Press.

III. Appendix

Appendix A.1

A.1 The Running Example "Conference Session"

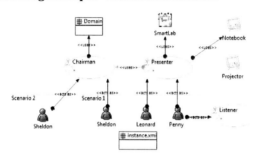

Figure A-1 CTML Model "Conference Session" in CTML Editor

$$CTML_{ConferenceSession} = \langle Coop, Conf \rangle$$

Cooperation Model

$$Coop = \langle \mathcal{R}, \mathcal{T}, \tau, \mathcal{TE}, L, \mathcal{DS}, \mathcal{ST}, dev, \mathcal{DM} \rangle$$

$$\mathcal{R} = \{Chairman\ (c), Presenter\ (p), Listener\ (l)\}$$

Figure A-2 Task Tree for Chairman with Abstract Task Names

Figure A-3 Task Tree for Presenter with Abstract Task Names

Figure A-4 Task Tree for Listener with Abstract Task Names

$$\mathcal{T} = \{er, wp, pa, at, sal, it, od, aod, wus, lr, in, clap, stpm, sp, sns, es, ep, rtq, aq\}$$

$$\tau(t) = \begin{cases} interactive & , t = clap \lor t = stpm \\ user & , else \end{cases}$$

Preconditions & Effects

Task	Type	Precondition	Abstract Syntax
Welcome Presenter	LOCATION	self.isIn(Presentation Zone)	$\lfloor(pz)\rfloor$
Present Agenda	LOCATION	self.isIn(Presentation Zone)	$\lfloor(pz)\rfloor$
Announce Talk	TASK	Listener.allInstances.Sit and Listen	$\lfloor(\forall,(l,sal))\rfloor$
Announce Open Discussion	TASK	Presenter.allInstances.End Presentation	$\lfloor(\forall,(p,ed))\rfloor$

Table A-1 Preconditions of the Role Chairman

Task	Type	Effect	Abstract Syntax
Enter Room	LOCATION	self.is(Presentation Zone)	$\lfloor(pz)\rfloor$
Leave Room	LOCATION	self.is(Outside)	$\lfloor(out)\rfloor$

Table A-2 Effects of the Role Chairman

Task	Type	Precondition	Abstract Syntax
Start Presentation	TASK	Chairman.oneInstance.AnnounceTalk	$\lfloor(\exists,(c,at))\rfloor$
Start Presentation	LOCATION	self.isIn(Presentation Zone)	$\lfloor(pz)\rfloor$
Start Presentation	DEVICE	self.Notebook.presentationStarted	$\lfloor(notebook, pSta)\rfloor$
Respond to Question	TASK	Chairman.oneInstance.OpenDiscussion	$\lfloor(\exists,(c,od))\rfloor$

Table A-3 Preconditions of the Role Presenter

Task	Type	Effect	Abstract Syntax
Introduce	DEVICE	self.Notebook.switchOn	$\lfloor(notebook, sOn)\rfloor$
Introduce	LOCATION	self.is(Presentation Zone)	$\lfloor(pz)\rfloor$
Set to Presentation Mode	DEVICE	self.Notebook.startPresentation	$\lfloor(notebook, startP)\rfloor$
Leave Room	LOCATION	self.is(Outside)	$\lfloor(out)\rfloor$

Table A-4 Effects of the Role Presenter

$$TE_c = (c, er)\lfloor(pz)\rfloor \gg \big(IS \gg (MT [> CS \gg (c, lr)\lfloor(out)\rfloor])\big)$$
$$IS = \lfloor(pz)\rfloor(c, wp)| = \|(pz)\rfloor(c, pa)$$
$$MT = \Big(\big(\lfloor(\forall,(l, sal))\rfloor(c, at) \gg SV\big) \gg \lfloor(c, od)\rfloor\Big)^*$$
$$SV = (c, sas)[> (c, it)$$
$$CS = \lfloor(\forall,(p, ed))\rfloor(c, aod)| = |(c, wus)$$

$$TE_p = IN \gg \Big(CE \gg \big(\lfloor(\exists,(c, at))\rfloor\lfloor(pz)\rfloor\lfloor(notebook, pSta)\rfloor(p, sp) \gg (NS[> EP])\big)\Big)$$
$$IN = (p, in)\lfloor(notebook, sOn)\rfloor\lfloor(pz)\rfloor$$
$$CE = (p, clap)| = |(p, stmp)\lfloor(notebook, startP)\rfloor$$
$$NS = \big((p, sns) \gg (p, es)\big)^*$$
$$EP = \Big((p, ep) \gg \big(\lfloor(\exists,(c, od))\rfloor(p, rtq) \gg (p, lr)\lfloor(out)\rfloor\big)\Big)$$

$$TE_l = (l, sal)| > \big((l, aq) \gg (l, lr)\big)$$

$$\mathcal{TE} = \{TE_c, TE_p, TE_l\}$$

Location Model

The location model used here is depicted in Figure 6-13.

$$L = \langle \mathcal{L}, \eta \rangle$$

$$\mathcal{L} = \left\{ \begin{array}{l} SmartLab\ (sl), Outside\ (out), PresentationZone(pz), \\ WhiteboardZone(wz), DoorZone\ (dz), RightChairsZone\ (rcz), \\ RearChairsZone\ (recz), LeftChairsZone\ (lcz), Chairs\ (c) \end{array} \right\}$$

$$\eta = \{(rcz, c), (recz, c), (lcz, c)\}$$

Devices

$$\mathcal{DS} = \{projector, notebook\}$$

$$projector = \left(\begin{array}{l} projector, \{on, off, pMOff, pMOn, final\}, \\ \{sOn, sOff, sPre, fPre, sPreM, fPreM\}, off, \{final\}, \delta_p \end{array} \right)$$

$$\delta_p = \left\{ \begin{array}{l} (off, sOn, on), (on, sOff, off), (off, end, final), (on, sPre, pMOn), \\ (pMOn, fPre, on)(pMOn, fPreM, pMOff), (pMOff, sPreM, pMOn) \end{array} \right\}$$

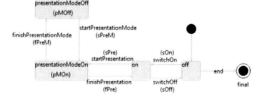

Figure A-5 Visual Representation of the State Chart for Projector

$$notebook = \begin{pmatrix} notebook, \{on, off, pStart, pStop, final\}, \\ \{sOn, sOff, startP, stopP, end\}, off, \{final\}, \delta_n \end{pmatrix}$$

$$\delta_p = \left\{ \begin{array}{l} (off, sOn, on), (on, sOff, off), (off, end, final), (on, startP, pSta), \\ (pSta, sOff, off), (pSta, stopP, pSto), (pSto, startP, pSta), (pSto, sOff, off) \end{array} \right\}$$

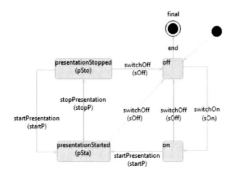

Figure A-6 Visual Representation of the State Chart for Notebook

$$ST = \{projector\}$$

$$dev = \{(p, notebook)\}$$

Domain Model

The domain model used here is depicted in Figure 6-15.

$$\mathcal{DM} = \langle \mathcal{Cl}, \mathcal{Ass}, \mathcal{Att} \rangle$$

$$\mathcal{Cl} = \{Notebook(o), Presenter(o), Pen(o), Presentation(o), Slide(o)\}$$

$$\mathcal{Ass} = \{notebook(o_1, o_2), stores(o_1, o_2), consistsOf(o_1, o_2), has(o_1, o_2), owns(o_1, o_2)\}$$

$$\mathcal{Att} = \{name(o, value), age(o, value), presented(o, value), title(o, value)\}$$

Configurations

$$Conf = \{Scenario1, Scenario2\}$$

Scenario 1

$$Scenario1 = \langle \mathcal{A}_{sc1}, Objects_{sc1} \rangle$$

$$\mathcal{A}_{sc1} = \{sh, le, pe\}$$

(Abbreviated for sh - Sheldon, le-Leonard, pe-Penny)

$$sh = (sh, out, \emptyset, \{c\}, \emptyset, c)$$

$$le = (le, out, \{le\_nb\}, \{p\}, \{(notebook, le\_nb)\}, p)$$

$$pe = (pe, rcz, \{pe\_nb\}, \{p, l\}, \{(notebook, pe\_nb)\}, p \gg l)$$

$$Objects_{sc1} = (\mathcal{O}, \mathcal{ass}, \mathcal{att})$$

The set of object names is:

$$O = \{Leonard, Pen, Slide\ 1, Slide\ 2, Towards\ ...\}$$

The set of associations of the objects is:

$$ass = \begin{cases} owns(le, Towards\ ...), consistsOf(Towards\ ..., Slide\ 1), \\ consistsOf(Towards\ ..., Slide\ 2) \end{cases}$$

The set of attributes of the objects is:

$$att = \begin{cases} name(le, Leonard), age(le, 28), presented(le, false), \\ name(Towards\ ..., Towards\ ...), name(Pen, Pen) \\ title(Slide\ 1, Intro), title\ (Slide\ 2, Outline) \end{cases}$$

Scenario 2

$$Scenario2 = \langle \mathcal{A}_{sc2}, Objects_{sc2} \rangle$$

$$\mathcal{A}_{sc2} = \{sh\}$$

(Abbreviated for *sh - Sheldon*)

$$sh = (sh, out, \emptyset, \{c\}, \emptyset, c)$$

$$Objects_{sc2} = (\emptyset, \emptyset, \emptyset)$$

Transformation to Intermediate Specification

$$IS_{CTML} = \langle TE_{CTML}, S_0, pre_H, pre_S, eff \rangle$$

The Initial State S_0 with respect to Scenario 1

$$S_0 = \mathcal{L}_0 \cup \mathcal{O}_0 \cup \mathcal{D}_0 \cup \mathcal{ST}_0 \cup T$$

$$\mathcal{L}_0 = \{location(sh, out), location(le, out), location(pe, rcz)\}$$

$$\mathcal{O}_0 = \begin{cases} attribute(name, le, Leonard), attribute(age, le, 28), \\ attribute(presented, le, false), ..., attribute(title, Slide2, Outline), \\ attribute(owns, le, Towards\ ...), attribute(consistsOf, Towards\ ..., Slide1), \\ attrbiute(consistsOf, Towards\ ..., Slide2) \end{cases}$$

$$\mathcal{D}_0 = \{deviceState(le_{nb}, notebook, off)\}$$

$$\mathcal{ST}_0 = \{deviceState(projector, projector, off)\}$$

$$T = \begin{cases} trans(projector, off, sOn, on), trans(projector, on, sOff, off), \\ ..., trans(projector, pMOff, sPreM, pMOn), trans(notebook, off, sOn, on), \\ trans(notebook, on, sOff, off), ..., trans(notebook, pSto, sOff, off) \end{cases}$$

The Transformation with respect to Scenario 1

Rule(s)	$TE_{CTML_{Sc1}}(CTML_{ConferenceSession}, Scenario2) =$
(1)	$\| (\Delta_a (sh), \Delta_a (le), \Delta_a (pe)) =$
(2)	$\| (\Delta_a (sh, c), \Delta_a (le, p), \Delta_a (pe, \gg (p, l))) =$
(3)	$\| (\Delta_a (sh, c), \Delta_a (le, p), \gg (\Delta_a (pe, p), \Delta_a (pe, l))) =$
(7)	$\| (\Delta_{te} (sh, TE_c), \Delta_{te} (le, TE_p), \gg (\Delta_{te} (pe, TE_p), \Delta_{te} (pe, TE_l)))$

Rule(s)	$\Delta_{te}(sh, TE_c) =$
	$\Delta_{te}\left(sh, \gg\left((c,er)\lfloor(pz)\rfloor, \gg\left(IS, [> (MT, \gg (CS, (c,lr)\lfloor(out)\rfloor))]\right)\right)\right) =$
(8)	$\gg\left(\Delta_{te}(sh,(c,er)\lfloor(pz)\rfloor), \Delta_{te}\left(sh, \gg\left(IS, [> (MT, \gg (CS, (c,lr)\lfloor(out)\rfloor))]\right)\right)\right) =$
(8)	$\gg\left(\Delta_{qt}(sh,(c,er)\lfloor(pz)\rfloor), \gg\left(\Delta_{te}(sh,IS), \Delta_{te}\left(sh, [> (MT, \gg (CS,(c,lr)\lfloor(out)\rfloor))]\right)\right)\right) =$
(12), (22)	$eff := eff \oplus \{((sh,c,er), eff_t)\}$ $eff_t = (\{x\}, \{location(x,sh)\}, \{location(pz,sh)\}, \{location(x,sh)\})$ $\gg\left(eff\left(\Delta_{qt}(sh,(c,er))\right), \gg\left(\Delta_{te}(sh,IS), \Delta_{te}\left(sh, [> (MT, \gg (CS,(c,lr)\lfloor(out)\rfloor))]\right)\right)\right) =$
(14),(23)	$\gg\left(eff((sh,c,er)), \gg\left(\Delta_{te}(sh,IS), \Delta_{te}\left(sh, [> (MT, \gg (CS,(c,lr)\lfloor(out)\rfloor))]\right)\right)\right) =$
(8)	$\gg\left(eff((sh,c,er)), \gg\left(\Delta_{te}(sh,IS), [> \left(\Delta_{te}(sh,MT), \Delta_{te}(sh, \gg (CS,(c,lr)\lfloor(out)\rfloor))\right)]\right)\right) =$
(8)	$\gg\left(eff((sh,c,er)), \gg\left(\Delta_{te}(sh,IS), [> \left(\Delta_{te}(sh,MT), \gg (\Delta_{te}(sh,CS), \Delta_{te}(sh,(c,lr)\lfloor(out)\rfloor))\right)]\right)\right) =$
(12), (22)	$eff := eff \oplus \{((sh,c,lr), eff_t)\}$ $eff_t = (\{x\}, \{location(x,sh)\}, \{location(out,sh)\}, \{location(x,sh)\})$ $\gg\left(eff((sh,c,er)), \gg\left(\Delta_{te}(sh,IS), [> \left(\Delta_{te}(sh,MT), \gg \left(\Delta_{te}(sh,CS), eff\left(\Delta_{te}(sh,(c,lr))\right)\right)\right)]\right)\right) =$
(14),(23)	$\gg\left(eff((sh,c,er)), \gg\left(\Delta_{te}(sh,IS), [> \left(\Delta_{te}(sh,MT), \gg \left(\Delta_{te}(sh,CS), eff((sh,c,lr))\right)\right)]\right)\right)$

Rule(s)	$\Delta_{te}(sh, IS) =$
	$\Delta_{te}\left(sh, | = |(\lfloor(pz)\rfloor(c,wp), \lfloor(pz)\rfloor(c,pa))\right) =$
(8)	$| = |\left(\Delta_{te}(sh, \lfloor(pz)\rfloor(c,wp)), \Delta_{te}(sh,, \lfloor(pz)\rfloor(c,pa))\right) =$
(12), (19)	$pre_S := pre_S \oplus \{((sh,c,wp), \{location(pz,sh)\})\}$ $| = |\left(pre_S\left(\Delta_{te}(sh,(c,wp))\right), \Delta_{te}(sh, \lfloor(pz)\rfloor(c,pa))\right) =$
(12), (19)	$pre_S := pre_S \oplus \{((sh,c,pa), \{location(pz,sh)\})\}$ $| = |\left(pre_S\left(\Delta_{te}(sh,(c,wp))\right), pre_S\left(\Delta_{te}(sh,(c,pa))\right)\right) =$
(14),(23)	$| = |\left(pre_S((sh,c,wp)), pre_S\left(\Delta_{te}(sh,(c,pa))\right)\right) =$

(14),(23)	$\| = \| \Big(pre_S\big((sh,c,wp)\big), pre_S\big((sh,c,pa)\big) \Big)$

Rule(s)	$\Delta_{te}\,(sh, MT) =$
	$\Delta_{te}\Big(sh, \big(\gg \big(\lfloor(\forall,(l,sal))\rfloor(c,at),\gg (SV,[(c,od)])\big)\big)^{*}\Big) =$
(9)	$\Big(\Delta_{te}\Big(sh, \gg \big(\lfloor(\forall,(l,sal))\rfloor(c,at),\gg (SV,[(c,od)])\big)\Big)\Big)^{*} =$
(8)	$\Big(\gg \Big(\Delta_{te}\big(sh,\lfloor(\forall,(l,sal))\rfloor(c,at)\big),\,\Delta_{te}\big(sh,\gg (SV,[(c,od)])\big)\Big)\Big)^{*} =$
(8)	$\Big(\gg \Big(\Delta_{te}\big(sh,\lfloor(\forall,(l,sal))\rfloor(c,at)\big),\gg \big(\Delta_{te}\,(sh,SV),\,\Delta_{te}\,(sh,[(c,od)])\big)\Big)\Big)^{*} =$
(15)	$pre_H := pre_H \oplus \{((sh,c,at),(\forall,\{(pe,l,sal)\}))\}$
	$\Big(\gg \Big(pre_H\big(\Delta_{te}\,(sh,(c,at))\big),\gg \big(\Delta_{te}\,(sh,SV),\Delta_{te}\,(sh,[(c,od)])\big)\Big)\Big)^{*} =$
(11)	$\Big(\gg \Big(pre_H\big(\Delta_{te}\,(sh,(c,at))\big),\gg \big(\Delta_{te}\,(sh,SV),[\Delta_{te}\,(sh,(c,od))]\big)\Big)\Big)^{*} =$
(14),(23)	$\Big(\gg \Big(pre_H\big((sh,c,at)\big),\gg \big(\Delta_{te}\,(sh,SV),[\Delta_{te}\,(sh,(c,od))]\big)\Big)\Big)^{*} =$
(14),(23)	$\Big(\gg pre_H\big((sh,c,at)\big),\gg \big(\Delta_{te}\,(sh,SV),[(sh,c,od)]\big)\Big)^{*}$

Rule(s)	$\Delta_{te}\,(sh, SV) =$
	$\Delta_{te}\Big(sh,[> \big((c,sas)(c,it)\big)\Big) =$
(8)	$[> \Big(\Delta_{te}\,(sh,(c,sas)),\Delta_{te}\,(sh,(c,it))\Big) =$
(14),(23)	$[> \Big((sh,c,sas),\Delta_{te}\,(sh,(c,it))\Big) =$
(14),(23)	$[> \big((sh,c,sas),(sh,c,it)\big)$

Rule(s)	$\Delta_{te}\,(sh, CS) =$
	$\Delta_{te}\Big(sh,\| = \| \big(\lfloor(\forall,(p,ed))\rfloor(c,aod),(c,wus)\big)\Big) =$
(8)	$\| = \|\Big(\Delta_{te}\big(sh,\lfloor(\forall,(p,ed))\rfloor(c,aod)\big),\Delta_{te}\,(sh,(c,wus))\Big) =$

(12), (15)	$pre_H := pre_H \oplus \{((sh, c, aod), (\forall, \{(pe, p, ed), (le, p, ed)\}))\}$ $| = | \left(pre_H\left(\Delta_{te}(sh, (c, aod))\right), \Delta_{te}(sh, (c, wus))\right) =$
(14),(23)	$| = | \left(pre_H((sh, c, aod)), \Delta_{te}(sh, (c, wus))\right) =$
(14),(23)	$| = | \left(pre_H((sh, c, aod)), (sh, c, wus)\right)$

Rule(s)	$\Delta_{te}(pe, TE_l) =$
	$\Delta_{te}\left(pe, | > \left((pe, l, sal), \gg ((l, aq), (l, lr))\right)\right) =$
(8)	$| > \left(\Delta_{te}(pe, (l, sal)), \Delta_{te}\left(pe, \gg ((l, aq), (l, lr))\right)\right) =$
(8)	$| > \left(\Delta_{te}(pe, (l, sal)), \gg \left(\Delta_{te}(pe, (l, aq)), \Delta_{te}(pe, (l, lr))\right)\right) =$
(14),(23)	$| > \left((pe, l, sal), \gg \left(\Delta_{te}(pe, (l, aq)), \Delta_{te}(pe, (l, lr))\right)\right) =$
(14),(23)	$| > \left((pe, l, sal), \gg \left((pe, l, aq), \Delta_{te}(pe, (l, lr))\right)\right) =$
(14),(23)	$| > \left((pe, l, sal), \gg ((pe, l, aq), (pe, l, lr))\right)$

Rule(s)	$\Delta_{te}(a, TE_p) =$, with $a \in \{le, pe\}$
	$\Delta_{te}\left(a, \gg \left(IN, \gg \left(CE, \gg \left(|(\exists, (c, at))||(pz)||(notebook, pSta)|(p, sp), [> (NS, EP))\right)\right)\right)\right) =$
(8)	$\gg \left(\Delta_{te}(a, IN), \Delta_{te}\left(a, \gg \left(CE, \gg \left(|(\exists, (c, at))||(pz)||(notebook, pSta)|(p, sp), [> (NS, EP))\right)\right)\right)\right) =$
(8)	$\gg \left(\Delta_{te}(a, IN), \gg \left(\Delta_{te}(a, CE), \Delta_{te}\left(a, \gg \left(|(\exists, (c, at))||(pz)||(notebook, pSta)|(p, sp), [> (NS, EP))\right)\right)\right)\right) =$
(8)	$\gg \left(\Delta_{te}(a, IN), \gg \left(\Delta_{te}(a, CE), \gg \left(\Delta_{te}(a, |(\exists, (c, at))||(pz)||(notebook, pSta)|(p, sp)), \Delta_{te}(a, [> (NS, EP)))\right)\right)\right) =$
(12), (15)	$pre_H := pre_H \oplus \left\{\left(\left(pre(pre(a, p, sp))\right), (\exists, \{(sh, c, at)\})\right)\right\}$ $\gg \left(\Delta_{te}(a, IN), \gg \left(\Delta_{te}(a, CE),\right.\right.$ $\left.\left. \gg \left(pre_H\left(\Delta_{te}(a, |(pz)||(notebook, pSta)|(p, sp))\right), \Delta_{te}(a, [> (NS, EP)))\right)\right)\right) =$
(12), (19)	$pre_S := pre_S \oplus \left\{\left((pre(a, p, sp)), \{location(pz, a)\}\right)\right\}$

	$$\gg\left(\Delta_{te}(a,IN),\gg\left(\Delta_{te}(a,CE),\right.\right.$$ $$\left.\left.\gg\left(pre_H\left(pre_S\left(\Delta_{te}(a,\lfloor(notebook,pSta)\rfloor(p,sp))\right)\right),\Delta_{te}(a,[>(NS,EP))\right)\right)\right)$$ $$=$$
(12), (18)	$$pre_S:=pre_S\oplus\{((a,p,sp),\{deviceState(d,notebook,pSta)\})\},with\ d$$ $$=\begin{cases}le\_nb,if\ a=le\\pe\_nb,if\ a=pe\end{cases}$$ $$\gg\left(\Delta_{te}(a,IN),\gg\left(\Delta_{te}(a,CE),\gg\left(pre_H\left(pre_S\left(pre_S\left(\Delta_{te}(a,(p,sp))\right)\right)\right),\Delta_{te}(a,[>(NS,EP))\right)\right)\right)$$ $$=$$
(14),(23)	$$\gg\left(\Delta_{te}(a,IN),\gg\left(\Delta_{te}(a,CE),\gg\left(pre_H\left(pre_S\left(pre_S((a,p,sp))\right)\right),\Delta_{te}(a,[>(NS,EP))\right)\right)\right)=$$
(8)	$$\gg\left(\Delta_{te}(a,IN),\gg\left(\Delta_{te}(a,CE),\gg\left(pre_H\left(pre_S\left(pre_S((a,p,sp))\right)\right),[>(\Delta_{te}(a,NS),\Delta_{te}(a,EP))\right)\right)\right)$$

Rule(s)	$\Delta_{te}(a,IN)=$, with $a\in\{le,pe\}$
	$\Delta_{te}(a,(p,in)\lfloor(notebook,sOn)\rfloor\lfloor(pz)\rfloor)=$
(13), (22)	$$eff:=eff\oplus\{(eff((a,p,in)),eff_t)\}$$ $$eff_t=(\{x\},\{location(x,a)\},\{location(pz,a)\},\{location(x,a)\})$$ $$eff\left(\Delta_{te}(a,(p,in)\lfloor(notebook,sOn)\rfloor)\right)=$$
(13),(21)	$$eff:=eff\oplus\{((a,p,in),eff_t)\}$$ $$eff_t=\begin{pmatrix}\{x,y\},\{deviceState(d,notebook,x),trans(notebook,x,sOn,y)\},\\\{deviceState(d,notebook,y)\},\{deviceState(d,notebook,x)\}\end{pmatrix}$$ $$,with\ d=\begin{cases}le\_nb,if\ a=le\\pe\_nb,if\ a=pe\end{cases}$$ $$eff\left(eff\left(\Delta_{te}(a,(p,in))\right)\right)=$$
(14),(23)	$$eff\left(eff((a,p,in))\right)$$

Rule(s)	$\Delta_{te}(a,CE)=$, with $a\in\{le,pe\}$
	$\Delta_{te}\left(a,|=|((p,clap),(p,stmp)\lfloor(notebook,startP)\rfloor)\right)=$
(8)	$|=|\left(\Delta_{te}(a,(p,clap)),\Delta_{te}(a,(p,stmp)\lfloor(notebook,startP)\rfloor)\right)=$
(14),(23)	$|=|((a,p,clap),\Delta_{te}(a,(p,stmp)\lfloor(notebook,startP)\rfloor))=$

(13),(21)	$eff := eff \oplus \{((a,p,stmp), eff_t)\}$
	$eff_t = \begin{pmatrix} \{x,y\}, \{deviceState(d,notebook,x), trans(notebook,x,startP,y)\}, \\ \{deviceState(d,notebook,y)\}, \{deviceState(d,notebook,x)\} \end{pmatrix}$
	$, with\ d = \begin{cases} le\_nb, if\ a = le \\ pe\_nb, if\ a = pe \end{cases}$
	$| = |\Big((a,p,clap), eff\Big(\Delta_{te}\big(a,(p,stmp)\big)\Big)\Big) =$
(14),(23)	$| = |\Big((a,p,clap), eff\big((a,p,stmp)\big)\Big)$

Rule(s)	$\Delta_{te}(a,NS) = \quad , with\ a \in \{le,pe\}$
	$\Delta_{te}\Big(a, \big((p,sns) \gg (p,es)\big)^*\Big) =$
(9)	$\Big(\Delta_{te}\big(a,(p,sns) \gg (p,es)\big)\Big)^* =$
(8)	$\Big(\gg \big(\Delta_{te}(a,(p,sns)), \Delta_{te}(a,(p,es))\big)\Big)^* =$
(14),(23)	$\Big(\gg \big((a,p,sns), \Delta_{te}(a,(p,es))\big)\Big)^* =$
(14),(23)	$\Big(\gg \big((a,p,sns), (a,p,es)\big)\Big)^*$

Rule(s)	$\Delta_{te}(a,EP) = \quad , with\ a \in \{le,pe\}$
	$\Delta_{te}\Big(a, \gg \big((p,ep), \gg (|[(\exists,(c,od))]|(p,rtq),(p,lr)|(out)|)\big)\Big) =$
(8)	$\gg \Big(\Delta_{te}(a,(p,ep)), \Delta_{te}\big(a, \gg (|[(\exists,(c,od))]|(p,rtq),(p,lr)|(out)|)\big)\Big) =$
(14),(23)	$\gg \Big((a,p,ep), \Delta_{te}\big(a, \gg (|[(\exists,(c,od))]|(p,rtq),(p,lr)|(out)|)\big)\Big) =$
(8)	$\gg \Big((a,p,ep), \gg \big(\Delta_{te}(a,|[(\exists,(c,od))]|(p,rtq)), \Delta_{te}(a,(p,lr)|(out)|)\big)\Big) =$
(12), (15)	$pre_H := pre_H \oplus \{((a,p,rtq),(\exists,\{(sh,c,od)\}))\}$
	$\gg \Big((a,p,ep), \gg \big(pre(\Delta_{te}(a,(p,rtq))), \Delta_{te}(a,(p,lr)|(out)|)\big)\Big) =$
(14),(23)	$\gg \Big((a,p,ep), \gg \big(pre((a,p,rtq)), \Delta_{te}(a,(p,lr)|(out)|)\big)\Big) =$
(13), (22)	$eff := eff \oplus \{((a,p,lr), eff_t)\}$
	$eff_t = (\{x\}, \{location(x,a)\}, \{location(out,a)\}, \{location(x,a)\})$
	$\gg \Big((a,p,ep), \gg \big(pre((a,p,rtq)), eff(\Delta_{te}(a,(p,lr)))\big)\Big) =$

(14),(23)	$\gg \Big((a,p,ep), \gg \big(pre((a,p,rtq)), eff((a,p,lr))\big)\Big)$

$$IS_{CTML} = \langle TE_{CTML}, S_0, pre_H, pre_S, eff \rangle$$

With

$$pre_H = \left\{ \begin{array}{c} ((sh,c,at),(\forall,\{(pe,l,sal)\})),\big((sh,c,aod),(\forall,\{(pe,p,ed),(le,p,ed)\})\big), \\ \Big(\big(pre\big(pre(le,p,sp)\big)\big),(\exists,\{(sh,c,at)\})\Big),\Big(\big(pre\big(pre(pe,p,sp)\big)\big),(\exists,\{(sh,c,at)\})\Big), \\ ((le,p,rtq),(\exists,\{(sh,c,od)\})),((pe,p,rtq),(\exists,\{(sh,c,od)\})) \end{array} \right\}$$

$$pre_S = \left\{ \begin{array}{c} ((sh,c,wp),\{location(pz,sh)\}),((sh,c,pa),\{location(pz,sh)\}), \\ ((le,p,sp),\{deviceState(le_{nb},notebook,pSta)\}), \\ ((pe,p,sp),\{deviceState(pe_{nb},notebook,pSta)\}), \\ \big((pre(le,p,sp)),\{location(pz,le)\}\big),\big((pre(pe,p,sp)),\{location(pz,pe)\}\big) \end{array} \right\}$$

$$eff(t) = \left\{ \begin{array}{ll} (\{x\},\{location(x,sh)\},\{location(pz,sh)\},\{location(x,sh)\}) & ,if\ t = (sh,c,er) \\ (\{x\},\{location(x,sh)\},\{location(out,sh)\},\{location(x,sh)\}) & ,if\ t = (sh,c,lr) \\ (\{x\},\{location(x,le)\},\{location(pz,le)\},\{location(x,le)\}) & ,if\ t = eff((le,p,in)) \\ (\{x\},\{location(x,pe)\},\{location(pz,pe)\},\{location(x,pe)\}) & ,if\ t = eff((pe,p,in)) \\ \binom{\{x,y\},\{deviceState(d,notebook,x),trans(notebook,x,sOn,y)\},}{\{deviceState(d,notebook,y)\},\{deviceState(d,notebook,x)\}} & ,if\ t = (le,p,in) \\ \binom{\{x,y\},\{deviceState(d,notebook,x),trans(notebook,x,sOn,y)\},}{\{deviceState(d,notebook,y)\},\{deviceState(d,notebook,x)\}} & ,if\ t = (pe,p,in) \\ \binom{\{x,y\},\{deviceState(d,notebook,x),trans(notebook,x,startP,y)\},}{\{deviceState(d,notebook,y)\},\{deviceState(d,notebook,x)\}} & ,if\ t = (le,p,stmp) \\ \binom{\{x,y\},\{deviceState(d,notebook,x),trans(notebook,x,startP,y)\},}{\{deviceState(d,notebook,y)\},\{deviceState(d,notebook,x)\}} & ,if\ t = (pe,p,stmp) \\ (\{x\},\{location(x,le)\},\{location(out,le)\},\{location(x,le)\}) & ,if\ t = (le,p,lr) \\ (\{x\},\{location(x,pe)\},\{location(out,pe)\},\{location(x,pe)\}) & ,if\ t = (pe,p,lr) \end{array} \right.$$

The Initial State S_0 with respect to Scenario 2

$$S_0 = \mathcal{L}_0 \cup \mathcal{O}_0 \cup \mathcal{D}_0 \cup \mathcal{ST}_0 \cup T$$

$$\mathcal{L}_0 = \{location(sh,out)\}$$

$$\mathcal{O}_0 = \emptyset$$

$$\mathcal{D}_0 = \emptyset$$

$$\mathcal{ST}_0 = \{deviceState(projector,projector,off)\}$$

$$T = \left\{ \begin{array}{c} trans(projector,off,sOn,on), trans(projector,on,sOff,off), \\ ..., trans(projector,pMOff,sPreM,pMOn) \end{array} \right\}$$

The Transformation with respect to Scenario 2

Rule(s)	$TE_{CTML_{Sc2}}(CTML_{ConferenceSession}, Scenario1) =$
(1)	$\Delta_a(sh) =$
(2)	$\Delta_a(sh,c) =$
(7)	$\Delta_{te}(sh,TE_c)$

		(shown before)

$$IS_{CTML} = \langle TE_{CTML}, S_0, pre_H, pre_S, eff \rangle$$

$$TE_{CTML} = \gg \left(eff\big((sh,c,er)\big), \right.$$

$$\gg \left(| = | \big(pre_S((sh,c,wp)), pre_S((sh,c,pa))\big), [\right.$$

$$> \left(\big(\gg (sh,c,at), \gg \big([> \big((sh,c,sas),(sh,c,it)\big), |(sh,c,od)|\big]\big)\right)^*, \right.$$

$$\left.\left.\left.\gg \big(| = | \big((sh,c,aod),(sh,c,wus)\big), eff\big((sh,c,lr)\big)\big)\right)\right)\right)$$

$$S_0 = \left\{ \begin{array}{c} location(sh,out), deviceState(projector,projector,off), \\ trans(projector,off,sOn,on), trans(projector,on,sOff,off), \\ ..., trans(projector,pMOff,sPreM,pMOn) \end{array} \right\}$$

$$pre_H = \emptyset$$

$$pre_S = \{((sh,c,wp),\{location(pz,sh)\}), ((sh,c,pa),\{location(pz,sh)\})\}$$

$$eff(t)$$
$$= \left\{ \begin{array}{ll} (\{x\},\{location(x,sh)\},\{location(pz,sh)\},\{location(x,sh)\}) & , if\ t = (sh,c,er) \\ (\{x\},\{location(x,sh)\},\{location(out,sh)\},\{location(x,sh)\}) & , if\ t = (sh,c,lr) \end{array} \right.$$